THE NORTHWEST WINE GUIDE

THE NORTHWEST WINE GUIDE

A BUYER'S HANDBOOK

ANDY PERDUE

SASQUATCH BOOKS
SEATTLE

Copyright© 2003 by Andy Perdue

Printed in the United States of America.
Published by Sasquatch Books
Distributed by Publishers Group West
09 08 07 06 05 04 03   6 5 4 3 2 1

Cover design: Rowan Moore/doublemranch.com
Cover photograph: Jason Koski
Interior design: Kate Basart
Copy editor: Don Graydon

Library of Congress Cataloging in Publication Data
Perdue, Andy.
        The northwest wine guide: a buyer's Handbook / Andy Perdue.
        p.   cm.
        Includes index.
        ISBN 1-57061-361-3
1. Wine and wine making—Northwest, Pacific. 2. Wineries—Northwest,
Pacific. I. Title.
        TP557.P45 2003
        641.2'2'09795—dc21   2002044649

Sasquatch Books
119 South Main Street, Suite 400
Seattle, WA 98104
(206) 467-4300
www.sasquatchbooks.com
books@sasquatchbooks.com

CONTENTS

Foreword

For most of the past two hundred years, the classic wines of Western Europe have stood as benchmarks of world-class quality. Regardless of variety, wines from France, Italy, and Germany had set worldwide standards of excellence. In the last half of the twentieth century, however, in various locations throughout the New World, innovative growers and winemakers have arrived to challenge the quality supremacy of these Old World producers and regions.

Among the challengers are the winegrowers and winemakers of the Pacific Northwest, headstrong individuals who firmly believe that their *terroirs* have the right soils and climates to make wines that rival the best of the classics. And they're right. Time and again we've seen the results of high-profile blind tastings where Washington Merlots or Oregon Pinot Noirs have upstaged the pricier Old World champs.

To casual observers this Northwest corner of the continent is an unlikely spot for powerful Cabernets and fragrant Chardonnays to call home. After all, the popular image of the area is that it's north, it's cold, and it's wet. Few people outside the region accurately understand the precious combination of natural factors that have come together to make up the *terroirs* of this new wine-growing area.

But Andy Perdue does, and with this book he helps to identify those producers who are optimizing the natural gifts of this region. Who better to comment on the conditions and wines of this region than Andy, a constant observer and dedicated student of all Northwest wines? His book takes some important steps in slaying myths and changing misguided thinking about the region, as well as being a handy field guide to finding a wine for tonight's dinner. Andy is one of the resident scholars of Northwest *terroirs,* developing insight and perspective through constant tasting and frequent outings to regional wineries. He knows the lay of the land and the personalities of the movers and shakers, he kicks sod and sniffs barrels, all the while looking for the causes and effects of this area's distinctive wine character. These pages are his refreshingly practical comment on the vinous buzz of the Northwest.

Through his close examination, we see a broad viticultural region in which vineyards are thriving in the valleys of the ancient mountains that run south to north up the West Coast of North America. These massive peaks block ocean storms and keep inland vineyards sunny and dry; indeed, eastern Washington's Columbia Valley and British Columbia's Okanagan Valley register only a frac tion of the rainfall of the Napa Valley. Here, the stressed Merl Chardonnay, and Cabernet Sauvignon vines yield wines of g fruit purity and sturdy structure. Similarly, in regions like Ore

Willamette Valley, winegrowers have responded by planting Pinot Noir and Pinot Gris, varieties better adapted to the cooler environment, with excellent results.

The natural setting wasn't the only factor that eventually pointed the way to achieving great wines from this area. It was also an attitude. Once bitten, Northwest winemakers never accepted a destiny that excluded them. In their minds, the existence of Western European benchmarks never ruled out the possibility of finding even better sites elsewhere. These are the people Andy has talked, swirled, tasted, and spat with. These are the characters that make these wines so real. You would do well to toss this book into the glove box for those wine-touring weekends, or clutch it as you peruse the wine shop shelves for the next exciting purchase. Its sensible, view-from-the-inside approach will be invaluable as you weave your way through the exciting discovery of these New World challengers.

—*Bob Betz, M.W.*
Vice President, Stimson Lane Vineyards and Estates
Winemaker and owner, Betz Family Winery

Introduction

Today is a great time to be a wine lover in the Pacific Northwest. Over the past decade, the Northwest has become one of the most exciting wine regions in the world. After playing second fiddle to California and the wine regions of Europe for years, the Northwest has gained worldwide recognition for producing wines of high quality, excellent value, and diversity. With each successive vintage, more and more wine professionals, collectors, and consumers alike are realizing the wine regions of Washington, Oregon, British Columbia, and Idaho can achieve greatness, that the wines produced here can stand alongside the best in the world.

Home to more than five hundred wineries, the Northwest offers a vast array of styles—robust Cabs and Merlots, hedonistic Syrahs, seductive Pinot Noirs, mouth-filling Chardonnays, crisp Pinot Gris and amazing dessert wines. In Washington's arid Columbia Valley, winemakers are crafting Cabernet Sauvignon, Merlot, and Syrah that will stand up with the best from France and California, and Washington's Rieslings and Gewürztraminers are generally recognized as being equal in quality to those of Alsace and Germany. Oregon's wines stand out as being among the best in the New World, with the sublime Pinot Noirs comparing well with those from France's Burgundy region and California's Russian River Valley. Idaho's wine industry has grown steadily over recent years. And perhaps the most exciting wine region to watch is British Columbia's Okanagan Valley, which gets more heat and light than Napa and Sonoma, yet grows cold enough for wineries to produce the region's world-famous ice wines.

This book is designed to help you navigate the exciting world of Northwest wines. Nearly 1,500 wines are reviewed and recommended here out of more than 5,000 tasted. They were reviewed under a variety of conditions, including double-blind judgings with *Wine Press Northwest* magazine's tasting panel, blind tastings at competitions, open tastings specifically for this book, wine festivals, in restaurants, and at wineries. To ensure a broad range of experience, I've tasted from barrels, from bottles submitted by wineries, and from bottles purchased at wine shops and grocery stores.

In this book, I don't cite specific vintages. It's not that vintages don't matter—they do. Immensely. But specific vintages are available only for a short period of time, so any reference to them i quickly outdated. Omitting the vintage allows me to provide broad picture of the strengths of each winery and to convey a se of how a winery performs over time with certain varietie styles. Multiple vintages of wineries' efforts have been eva whenever possible so each producer's best and most reliab are reviewed.

This guide will get you started in your exploration of Northwest wine. Take it with you to wine shops, grocery stores, wine-tasting trips—even restaurants. Wine appreciation is a journey. I hope you enjoy it as much as I do.

Prices

Each dollar sign ($) after a wine represents a range of $15. (Canadian prices have been converted to U.S. dollars.) Therefore:
$ = $15 and under
$$ = $16-$30
$$$ = $31-$45
$$$$ = $46-$60
$$$$$ = $61-$75
$$$$$$ = $76-$90

Acknowledgments

As a wine takes many seasons to develop and mature from the vine to the cellar, so has this book been a labor of time and effort. I could not have even begun to think of taking on this odyssey without my wife, Melissa, who keeps me focused when the goal seems so distant, indulges my crazy ideas, and loves me unconditionally regardless of what life puts before us.

My parents, Ed and Mona Perdue, have taught me the value of hard work and creativity; my brother, Joe, has been my role model for perseverance and work ethic; and my in-laws, Chip and Jean O'Neil, have supported and fostered my interest in wine. My fellow *Wine Press Northwest* tasting panelists—Eric Degerman, Coke Roth, Hank Sauer, Paul Sinclair, and Bob Woehler—have tasted thousands of wines with me and shared their opinions and insights. Bob, in particular, awakened my initial interest in wine with his wine column in the *Tri-City Herald*. My boss, Cheryl Dell, has been a great supporter of this book from the beginning.

Jean Yates of the Avalon of Oregon wine shop in Corvallis and Dan Paynter of the Pacific Northwest Wine Club helped me gather and taste several hundred Oregon wines, and Jamie Peha and Steve Burns of the Washington Wine Commission aided me in tracking down many hard-to-find wines.

Many thanks to wine writer Heidi Yorkshire, who recommended me to Sasquatch Books. Joan Gregory, former managing editor of Sasquatch, nurtured this project from the beginning, and Heidi Schuessler, managing editor of Sasquatch, saw it through to the finish. And special thanks to Bob Betz, M.W., one of the kindest and classiest people I've had the pleasure to know, who provided the foreword.

Wine-Appreciation Tips

You don't have to be a snob to enjoy and appreciate wine. You don't have to have a thousand-bottle cellar, a vertical of Leonetti, or a fat bank account. The joy is in the glass, and while it's easy to spend a lot of money on this passion, it isn't a necessity.

Here are a few ways to enhance and encourage wine appreciation:

Swirl, sniff, and sip. Swirling wine in the glass releases esters that will reveal more about the wine. If you're afraid of spilling, put your glass on a flat surface and move the base in a circle. After you give the wine a good swirl, stick your nose down into your glass and take a long, even sniff. Next, take a good bit of wine into your mouth and swish it around your entire mouth. Try to suck in a little air while you do this. It makes a gross "sucking" sound, but it will introduce more oxygen into the wine and enhance the flavors.

Take notes. This may sound geeky-nerdy, but writing down what you like (and don't like) about a wine will help you learn about a grape variety, wine, winemaker, and region.

When you find a wine you like, buy a few bottles. You never know when you'll find any more of a wine that speaks to you. If you want to see how a wine ages, buy a case and drink one bottle per year. It's a lot of fun to track a wine's progression.

Share with your friends and family. Encouraging others to enjoy wine will give you an outlet to communicate your passion. And they'll know what to get you for your birthday.

Throw a wine party. Here's a quick way to try a lot of different wines: Invite ten friends to bring a bottle of their favorite wines and an appetizer to your home. Everyone will get to try different wines, eat new dishes, and enjoy each other's company.

Stemware makes a difference. While some wine is meant to be drunk out of a paper bag, the fine wines of the Pacific Northwest are not. Proper stemware will enhance the wine-tasting experience. The most famous stemware producer is an Austrian company called Riedel (pronounced REE-dull). Its research shows that different shapes enhance different wines, so a Burgundy glass is best for Pinot Noir and a Bordeaux glass is perfect for Cabernet Sauvignon. This can get expensive in a hurry, but if you invest in a few good crystal glasses, you'll find yourself appreciating the wine more. If you're in a fine restaurant that tries to give you substandard stemware, ask for something better.

Don't overdo it. The point of wine appreciation is not to get tipsy. If you're tasting a lot of wine for educational purposes, spit. It sounds gross, but it beats a headache or losing your driver's license. And remember: Always drive responsibly.

Wine-and-Food Pairing

Successfully pairing food and wine is not a great mystery. The rule of thumb once was that red wine goes with meat and white wine goes with fish. It's still a good idea, but it isn't necessarily gospel. Throughout this guide, I offer many food-pairing suggestions, so consider them when trying to decide what to serve with a particular wine.

Here are a few ideas and guidelines:

- Northwest seafood goes well with a lot of our white wines—and a few reds. Shellfish, salmon, and halibut are exquisite matches with Oregon Pinot Gris and Washington Sauvignon Blanc, and they go well with some lesser-known varieties, including Madeleine Angevine, Ehrenfelser, and Semillon. A fruity Pinot Noir sometimes works with salmon. And a good, crisp Chardonnay can be heavenly.

- Consider sauces when pairing wines. A dish with a hearty red sauce is more likely to pair well with robust red wines, and cream sauces tend to match better with white wines.

- Regional dishes do well with regional grape varieties. If you're serving a hearty Italian dish, a Northwest Sangiovese might just be the ticket. Spicy German cuisine could pair with a dry Riesling or Gewürztraminer. And a heavy French-inspired dish would be exquisite with a Cabernet Sauvignon.

- Oaky wines aren't always the best food matches. What should you pair with an oaky, buttery Chardonnay? It's actually difficult to say, since little will get through the viscous, oily flavors of a full-blown California-style Chardonnay. Big, oaky wines are show-pieces, so perhaps start out the evening by sharing a glass with your guests before any food is served.

- Cook 'em rare and drink 'em young. This is more of a personal preference, but if you're serving a big, young Washington Merlot, a rare or medium-rare cut of beef or lamb can cut right through the mouth-puckering tannins and allow the delicious fruit to marry with the flavors of the meat.

- Take chances. Opening a bottle of wine to see how it matches with a particular dish is a sure way to find out if it does. And if it doesn't, open a different bottle. Learning is at least half the fun.

- Drink what you like. If you can't stand Pinot Noir but you're told it will be the best match for a particular dish, consider something else that will enhance your meal and experience.

Wine-Buying Tips

Finding the kind of wine you like is one of the joys of wine appreciation, and the wide range of grape varieties and styles will give you plenty of research opportunities.

Here are a few tips to make wine buying an enjoyable experience:

If you're new to wine enjoyment, it's safe to start with a sweeter wine. Bold reds and bone-dry whites can seem unapproachable to the uninitiated, so look for off-dry white varieties such as Riesling, Gewürztraminer, or Chenin Blanc. Some wines that would seem sweeter but often are bone dry include Sauvignon Blanc, Pinot Gris, or Viognier.

Don't let pronunciation problems get in the way. Some of the most aromatic and beautiful wines have names that are difficult to pronounce. This is just one reason Chardonnay is the most popular wine in North America. Don't be frightened by such tongue twisters as Gewürztraminer, Viognier, and Sangiovese.

If you have questions about wine, ask a wine expert. Neighborhood wine shops are some of the best sources of information, not only about Northwest products but also about wines from around the world. Wine shop owners aren't usually in the business just for the money but because they love wine—and love to talk about it. Many right-thinking grocery stores employ wine stewards, who can be very helpful.

Wines from the New World (which includes the Northwest) usually are identified by their grape variety, such as Merlot, Chardonnay, or Cabernet Sauvignon. Wines from the Old World (including France, Italy, Germany, and Spain) often are identified by region. This can be confusing because, for example, a red wine from the Bordeaux region of France might be Cabernet Sauvignon, Merlot, Cabernet Franc, or a blend of all three (plus a couple of others). But the label doesn't say. A red wine from Burgundy is always Pinot Noir. And a red wine from the Chianti region is primarily Sangiovese, though it might have other grapes blended with it.

Light and heat are harmful to wine. Good wine shops will protect against both, but beware of wines at grocery stores that have been left under ultraviolet lights or near a window that gets a lot of sun. In fact, it wouldn't hurt to grab a bottle that is behind the display bottle and away from light.

Some wines are just plain confusing. Sparkling wine, for example: Brut is dry, but Extra Dry is sweet. Ports also can be riddles. There are Vintage Ports, Nonvintage Ports, Late Vintage Ports, Tawny Ports, and Ruby Ports. Finding your way through these mazes, however, can be quite fun.

Wine Terminology

Wine appreciation has its own language, which contains words from different languages, especially French. Here are a few you're likely to run across:

Acidity: This is the tart, refreshing element in wine. It's often measured in pH, in which the number gets lower as the level of acidity gets higher. Water, for example, is around 7 pH, while most wines are between 4 and 3. If a wine is too high in pH (low in acidity), it can seem flabby and is less likely to pair well with food. For dessert wines, especially ice wines, acidity is vital for keeping the high sugar levels balanced.

Appellation: This is a French term for a grape-growing area, known officially in the United States as an AVA. In the Pacific Northwest, there are more than a dozen appellations.

AVA: This means American Viticultural Area, a region approved by the federal Bureau of Alcohol, Tobacco, and Firearms. To gain AVA status, a region must be shown to contain unique grape-growing qualities.

Barrels: Oak barrels are used to age wine. A newer barrel will impart certain flavors into a wine and will draw out some of the tannins. There are two primary sources for barrels: French (very expensive) and American (not as expensive). American oak comes primarily from Missouri, but it also can come from Minnesota, Pennsylvania, and Oregon, as well as other states. Winemakers also will purchase barrels made of oak from Hungary or Russia, as well as from other European countries. Most winemakers use a mixture of barrels from different producers (called coopers) and of different ages, as this can add a little more complexity to the finished product. High-end producers often use only expensive French oak barrels, which consumers will see in the price. Many Oregon Pinot Noir producers use only French oak.

Blanc de Blanc / Blanc de Noir: French terms that mean "white of white" and "white of black." A Blanc de Blanc is a white wine made from white wine grapes, such as Chardonnay. A Blanc de Noir is a white wine made from red grapes, such as Pinot Noir. The terms normally are associated with sparkling wines, but consumers will find them on still wines, too. To keep a wine that uses red grapes from looking red, the skins are removed after the juice is pressed. The color of the wine comes from the skins.

Blend: The French have known for centuries that many wines are better together than alone. Nowhere is this more famous than in Bordeaux, where Cabernet Sauvignon, Merlot, Cabernet

Franc, Malbec, and Petit Verdot are blended to produce spectacular wines. In the Pacific Northwest, many wines are blended, with perhaps the most famous being the Cab–Merlot marriage. In fact, even wines that state just one variety on the label may be a blend because U.S. law allows as much as 25 percent of a wine to be another variety. So just because you have a bottle of Merlot doesn't mean there isn't a little Cabernet Sauvignon in it. Interestingly, white wines occasionally are blended with reds. For example, Viognier sometimes is blended into Syrah during fermentation. This can add a bit of perfuminess to the wine but doesn't affect the color because the pigments in the red Syrah grape are absorbed into the white Viognier juice.

Botrytis (bo-TRY-tus): This fungus, affectionately known as "noble rot," occurs when humidity or dampness is present in a vineyard. A winery will hope for botrytis when it is trying to make a dessert wine, as the fungus will attack the grapes, pierce their skins, and drain the liquid, leaving a shriveled mess that is loaded with sugar. When harvested and pressed, the resulting wine will be sweet and spicy. The most famous version of botrytis occurs in the Sauternes region of France, where bottles of Chateau d'Yquem's Sauternes can fetch hundreds of dollars.

Clones: A clone is a version of a specific grape variety. For example, there are many, many clones of Pinot Noir. Oregon vintners are fanatical about clones and have done as much research on how specific clones perform as any group outside of France. They've found that certain clones of Pinot Noir, for instance, ripen better in certain soil types. Clones can vary dramatically in taste, and many Oregon vintners will blend different clones of Pinot Noir or Chardonnay to gain more complexity.

Cuvée (coo-VAY): This is a fancy French term for "blend." It's most often used with sparkling wines, but consumers also will see it with red Bordeaux-style blends or even Pinot Noirs that blend different vineyards or clones.

Fining / Filtering: Often, wine lovers will see references to "unfined and unfiltered" on a wine bottle or description. There is much controversy surrounding the practice of fining and filtering wines. To "fine" a wine means to clarify it so it doesn't appear hazy or cloudy. Winemakers use a number of methods to do this, including allowing sediment in the wine to settle to the bottom of a barrel or tank, then transferring most of the wine to another vessel. Egg whites also are used to fine a wine because the tiny particles in the wine will stick to the egg whites. To "filter" a wine means to actually push the wine through a filter to strain sediments out of the wine. Many winemakers believe filtering can rob a wine of its character. Others disagree. If you finish a bottle of wine and there is muddy sediment in the bottom of the bottle, it probably was unfiltered.

Finish: A wine's finish is the residual flavor left in the mouth after the wine is swallowed. The length of a wine's finish is an indication of its fruitiness and complexity. Tannins and acidity can seem to extend a wine's finish, but it's the complexity of the wine that is the true measure of finish—and greatness.

Gravity-flow facility: This is a trend primarily in Oregon (though a few gravity-flow wineries are found elsewhere in the Pacific Northwest). Many vintners believe that gentle handling of the wine will make a difference in the final product. They will go so far as to build multistory buildings so each stage of the winemaking (crush, press, fermentation, barrel aging, bottling, etc.) is done at a lower level and handled by gravity rather than pumps. This is particularly important with Pinot Noir, the most fickle of wines, which must be handled with care and delicacy. Examples of gravity-flow facilities include Domaine Drouhin Oregon, WillaKenzie Estate and Domaine Serene in Oregon, and Hainle Vineyards in British Columbia.

Ice wine: One of the rarest of wine delicacies, ice wine is produced when the grapes are left on the vine until they freeze. They are then harvested (usually in the middle of the night), pressed (a daunting task because they're as hard as marbles), and fermented (which can take weeks because of the sugar levels). The sweetness comes not only from how late they are harvested—as early as December and as late as January or even February), but also because the freezing causes the liquid in the grape to turn to ice. Thus, what is squeezed out has extremely high sugar levels. Most Northwest ice wine is produced in British Columbia, where temperatures must reach at least –9° Centigrade (about 17° Fahrenheit) for a certain number of hours. In B.C., wineries are not allowed to artificially freeze their grapes. However, this is practiced in the United States, especially in Oregon and California, where it rarely gets cold enough to make ice wine. These artificially frozen ice wines usually are inferior to natural B.C. ice wines.

Malolactic fermentation: Also known as "ML," this is a secondary fermentation that often is allowed to occur in the Pacific Northwest. In the early days of the Washington wine industry, the wines were seen as too tart and acidic. Malolactic fermentation alleviated this by converting harsh malic acids into softer lactic acids, thus reducing the tartness in the wines. A good example of this is a creamy Chardonnay.

Mead: Not all wine is made from grapes. Mead, for example, is made from honey. It is part of ancient lore and is believed to be older than beer or wine. According to legend, the term "honeymoon" comes from the consumption of mead (honey wine) as a fertility drink on a couple's wedding night.

Meritage: A Meritage is a red or white Bordeaux-style blend. The term was invented by a U.S.-based organization that formed in the late 1980s. The wines must be a blend, and the name, which rhymes with "heritage," can only be used by wineries that are members of the Meritage group. Red wines can include Cabernet Sauvignon, Merlot, Cabernet Franc, Petit Verdot, Malbec, and three obscure Bordeaux grapes. A white Meritage is a blend of Semillon and Sauvignon Blanc.

Residual sugar: This is a measurement of sweetness in a wine. Most wines are bone dry or have imperceptible levels of sugar. Off-dry wines might have 1 or 2 percent residual sugar, and a late-harvest wine might have 5 to 7 percent. A British Columbia ice wine might have as much as 27 percent.

Sur lie: When a wine is fermented, yeast converts sugar to alcohol. Eventually, the yeast finishes its job and dies, and the resulting sediment settles in the bottom of the barrel or tank. Stirring the sediment, called "lees," can add an element of creamy complexity to a wine. This method, known by its French term *sur lie*, is most often used with Chardonnay and Semillon. Eventually, the sediment is filtered out.

Tannin: Tannins are compounds that can cause a drying effect while drinking red wine. Tannins aren't present in white wines because they come from the skins and seeds of the grapes, which are discarded before a white wine ferments. Tannins can give a wine good backbone, though too much can overwhelm a wine and cause astringency.

Terroir: An overused—and misused—term in recent years, this French word loosely translates to "soil" but means so much more. *Terroir* (pronounced tehr-WAHR) refers to how specific grape varieties perform in certain locations. Soil type and weather conditions play a factor. Wine experts believe a wine expresses its *terroir*. For example, the hot days and cool nights on Washington's Red Mountain help Cabernet Sauvignon there get very ripe and hold onto more acidity than Cabernet Sauvignon from some famous California wine regions.

Varietal / Variety: There are many varieties of grapes. Thousands of them. Wine lovers are primarily interested in grapes from the *Vitis vinifera* family, such as Merlot, Chardonnay, and Syrah. The origins of these classic wine grapes can be traced to

Europe, and the vines have been exported around the globe over the past three centuries. Non-vinifera grapes, including such North American varieties as Concord or Niagara, also are used to make wine, though usually because the vines can survive better in cold winters. Invariably, wines made from North American grapes or crossings of European and North American grapes (called hybrids) are vastly inferior to wines made from vinifera grapes. In this book "variety" is used as a noun and "varietal" is used as a modifier.

Veraison. This is a French term that means "change" and signals when wine grapes change color as harvest nears. In Washington, for example, many red wine grapes will start to change color in early August, depending on how warm the summer was.

Vineyard-designated: These are wines that come from a single vineyard. While many wines will come from one location, vineyard-designated wines include the vineyard's name on the label as a way to distinguish the wine for discerning consumers. This is a growing trend in the Pacific Northwest as the industry matures and winemakers and grape growers learn more about *terroir.*

Vintage: The vintage is the year the grapes were grown. Vintage is vital because weather makes each year different. A spring frost can damage vines, a cool summer can mean late-ripening fruit, and a rainy harvest can ruin an entire year's work. Washington probably has the fewest problems of any of the Northwest wine regions because the summers usually are long and warm and the harvests are devoid of rain. In British Columbia, grapes for ice wines occasionally are picked in January or even February. However, the wine still will be from the vintage in which the grapes were grown, not necessarily when they were harvested.

VQA: This stands for Vintners Quality Alliance and is a Canadian system that attempts to ensure a wine's quality. Most British Columbia wines are part of the VQA system, and 95 percent of wines that go through the VQA system are deemed commercially acceptable. A handful of wineries, however, have chosen not to participate in the VQA system. This doesn't say anything bad about the quality of their wines. In fact, some non-VQA wines are among the best in the province.

Top Northwest Wineries

As in every wine region in the world, some Pacific Northwest wineries specialize in certain styles or varieties of wines, while others excel in many areas. Depending on the region they're in, these wineries may produce a wide variety of wines, often at different price levels. For example, Chateau Ste. Michelle produces several Merlots, Chardonnays, and Cabernets, including its mainline wine, a reserve, and several vineyard-designated versions.

If you want top quality in a broad range of wines, look to these wineries.

Barnard Griffin, Richland, Washington
Chateau Ste. Michelle, Woodinville, Washington
Columbia Crest, Paterson, Washington
Hogue Cellars, Prosser, Washington
Jackson-Triggs Vintners, Oliver, B.C.
Kiona Vineyards Winery, Benton City, Washington
L'Ecole No. 41, Lowden, Washington
Sumac Ridge Estate Winery, Summerland, B.C.
Willamette Valley Vineyards, Turner, Oregon
Woodward Canyon Winery, Lowden, Washington

Good Bargains

The Northwest is known as a haven for good wines of great value, perhaps with the exception of Oregon Pinot Noir (and there are even a few of those around if you look hard enough).

While Washington wineries' prices have risen through the years as the industry has developed and improved, there still are plenty of bargains to be had. And British Columbia and Idaho are replete with great prices.

The following wineries have well-earned reputations for producing delicious wines at hard-to-beat values.

Bridgeview Winery, Cave Junction, Oregon
Columbia Crest, Paterson, Washington
Covey Run Vintners, Woodinville, Washington
Gray Monk Cellars, Okanagan Centre, B.C.
Hogue Cellars, Prosser, Washington
Jackson-Triggs Vintners, Oliver, B.C.
Pend d'Oreille Winery, Sandpoint, Idaho
Powers Winery, Kennewick, Washington
Snoqualmie Vineyards, Prosser, Washington
Ste. Chapelle, Nampa, Idaho
Tinhorn Creek Vineyards, Oliver, B.C.
Washington Hills Cellars, Sunnyside, Washington

The Varieties of Northwest Wine

The Pacific Northwest is a microcosm of the world of wine. Eastern Washington successfully grows the grape varieties of France's Bordeaux, Alsace, and Rhône Valley regions; Oregon's Willamette Valley is dedicated to the grapes that made Burgundy famous; and British Columbia crafts ice wines like those of Germany and Austria. Throughout the microclimates of the Northwest, the noble varieties of the world thrive, be it France or Germany, Italy or Spain, Austria or Portugal.

In this section you will find introductions of the most significant grape varieties grown in the Northwest, along with a list of the top producers for each.

CABERNET FRANC

In most of the wine world, Cabernet Franc is often overlooked. Used primarily as a blending grape in Bordeaux and California, Cabernet Franc is finding its own voice in the Northwest, and for good reason. Done well, it exhibits all the wonderful aromas and flavors of Cabernet Sauvignon without the often-biting tannins. Cabernet Franc is bottled as a separate variety primarily in British Columbia and Washington, a trend that wine lovers hope will continue.

Here are a few of the top wineries producing great Cabernet Franc:

Abacela Vineyards, Roseburg, Oregon
Inniskillin Okanagan, Oliver, B.C.
Lost Mountain Winery, Sequim, Washington
Patrick M. Paul Vineyards, Walla Walla, Washington
Sorensen Cellars, Port Townsend, Washington
Sumac Ridge Estate Winery, Summerland, B.C.

CABERNET SAUVIGNON

Cabernet Sauvignon (nickname: Cab) is the king of red wines. Traditionally the basis for the great red Bordeaux of France, Cab helped California's Napa Valley rise to prominence in recent decades. Fortunately, it also excels in the Pacific Northwest, especially Washington's Columbia Valley.

Cab can take on a number of forms, from sleek and elegant to bold and brash. It is, perhaps, the most ageable wine, though most Northwest Cab is ready to consume soon after it's released.

In Washington's arid Columbia Valley, the most prized regions ⊔r growing Cab are Red Mountain, the Horse Heaven Hills, the ⊔hluke Slope, and the Walla Walla Valley.

In addition to Washington, other Northwest regions that are emerging as Cab-producing areas are Oregon's Rogue Valley, Idaho's Snake River Valley, and British Columbia's southern Okanagan Valley, particularly the Black Sage Bench.

As you explore Northwest Cabernet Sauvignon, start with these top producers:

Andrake Cellars, Olympia, Washington
Columbia Crest, Paterson, Washington
Dunham Cellars, Walla Walla, Washington
Kettle Valley Winery, Naramata, B.C.
L'Ecole No. 41, Lowden, Washington
Leonetti Cellar, Walla Walla, Washington
Quilceda Creek Vintners, Snoqualmie, Washington
Reininger Winery, Walla Walla, Washington
Sandhill Winery, Benton City, Washington
Soos Creek Wine Cellars, Kent, Washington
Sorensen Cellars, Port Townsend, Washington
Woodward Canyon Winery, Lowden, Washington

CHARDONNAY

America's favorite wine is Chardonnay, and nearly every winery makes it because winemakers are guaranteed to be able to sell it, no matter how mediocre it might be. As is true elsewhere, Northwest Chardonnays range from the fat and buttery to the lean and crisp. Washington's Columbia Valley would appear to have the upper hand in producing the Northwest's consistently best Chardonnays, but Oregon vintners are doing the most serious work with clonal selection and are beginning to emerge as having the greatest potential to match their Burgundian cousins with great Chardonnay.

Here are some of the region's most consistent producers:

Arbor Crest Wine Cellars, Spokane, Washington
Chateau Ste. Michelle, Woodinville, Washington
Columbia Crest, Paterson, Washington
Domaine Drouhin Oregon, Dundee, Oregon
Eola Hills Wine Cellars, Rickreall, Oregon
Gordon Brothers Cellars, Pasco, Washington
Pend d'Oreille Winery, Sandpoint, Idaho
Woodward Canyon Winery, Lowden, Washington

GEWÜRZTRAMINER

Hard to pronounce, easy to love, this classic white grape is commonly associated with the Alsace region of France. Gewürztraminer is wildly aromatic, with notes of grapefruits, oranges, ar nutmeg, and often is just slightly sweet. It's also notoriously low acidity, so many Gewürztraminers are delicious sippers and are especially enjoyable at the end of a hot day or as a brunch wine. Those with good acidity will pair well with spicier dishes, such as mild curries, Thai, or Tex-Mex, and are also a classic with Thanksgiving fare, such as turkey.

Gewürztraminer was one of the early stars in the Pacific Northwest because it performs well in cooler climates, and many delicious examples are still produced, including those by:

Canoe Ridge Vineyards, Walla Walla, Washington
Hogue Cellars, Prosser, Washington
Seth Ryan Winery, Benton City, Washington
Sumac Ridge Estate Winery, Summerland, B.C.
Tinhorn Creek Vineyards, Oliver, B.C.
Tyee Wine Cellars, Corvallis, Oregon
Weisinger's of Ashland, Ashland, Oregon
Wild Goose Vineyards, Okanagan Falls, B.C.

ICE WINE

Ice wine is a sweet nectar, a gift from Mother Nature. It is made when grapes are left on the vines well past traditional harvest dates—sometimes early into the next year—until winter conditions freeze them. When this happens, winery workers trudge through the snow in the middle of the night to pick the marblelike fruit so it can be pressed to create an ultra-sweet dessert wine.

The best ice wines hold their acidity so the wine shows balance of fruit and sugar without tasting too much like syrup. And true ice wines occur naturally—that is, they are left to freeze on the vine rather than picked and frozen in a cold room.

British Columbia is the Northwest's premier producer of ice wine, and consumers can count on these to be true ice wines. A handful of Washington wineries also will make ice wines when conditions allow. Though ice wine can be made with any grape variety (including reds), the most successful are Riesling and a rare variety called Ehrenfelser.

Here are a few producers to start with:

Gehringer Brothers Estate Winery, Oliver, B.C.
Hawthorne Mountain Vineyards, Okanagan Falls, B.C.
Hyatt Vineyards, Zillah, Washington
Jackson-Triggs Vintners, Oliver, B.C.
Kiona Vineyards Winery, Benton City, Washington
Mission Hill Family Estate, Westbank, B.C.
Quails' Gate Estate Winery, Kelowna, B.C.
Summerhill Estate Winery, Kelowna, B.C.
Tinhorn Creek Vineyards, Oliver, B.C.

LATE HARVEST

Appreciation for sweeter wines can present a paradox. Late Harvest wines are often entrées for wine appreciation, then are eschewed for dry whites and reds. But then a funny thing happens: Sweeter wines—especially serious efforts rather than sugar bombs—become sought after, even treasured. Some of the world's greatest wines—Sauternes from Bordeaux—are the most expensive.

In the Northwest, several wineries will make Late Harvest wines to attract both ends of the spectrum. And often they are great bargains that are perfect for enjoying at the end of a summer day, in the hot tub, or with dessert.

Looking to indulge in a high-quality Late Harvest? Here are a few wineries to look for:

Bainbridge Island Winery, Bainbridge Island, Washington
Claar Cellars, Pasco, Washington
Eola Hills Wine Cellars, Rickreall, Oregon
Hogue Cellars, Prosser, Washington
Tualatin Estate, Turner, Oregon

LEMBERGER

Outside of Washington, Lemberger is hardly heard of. This wonderfully jammy fruit has nothing to do with stinky cheese and is traditionally at home in Austria, where it's known as Blaufrankish. That explains why some Northwest wineries have tried to market their Lemberger under other names, such as Blue Franc.

Find a good Lemberger, and you'll find it to be fruit-driven and eminently food-friendly. Here are a few to look up:

Hawthorne Mountain Vineyards, Okanagan Falls, B.C.
Hogue Cellars, Prosser, Washington
Kiona Vineyards Winery, Benton City, Washington
Oakwood Cellars, Benton City, Washington
Thurston Wolfe Winery, Prosser, Washington

MERLOT

This luscious and versatile red wine finds its traditional home in France's Bordeaux region, usually blended with Cabernet Sauvignon and Cabernet Franc. And while plenty is grown throughout the New World, Washington Merlot is generally recognized as one of the very best.

Merlot can be supple and approachable or big and biting hallmark is bright, rich fruit and food-friendly flavors of che raspberries, sweet spices, chocolate, and herbs.

In addition to Washington, other emerging Northwest Merlot regions include Oregon's Rogue Valley, Idaho's Snake River Valley, and British Columbia's Okanagan Valley.

To begin your exploration of Northwest Merlot, start with these top producers:

Andrake Cellars, Olympia, Washington
Barnard Griffin, Richland, Washington
Canoe Ridge Vineyard, Walla Walla, Washington
Cañon de Sol Winery, Benton City, Washington
Chateau Ste. Michelle, Woodinville, Washington
Chinook Wines, Prosser, Washington
Columbia Crest, Paterson, Washington
E. B. Foote Winery, Burien, Washington
Hells Canyon Winery, Caldwell, Idaho
L'Ecole No. 41, Lowden, Washington
Leonetti Cellar, Walla Walla, Washington
Northstar, Walla Walla, Washington
Reininger Winery, Walla Walla, Washington
Tamarack Cellars, Walla Walla, Washington
Walla Walla Vintners, Walla Walla, Washington
Wineglass Cellars, Zillah, Washington

PINOT GRIS

Virtually unknown elsewhere in the world, Pinot Gris is the defining white wine in Oregon, even displacing Chardonnay in total acres. Thank goodness—because this crisp, fruit-laden wine goes so well with the fresh seafood that is prevalent in Portland restaurants. It's noted for its tropical and citrus fruit aromas and flavors and shows off a few buttery notes even when it gets nowhere near oak.

Pinot Gris is starting to catch on in Washington, British Columbia, and Idaho, but Oregon is where this budding star shines. Here are a few wineries making delicious Gris:

Adelsheim Vineyard, Newberg, Oregon
Elk Cove Vineyards, Gaston, Oregon
Flerchinger Vineyards, Hood River, Oregon
King Estate, Eugene, Oregon
Red Rooster Winery, Naramata, B.C.
Rex Hill Vineyards, Newberg, Oregon
Winter's Hill Vineyard, Lafayette, Oregon

PINOT NOIR

Perhaps the most difficult wine to grow, craft, and learn to love is the noble red grape of Burgundy. But, oh, when you find a great Pinot, you may well spend the rest of your life searching for a holy grail of sorts. Selecting a region's top producers is almost impossible because of the more than two hundred Northwest wineries that make Pinot Noir, there are at least as many opinions about true varietal style. In the Northwest—and perhaps anywhere in the world outside Burgundy—Oregon is the proudest producer of Pinot Noir. Just like the grape, the Willamette Valley can be maddening: In dry vintages, the wines are seductive and powerful, but if Mother Nature dampens the harvest, Pinot lovers will be disappointed with all but the best or most fortunate producers. British Columbia's Okanagan Valley is emerging as a region that can produce good Pinot Noir. The central Okanagan is cool and dry enough to have the potential for stellar wines. Almost no Pinot Noir is made in Washington or Idaho.

Searching for great Pinot Noir is more than a journey—it's an odyssey. To begin yours, consider these wineries:

Amity Vineyards, Amity, Oregon
Beaux Frères, Newberg, Oregon
Belle Pente Winery, Carlton, Oregon
Benton-Lane Winery, Monroe, Oregon
Blue Mountain Vineyards, Okanagan Falls, B.C.
Brick House Wines, Newberg, Oregon
CedarCreek Estate Winery, Kelowna, B.C.
Cristom, Salem, Oregon
Domaine Drouhin Oregon, Dundee, Oregon
Ken Wright Cellars, Carlton, Oregon
Patricia Green Cellars, Newberg, Oregon
Penner-Ash Cellars, Newberg, Oregon
Rex Hill Vineyards, Newberg, Oregon
Winter's Hill Vineyard, Lafayette, Oregon
Witness Tree Vineyards, Salem, Oregon

PORT

Port is a dessert wine—often red—that is made by stopping fermentation with brandy. The result is a sweet wine that is high in alcohol. A little goes a long way, and Ports often get better with age. They're a great way to finish off a long winter's day, and they pair well with chocolate, Stilton and, of course, cigars.

Few Northwest wineries make Ports, and those doing the best job include:

Hinzerling Winery, Prosser, Washington

Laurel Ridge Winery, Carlton, Oregon
Tefft Cellars, Outlook, Washington
Thurston Wolfe Winery, Prosser, Washington
Wild Goose Vineyards, Okanagan Falls, B.C.
Wind River Cellars, Husum, Washington

RED BLENDS

In Bordeaux, few red wines are 100 percent of one grape variety. Instead, they are blends of Cabernet Sauvignon, Merlot, Cabernet Franc, Petit Verdot, and Malbec. In the Northwest, vintners often will blend varieties together with great success. For example, the fruitiness of Merlot and the richness of Cabernet Sauvignon can prove to be better together than apart.

Blends can be known by various names, such as the name of the grapes used (Cab–Merlot) or words that have significance, such as cuvée (indicating a blend) or Meritage.

Northwest wineries that understand the importance of blends and are creating world-class reds as a result include:

Andrew Will Winery, Vashon, Washington
Cadence Winery, Seattle, Washington
DeLille Cellars, Woodinville, Washington
Fidelitas, Kennewick, Washington
Hedges Cellars, Benton City, Washington
L'Ecole No. 41, Lowden, Washington
Pend d'Oreille Winery, Sandpoint, Idaho
Sumac Ridge Estate Winery, Summerland, B.C.
Waterbrook Winery, Walla Walla, Washington
Weisinger's of Ashland, Ashland, Oregon

RIESLING

When the industry was in its infancy, Riesling was king in Washington. That's because most thought the Evergreen State was too cold to grow anything else. While that has been proven to be a folly, the Northwest continues to excel with this classic German and Alsatian variety. And when Mother Nature gets cranky with Washington vintners, Riesling proves to be a savior that can thrive in the most bitter winters.

In fact, Riesling does well throughout the Northwest and also makes wonderful dessert wines. Here are a few Riesling producers to keep an eye out for:

Bookwalter Winery, Richland, Washington
Chateau Ste. Michelle, Woodinville, Washington
Jerchinger Vineyards, Hood River, Oregon
gue Cellars, Prosser, Washington

Indian Creek Winery, Kuna, Idaho
Kiona Vineyards Winery, Benton City, Washington
Pinot Reach Cellars, Kelowna, B.C.
Ste. Chapelle, Caldwell, Idaho

SANGIOVESE

Italy's most famous grape—the main component of the humble Chianti and the superb Super-Tuscan—is finding a home in the Northwest, particularly Washington's Columbia Valley. Though unlikely to be anything more than a minor player, Sangiovese nonetheless plays a strong role by offering a delicious and food-friendly alternative to Cabernet Sauvignon and Merlot.

Wineries that are doing a great job with Sangiovese include:
Columbia Winery, Woodinville, Washington
Leonetti Cellar, Walla Walla, Washington
Tefft Cellars, Outlook, Washington
Three Rivers Winery, Walla Walla, Washington
Thurston Wolfe Winery, Prosser, Washington
Walla Walla Vintners, Walla Walla, Washington

SAUVIGNON BLANC

This suave white wine has gained fame and following in recent years, especially in France, California, and New Zealand. It is especially prized when it exhibits aromas of mulberries and—believe it or not—cat pee. In the Northwest, Sauvignon Blanc tends to be more fruit-driven and elegant and is a delicious match with our region's fresh seafood. For marketing purposes, Sauvignon Blanc also is known as Fumé Blanc.

When exploring Northwest Sauvignon Blancs, here are a few wineries to start with:
Barnard Griffin, Richland, Washington
Chateau Ste. Michelle, Woodinville, Washington
Mission Hill Family Estates, Westbank, B.C.

SEMILLON

Lost amid the national thirst for Chardonnay and the Northwest's interest in Pinot Gris and Riesling, Semillon quietly has built a base of fans who enjoy a versatile, delicious, and food-friendly white wine. Semillon is one of two key white grapes (with Sauvignon Blanc) in classic White Bordeaux, and Washington in particular ca produce Semillon as good as any in the world. Often richly str tured with fig and tropical notes, Semillon can imitate Chardor if aged in oak. It pairs well with seafood and chicken.

Some of the Northwest's top Semillon producers are:

L'Ecole No. 41, Lowden, Washington
Washington Hills Cellars, Sunnyside, Washington
Woodward Canyon Winery, Lowden, Washington

SPARKLING WINES

Often associated with celebrations, sparkling wines actually are quite agile food wines that are appropriate under many circumstances. Made famous in France's Champagne region, sparkling wines are made using many methods. The best and most labor-intensive is *methode champenoise,* in which the second fermentation—the one that creates the bubbles—occurs in the bottle.

Only a handful of Northwest wineries specialize in sparkling wines, and a few others make them as part of their lineups. If you love bubblies, here are a few to seek out:

Argyle Winery, Dundee, Oregon
Domaine Meriwether, Eugene, Oregon
Domaine Ste. Michelle, Paterson, Washington
Pinot Reach Cellars, Kelowna, B.C.
Ste. Chapelle, Caldwell, Idaho
Sumac Ridge Estate Winery, Summerland, B.C.
Summerhill Estate Winery, Kelowna, B.C.

SYRAH

Syrah is the red grape that defines the northern Rhône Valley in France as well as much of the continent of Australia (where it's called Shiraz). And it is beginning to define the Pacific Northwest, particularly Washington's Columbia Valley. The Syrahs coming out of Red Mountain and the Yakima and Walla Walla Valleys are powerful yet approachable and may just be the best red grapes for the region.

Outside of Washington, Oregon's Rogue Valley and British Columbia's southern Okanagan Valley have great potential for producing lush, ripe Syrah. And in Idaho, Snake River Valley vintners also are bullish on the grape.

Many grape growers and wineries are jumping on the Syrah bandwagon, so consumers will have little problem finding delicious examples. Those crafting consistently great Syrah include:

Betz Family Winery, Woodinville, Washington
Cayuse Vineyards, Walla Walla, Washington
Columbia Winery, Woodinville, Washington
DeLille Cellars, Woodinville, Washington
L'Ecole No. 41, Lowden, Washington
Lost Mountain Winery, Sequim, Washington
McCrea Cellars, Rainier, Washington
Reininger Winery, Walla Walla, Washington

VIOGNIER

This classic white grape of France's Rhône Valley has become extremely fashionable in the Northwest—and for good reason. It's a delicious and food-friendly wine that shows off exotic aromatics and delicious flavors. Viognier sometimes is blended into Syrah during the early winemaking process, giving the classic Rhône red even more provocative aromas. Those looking for an alternative to Chardonnay will find Viognier an excellent match with shellfish, salmon, chicken, and more.

Viognier seems to perform well in the Northwest, so you can expect to find more and more wineries producing it. Here are a few to start with:

Griffin Creek, Turner, Oregon
McCrea Cellars, Rainier, Washington
Waterbrook Winery, Walla Walla, Washington

WHITE BLENDS

Though not as fashionable as single-variety whites, many wineries find success with white blends. One of the most delicious is Semillon and Chardonnay, first made popular in Australia. Of equal interest are classic white Bordeaux-style blends using Semillon and Sauvignon Blanc. Often, these blends will fill in holes (such as flavors, acidity, or mouth feel) that each variety by itself might have, so consumers end up with a much more enjoyable wine that is more likely to pair well with food.

If you want to explore white blends, these wineries are good places to start:

Columbia Crest, Paterson, Washington
DeLille Cellars, Woodinville, Washington
McCrea Cellars, Rainier, Washington
San Juan Vineyards, Friday Harbor, Washington
Sumac Ridge Estate Winery, Summerland, B.C.
Thurston Wolfe Winery, Prosser, Washington
Woodward Canyon Winery, Walla Walla, Washington

WASHINGTON WINES & WINERIES

Washington, the nation's second-largest wine-producing state, has gained global prominence—and for good reason: It might just be the best place on Earth to grow wine grapes.

Many people still envision the Evergreen State as a place of gray skies, constant drizzle, and great coffee. Often overlooked is arid Eastern Washington, a vast, inhospitable-looking desert that is practically devoid of precipitation and perfect for growing world-class wine grapes.

In the early days of the Washington wine industry, naysayers from California thought Washington was too cold, too wet, and too far north to grow serious wine grapes. However, Washington is at the same latitude as the great wine-growing regions of France and Germany and in summer has long, hot days and cool nights.

With the success and growth of the industry, Washington has shown itself to be a top wine region. A total of more than two hundred wineries now dot every corner of the state. Nearly all the grapes are grown in the Columbia Valley, though only about half the wineries are near the vineyards. The rest are in and near Seattle, stretched along the Interstate 5 corridor, and in the Spokane area. It is unusual to have so many wineries so far away from where the grapes are grown, but it's also convenient for those living in the major population areas of Seattle and Spokane.

In the 1960s and 1970s, Washington was best known for white wines, including Riesling, Gewürztraminer, and Chenin Blanc, because most thought that was what would grow here. But in the '80s and '90s, classic Bordeaux varieties took root, with Merlot becoming the dominant red grape, and the state's most famous. Other red varieties of note include Cabernet Sauvignon, Cabernet Franc, Lemberger, Sangiovese, and Syrah. The last-named has become a darling in recent years and may well prove to be the red grape most suited for Washington.

For white wines, Chardonnay is king (as it is in California). But other varieties have gained footholds, including Semillon, Sauvignon Blanc, Pinot Gris, and Viognier. Riesling and Gewürztraminer continue to have a strong, even growing, following.

The federal government has granted Washington five American Viticultural Areas (AVAs), or appellations. The largest by far is the Columbia Valley, which contains three appellations within it.

Washington Appellations

Columbia Valley. This huge area stretches from Wapato in the west to Walla Walla in the east. The Columbia Valley dips into Oregon from The Dalles to Milton-Freewater. It holds more than 99 percent of the state's vineyards and has room for much more.

Yakima Valley. Washington's oldest appellation is the western part of the Columbia Valley, stretching from Wapato to Benton City. It tends to be a little cooler than other areas of the Columbia Valley and could end up being a key area for growing Syrah.

Red Mountain. Washington's newest and smallest appellation is in the eastern Yakima Valley near Benton City. It's neither red nor a mountain. Rather, it's a west-facing ridge that is one of the warmer viticulture sites in the state. It holds just a few hundred acres of grapes and is prized for its red varieties.

Walla Walla Valley. The eastern part of the Columbia Valley is home to some of the state's most celebrated wineries. The appellation dips into Oregon where, in fact, some of the region's top vineyards are located. The valley is warm, and its namesake city has rejuvenated itself into a fine destination.

Puget Sound. Though large in area, this appellation around Seattle actually holds few grapes. Vineyards are scattered on Bainbridge Island, the San Juans, the Olympic Peninsula, and near the Canadian border. This is cool-climate viticulture that produces wines of distinction that often pair well with seafood.

Washington Subappellations and Regions of Interest

While not appellations at this time, these key grape-growing areas may well earn AVA status one day.

Wahluke Slope. This area west of the Hanford Nuclear Reservation is gaining prominence as vineyards replace orchards. The grapes are prized because it's a warm area that produces wines of depth and distinction.

Canoe Ridge and Alderdale. In the eastern Columbia Gorge, these two ridges are proving to be great grape-growing areas. They are warm and consistently produce properly ripened grapes. Several top wineries see a strong future for this area.

Columbia Gorge. Continuing west from Alderdale are several smaller pockets of vineyard that hold great potential. Though only a small amount of Zinfandel is planted in the Northwest, much of it is in the Gorge, and it's proving to be a great place to grow Zin because of its warmth.

Horse Heaven Hills. Primarily known for its dryland wheat farming, this area south of the Yakima Valley is home to some key vineyards.

Columbia–Cascade. This young wine region in the center of th state around Wenatchee is emerging as vineyards replace orchar

Already, more than a dozen wineries have popped up, and this small band of vintners is proving itself with high-quality early efforts.

Key Washington Vineyards

Klipsun Vineyard (Red Mountain). The state's most prominent vineyard is best known for growing fabulous Cabernet Sauvignon, Merlot, and Sauvignon Blanc. It supplies grapes to no fewer than fifteen wineries throughout the Northwest. Wines made with Klipsun fruit tend to be tight in their youth and to blossom with age.

Champoux Vineyards (Horse Heaven Hills). Pronounced "shampoo," this is the famed Mercer Ranch Vineyard that was planted in the early 1970s. Paul Champoux now owns and runs the vineyard. He has four winery partners (Andrew Will, Quilceda Creek, Powers, and Woodward Canyon) and also sells grapes to more than a dozen other wineries.

Boushey Vineyard (Yakima Valley). Dick Boushey focuses almost exclusively on red grapes. His Syrah is used by some of the state's top small producers. Any Boushey Vineyard–designated wine is well worth seeking out.

Cold Creek Vineyard (near the Wahluke Slope). Owned by Stimson Lane, this vineyard north of the Yakima Valley sends nearly all its fruit to Chateau Ste. Michelle. It produces classic varieties and is best known for achieving some of the most powerful Chardonnays in the Northwest.

Sagemoor Vineyards (Columbia Valley). This is one of the state's oldest vineyards; grapes from this site north of Pasco are used by many of Washington's top producers. Look for vineyard-designated wines from Bacchus and Dionysus, which are part of Sagemoor.

Seven Hills Vineyard (Walla Walla Valley). Technically speaking, this vineyard is in Oregon (just barely), but it's most often associated with Washington because its grapes are used by many Walla Walla Valley producers. Wines from Seven Hills Vineyard grapes tend to be rich, deep, and lusty.

Ciel du Cheval (Red Mountain). Just across the road from Kiona Vineyards Winery, Ciel du Cheval is known for growing Syrah and Cabernet Sauvignon of great distinction. A Ciel du Cheval–designated wine is a guarantee of quality. Two key wineries, DeLille Cellars and Quilceda Creek Vintners, think so much of the site that they planted their own vines on previously unused portions of the vineyard.

Red Willow Vineyard (Yakima Valley). Owner Mike Sauer has a long and storied relationship with Columbia Winery in Woodinville. Sauer and winemaker David Lake have worked together since the early '80s to produce many celebrated red wines. Perhaps of greatest importance, Sauer planted the state's first significant Syrah vineyard, in the mid-'80s.

Celilo Vineyard (Columbia Gorge). This vineyard near Husum grows vaunted Chardonnay that is sought by top Washington and Oregon wineries, including Woodward Canyon and Ken Wright Cellars.

AMBROSIA BY KRISTY

SEATTLE AREA   ESTABLISHED 1997

Kristina Anderson of University Place, near Tacoma, launched her mead-only operation in the mid-'90s and can hardly make her sweet honey wine fast enough to keep up with the market. As a history major in college, Anderson learned about mead but couldn't find any. After a friend gave her some homemade mead, she was hooked and launched Ambrosia by Kristy.

BEST BETS

Honey wine $ This sweet, refreshing mead is a distinctive drink with wonderfully bright aromas and silky flavors. Serve chilled or simmered with spices.

WHERE TO BUY: GROCERY STORES

4921 85th Ave. W., University Place, WA 98467; 253-307-5156; www.amead.com. Not open to the public.

ANDRAKE CELLARS

SEATTLE AREA   ESTABLISHED 1997

Owner/winemaker Bob Andrake crafts thick, concentrated Bordeaux-style wines, primarily from top Red Mountain vineyards. Using only free-run juice (juice taken from crushed grapes before they are pressed), Andrake's wines are built to last and, in fact, don't always show their best right away. If you have patience, a cellar, and a taste for great reds, buy Andrake wines whenever possible. And the juice he presses goes into his second label, Hurricane Ridge.

BEST BETS

Cabernet Sauvignon $$$ A perfect example of what Andrake strives to achieve, this big red is an age-worthy wine showing off concentrated aromas of black currants, blackberries, bittersweet chocolate, and chewy tannins. Enjoy now with a fat-rippled steak or cellar for a decade or more.

Merlot $$ Andrake doesn't rely on a lot of oak to bowl over wine lovers, and this jammy Merlot is a good example with its extracted berry flavors, smoky vanilla undertones, light spice, and rich tannins.

Reserve Cuvée $$$ A Bordeaux-style blend that shows off Andrake's winemaking technique. It's a bold yet elegant red with rich, concentrated flavors, superb balance, and excellent cellar potential.

WHERE TO BUY: WINERY, WINE SHOPS

4309 Glen Terra Drive S.E., Olympia, WA 98506; 360-943-3746. Open by appointment.

ANDREW WILL WINERY

SEATTLE AREA   ESTABLISHED 1989

In a secluded corner of Vashon Island, Chris Camarda crafts some of Washington's most highly regarded Bordeaux-style wines. Camarda, who has served as mentor to some of the state's brightest young winemakers, focuses on vineyard-designated wines, primarily from some of the state's best vineyards, including Pepper Bridge, Seven Hills, Klipsun, Ciel du Cheval, and Champoux. He is a partner in the latter, along with Quilceda Creek, Powers, and Woodward Canyon. Camarda also crafts Syrah, Sangiovese, a table wine, and Pinot Gris. Keep an eye out for his newest label, Cuvée Lucia, which features many of his non-Bordeaux style wines.

BEST BETS

Champoux $$$ Camarda is moving toward Bordeaux blends that will be named after the vineyard, not the grape variety. This is the first, and it's typical Champoux: dense, rich, and powerful. The blend of Cabernet Sauvignon, Merlot, and Cabernet Franc will pair well now with a rare ribeye or age gracefully for a decade or more.

Sorella $$$$ A blend primarily from Champoux Vineyard fruit, this is a rich, elegant red with surreal aromas and complex flavors. The pinnacle of Andrew Will.

Sheridan Vineyard Cabernet Sauvignon $$$ From Sheridan Vineyard in the Yakima Valley, this is a richly aromatic wine with light vanilla aromas, massive black fruit, and black pepper undertones.

Klipsun Vineyard Cabernet Sauvignon $$$ Telltale blackberry and vanilla aromas with rich, penetrating flavors. Buy this for your cellar, as it will really show its stuff a half-decade or more after vintage.

Ciel du Cheval Cabernet Sauvignon $$$ A delicate and elegant wine from a classic vineyard on Red Mountain. Delightful cherry and violet aromas with tangy berry, blueberry, and smoky vanilla flavors. A great wine that should be paired with the finest cuts of beef.

WHERE TO BUY: WINE SHOPS

12526 S.W. Bank Road, Vashon, WA 98070; 206-463-3290. Not open to the public.

ARBOR CREST WINE CELLARS

SPOKANE   ESTABLISHED 1982

It's exciting to witness the emergence of a talented young winemaker. This is the case with Kristina Mielke-van Löben Sels, the second generation to make wine at Arbor Crest. The winery gained a following for its top-grade Sauvignon Blanc, though the "A" list has expanded since Kristina took over winemaking duties in 1999. In addition to some of the Northwest's best Chardonnays, Arbor Crest is crafting world-class reds, including Cabernet Franc, Merlot, and Syrah.

BEST BETS

Chardonnay $ One of the best steals in Washington white wines is this perfectly balanced Chardonnay. Light oak treatment gives backbone while allowing the fabulous fruit to show through. And don't forget the Conner Lee Vineyard Chardonnay.

Cabernet Franc $ This often-overlooked red offers huge aromas and rich black fruit flavors with sweet, supple tannins.

Merlot $$ An outstanding wine with bright, approachable fruit, complex flavors, and a smooth finish. A great match with lamb, beef, or pasta.

Syrah $$ A tremendous wine with inviting aromas, succulent fruit, layers of complexity, and light oak undertones.

WHERE TO BUY: WINERY, WINE SHOPS, GROCERY STORES

4705 N. Fruithill Road, Spokane, WA 99217; 509-927-9463; www.arborcrest.com. Open daily.

AUSTIN ROBAIRE VINTNERS

SEATTLE AREA   ESTABLISHED 1999

The Boeing Wine Club continues to give Washington many top winemakers, and Ron Yabut is a club graduate. The Boeing engineer and his wife, Lorraine, released their first wine, a delicious Cabernet Sauvignon, in 2001 and will expand into Syrah, Nebbiolo, Pinot Noir, and a Viognier-Chardonnay blend in future releases. Like many boutique Woodinville wineries, Austin Robaire has gotten its start in a business park and welcomes visitors by appointment.

BEST BETS

Cabernet Sauvignon $$ An appealing red with rich berry, currant, and vanilla aromas, and mouth-filling flavors with wonderful depth and a pleasing finish. Drink now with a thick steak or hold for a half-decade or longer.

WHERE TO BUY: WINERY, WINE SHOPS

19501 144th Ave. N.E., Suite D-800, Woodinville, WA 98072; 206-406-0360; www.austinrobaire.com. Open by appointment.

BADGER MOUNTAIN VINEYARD / POWERS WINERY

TRI-CITIES   ESTABLISHED 1982

The father-son duo of Bill and Greg Powers offers two styles of wines. The flagship Powers brand offers high-quality, cost-conscious reds and whites, while the Badger Mountain wines are 100 percent organic with limited sulfites. The winery's lineup is a dizzying array of Cabernet Sauvignon, Merlot, Syrah, Pinot Noir (from Columbia Valley fruit), Cabernet Franc, Chardonnay, Sauvignon Blanc, Muscat Canelli, and more. The wines are consistently good and often excellent while priced for everyday enjoyment.

BEST BETS

Cab–Merlot $ Flavorful blend of two favorites, this is approachable and delicious, with good tannins for food matching.

Mercer Ranch Vineyard Cabernet Sauvignon $$ A classy Cab from a classic Columbia Gorge vineyard, this is a rich red with superior fruit and oak integration that may be the best Powers wine. This tends to be a little tight in its youth, so consider cellaring.

Muscat Canelli $ Perhaps the most popular Powers wine, this perfect brunch sipper offers lovely aromatics, nice sweetness, and exotic fruit flavors.

Quinta da Ranco Mercer Port $$ A red dessert wine from the old Mercer Ranch Vineyard (now called Champoux Vineyard), this is one of the best winter sippers you'll find. Match with Stilton.

WHERE TO BUY: WINERY, WINE SHOPS, GROCERY STORES

1106 S. Jurupa St., Kennewick, WA 99338; 509-627-4986; www. badgermtnvineyard.com. Open daily.

BAINBRIDGE ISLAND VINEYARDS & WINERY

PUGET SOUND   ESTABLISHED 1977

The driving force behind establishing the Puget Sound viticultural area, Gerard and Jo Ann Bentryn are fiercely proud of their ability to grow and craft delicious wines entirely from estate-grown grapes. The Bentryns focus on small lots of cool-climate varieties, which they produce with love and care. They also make strawberry and raspberry wines from island-grown fruit.

BEST BETS

Late Harvest Siegerrebe $$ This rare wine may be one of the best dessert wines in the Pacific Northwest. Spiciness from botrytis (noble rot) combines with flavors of richly honeyed nectarines, pears, apricots, and more.

Müller-Thurgau $ Bainbridge Island makes two styles of wine from Germany's most popular grape. One is dry with a hint of oak aging. The other is off-dry and shows some of its Riesling origins with orchard fruit flavors. Both match well with shellfish, chicken, pork, or turkey.

Ferryboat White $ This popular blend of four varieties is slightly sweet with crisp fruit aromas and flavors and is a perfect picnic wine.

Strawberry $ Released each year in time for Christmas, this spectacular fruit wine is a delicious after-dinner sipper that complements French vanilla ice cream.

WHERE TO BUY: WINERY, WINE SHOPS

682 Hwy. 305, Bainbridge Island, WA 98110; 206-842-9463. Seasonal hours.

BALCOM & MOE WINES

TRI-CITIES   ESTABLISHED 1985

Longtime grape grower Maury Balcom is a third-generation farmer who manages 150 acres of grapes and 3,000 acres of other crops in the Columbia Basin. He produces several styles of classic wine varieties, all of which are highly regarded by discerning consumers.

BEST BETS

Sangiovese $$ A delicious red showing berry aromas with herbal hints and flavors of chocolate, cherry, and berry. A smooth, easy-drinking wine to enjoy with lasagna.

Cabernet Sauvignon $$ A first-class red that provides rich oak and berry aromas and lush, deep, complex flavors, including blackberries, black currants, vanilla, and sweet spice. Match with lamb or prime rib.

Merlot $$ A rich, flavorful wine showing off classic varietal tendencies, including long blackberries, sweet oak spices, cherries, and vanilla. Plenty of tannins and fine balance give this good ageability.

WHERE TO BUY: WINERY, WINE SHOPS, GROCERY STORES

2520 Commercial Ave., Pasco, WA 99301; 509-547-7307. Open by appointment.

BARNARD GRIFFIN

TRI-CITIES   ESTABLISHED 1983

For a guy who has been making wine as long as anyone in Washington, Rob Griffin maintains youthful looks and energy. Griffin came to Washington in 1977 to make wine for Preston Premium Wines, then moved to Hogue Cellars when it started in the early '80s. He and his wife, Deborah Barnard, began making their own brand while he was at Hogue, which he left in the early '90s to focus on his own winery. Barnard Griffin wines are consistently some of the best in the North-

west. And because they tend to be underpriced for the quality, these wines are among the best bargains around.

BEST BETS

Cabernet Sauvignon $$ Year in and year out, Rob Griffin's Cabs are richly aromatic, with great structure, fruit, and oak integration.

Fumé Blanc $ This dry-style Sauvignon Blanc shows plenty of fruit melding with bright herbal notes and a rich mouth feel.

Syrah $$$ One of the best Syrahs you're likely to come across, this is a big, thick red with tons of character and complexity. It tends to be in short supply, so buy it when you can.

Zinfandel $$$ Zin is a rarity in the Northwest, and this beauty from Columbia Gorge grapes has all the lush fruit of a California Zin with plenty of structure.

WHERE TO BUY: WINERY, WINE SHOPS, GROCERY STORES

878 Tulip Lane, Richland, WA 99352; 509-627-0266; www.barnard griffin.com. Open daily.

BETZ FAMILY WINERY

SEATTLE AREA   ESTABLISHED 1997

One of the classiest characters in the Washington wine industry is Bob Betz, a longtime executive for Stimson Lane who has been a driving force behind such Chateau Ste. Michelle international collaborations as Col Solare and Eroica. Betz, who earned the prestigious Master of Wine degree in 1998, launched his own small operation to express his style of winemaking. He and his wife, Cathy, focus on red wines from Washington's Columbia Valley, and the results are cellar-worthy efforts of great promise and intensity. Additionally, the Betzes import Italian olive oil and balsamic vinegar.

BEST BETS

Cabernet Sauvignon $$$ A big, classic wine showing off the best of the king of red wine. Black fruit abounds with layers of complexity and well-managed oak. Big tannins give it plenty of structure.

La Serenne $$ This Syrah from venerable Red Mountain is a rich, luscious wine with huge, ripe black fruit, and minimal oak that allows the variety to shine. Named for a French term for the grape.

Clos de Betz $$ A Bordeaux-style blend with more Merlot than Cabernet Sauvignon that shows off bright fruit and spice aromas and a rich, complex mouth feel.

WHERE TO BUY: WINERY, WINE SHOPS

18512 142nd Ave. N.E., Woodinville, WA 98072; 425-415-1751; www.betzfamilywinery.com. Open by appointment.

BLACK DIAMOND WINERY

OLYMPIC PENINSULA   ESTABLISHED 2000

In the hills high above Port Angeles, Sharon Adams crafts a variety of tasty fruit and grape wines. When estate vineyards begin to bear, she'll add Müller-Thurgau, Madeleine Sylvaner, and Madeleine Angevine to her repertoire. Though she specializes in fruit wines, don't overlook her delicious Syrah from Columbia Valley grapes.

BEST BETS

Syrah $$ A rich, jammy red with classic plum and blackberry flavors and hints of vanilla. A tasty, approachable wine to enjoy with lamb or beef.

Red Currant $ Taste this blind and you might mistake it for a grape wine. It explodes with bright, delicious fruit and is smooth across the palate. A superb match for poultry.

Apricot $$ Bright stone fruit aromas lead to a tasty wine with nice mouth weight. A good brunch wine.

Loganberry $ Terrific aromas of blackberries and smooth, fruit-driven flavors with good crispness.

WHERE TO BUY: WINERY, WINE SHOPS

2976 Black Diamond Road, Port Angeles, WA 98363; 360-457-0748; http://pages.prodigy.net/sharonlance. Seasonal hours.

BLACKWOOD CANYON VINTNERS

RED MOUNTAIN   ESTABLISHED 1983

Mike Moore is undoubtedly the most controversial character in the Washington wine industry. He's a maverick who crafts wines his own way, and he doesn't much care what his neighbors think. His philosophy is to produce, on low-yielding, stressed vines, grapes that become long-lived, concentrated wines. He generally doesn't release his creations for at least ten years after vintage, and Moore has many fans for his unusual styles of wine. Moore also makes no fewer than four wine vinegars that are among the best you'll find.

BEST BETS

Reserve Chardonnay $$$ Like an old Burgundy, this rich, sumptuous wine shows butterscotch and baked apple aromas with thick, creamy flavors and a long, acidic finish. A good match for big, ripe cheeses.

Pinnacle $$$$ A botrytised Riesling that may shock you with its deep garnet color, this is heavily accented with honey and spice. The flavors are rich yet smooth from fifteen-plus years of aging.

Penultimate $$$$$$ Another dessert wine that is tawny in color and rich in aromas of honey and carmelized brown sugar, with smooth, long flavors.

Chardonnay Vinegar $ A wine vinegar that is so good you might want to sit around and sip it. Rich in acidity with thick, lush flavors.

WHERE TO BUY: WINERY

53258 N. Sunset Road, Benton City, WA 99320; 509-588-6249. Open daily.

BONAIR WINERY

YAKIMA VALLEY   ESTABLISHED 1985

Gail and Shirley Puryear have been making wine and enjoying the work for nearly two decades. In their upper Yakima Valley winery, they welcome guests with a wide variety of wines to fit every palate, from rich Cabs and Merlots to the popular Bonnie Bonair and even a couple kinds of mead (honey wine). Enjoy the wines, the lush picnic grounds, and the happy folks behind the tasting bar and on the tractor.

BEST BETS

Frankensauv $ This blend of Cabernet Franc and Cabernet Sauvignon is a rich, spicy red with bright fruit aromas and flavors, hints of chocolate, and a long, smooth finish. Try this with barbecued ribs or Tex-Mex.

Morrison Vineyard Cabernet Sauvignon $$ Inviting black fruit and coffee greet the nose, and dark, smooth flavors meld with long, supple tannins and solid acidity. A big wine for a thick steak

Bonnie Bonair $ This blend of Gamay and Cabernet Sauvignon is left with about 2.5 percent residual sugar and, despite being a red wine, is best served chilled. It's a fun, unpretentious wine with attractive raspberry and strawberry notes and will pair well with barbecued meats.

Late Harvest Riesling $ This is one of two tasty Rieslings the Puryears produce. With 6 percent residual sugar, it's a dandy sipper with grapefruit and sweet apple aromas, and just an underlying hint of classic petrol notes. The sugar is expertly backed up with crisp acidity. Enjoy this on its own or with cheesecake.

WHERE TO BUY: WINERY, WINE SHOPS, GROCERY STORES

500 S. Bonair Road, Zillah, WA 98953; 509-829-6027; www.bonair wine.com. Open daily. December–February open weekends.

BOOKWALTER WINERY

COLUMBIA VALLEY   ESTABLISHED 1983

Jerry and Jean Bookwalter helped establish Washington as a viable wine-producing region in the 1980s and early '90s, with Jerry also managing the venerable Sagemoor Vineyard in the Columbia Valley. And just when it seemed that the industry had passed them by, their son John joined the business and revitalized the winery. Today, Bookwalter produces consumer-friendly whites and top-rated reds and is considered a winery to watch.

BEST BETS

Merlot $$ A seductive red that is everything one could hope for in a Washington Merlot. It's richly endowed with cherry and berry aromas and flavors with underlying vanilla and spice notes. Pair with beef, pasta, or lamb.

Cabernet Sauvignon $$$ A deep, complex wine with classic aromas of black currants, pencil shavings, and black olives, and a rich, balanced palate. Enjoy with prime rib.

Johannisberg Riesling $ An off-dry white that provides succulent aromas and flavors of peaches, pears, and apples. A good dose of sugar is expertly balanced with cleansing acidity. Enjoy with a cheese plate or chicken.

Muscat Blanc $ A hugely popular and wildly aromatic wine; it has rich white floral and orchard fruit and plenty of sweetness. This is a picnic or hot tub wine.

WHERE TO BUY: WINERY, WINE SHOPS, GROCERY STORES

894 Tulip Lane, Richland, WA 99352; 509-627-5000; www.bookwalter wines.com. Open daily.

BUNCHGRASS WINERY

WALLA WALLA VALLEY   ESTABLISHED 1997

Lifelong Walla Walla resident Roger Cockerline began making wine in the early '80s and soon after planted a small Merlot vineyard, later adding Cabernet Franc. After retiring from teaching, he opened the winery and is the valley's smallest producer, making about 300 cases per year; most of the vintage sells out immediately.

BEST BETS

Founder's Blend $$ This Bordeaux-style red blend of Cabernet Franc, Merlot, and Cabernet Sauvignon is a classic, with cassis and black fruit aromas and delicious, approachable dark fruit flavors.

Cabernet Sauvignon $$$ Rich and smooth, this red wine is highlighted by flavors of blackberries, cracked peppercorns, and dark chocolate.

Good tannin structure and acidity give it backbone for aging potential.

WHERE TO BUY: WINERY, WINE SHOPS

151 Bunchgrass Lane, Walla Walla, WA 99362; 509-525-1492. Open by appointment.

BUTY WINERY

WALLA WALLA   ESTABLISHED 2000

Pronounced "beauty," this boutique winery is off on the right foot with its first offerings, a Semillon–Sauvignon Blanc blend and a Merlot–Cabernet Franc. In future releases, look for Syrah and Chardonnay from this bright young star.

BEST BETS

Semillon–Sauvignon Blanc $$ This classic white Bordeaux blend is a richly structured wine with layered flavors of figs, pears, and kiwis. The creamy mouth feel and solid acidity give it a big finish. Enjoy with halibut, salmon, or chicken.

Merlot–Cabernet Franc $$$ From Woodward Canyon Vineyard in the western Walla Walla Valley, this is a big, toasty wine with penetrating flavors of cherry, blackberry, and plum. Supple tannins and a smooth finish make this a good match for beef, lamb, and venison.

WHERE TO BUY: WINERY, WINE SHOPS

535 E. Cessna Ave., Walla Walla, WA 99362; 509-527-0901; www.butywinery.com. Open by appointment.

CADENCE WINERY

SEATTLE AREA   ESTABLISHED 1998

Ben Smith and Gaye McNutt are crafting some of Washington's most exciting red blends. Smith, a "graduate" of the Boeing Wine Club, focuses on Bordeaux-style blends named for the vineyards from which the fruit comes, rather than for the grapes. Cadence works with top vineyards, including Ciel du Cheval, Klipsun, and Tapteil, all on Red Mountain. The couple plans to plant an estate vineyard, also on Red Mountain. Join Cadence's mailing list, as the wine could become scarce in years to come.

BEST BETS

Ciel du Cheval Vineyard $$$ A balanced blend of Cabernet Sauvignon, Merlot, and Cabernet Franc produces a powerful, elegant wine with ripe fruit up front, a jammy midpalate, and a deep, rich finish. A model red that shows off what Washington can produce.

Tapteil Vineyard $$$ Darker and more brooding than the Ciel du Cheval, this wine offers penetrating blackberry fruit with vanilla undertones and dense, rich tannins. Put this one away for a few years or match it up with a thick steak.

WHERE TO BUY: WINERY, WINE SHOPS

2920 Sixth Ave. S., Seattle, WA 98134; 206-790-8736; www.cadencewinery.com. Open by appointment.

CAMARADERIE CELLARS

OLYMPIC PENINSULA   ESTABLISHED 1992

Everything about Camaraderie Cellars says elegance, beginning with the gentle spirit of owners Don and Vicki Corson and following through to the powerful yet delicate wines produced at the winery in the hills southwest of Port Angeles. Don Corson began making wine in 1981 with a few friends and took his deep interest to a professional level a decade later. Like many top smaller wineries, Camaraderie focuses on a few high-quality wines, and Corson's passion is Bordeaux styles. Camaraderie's wines are built on grapes from high-quality vineyards, including the legendary Mercer Ranch Vineyard, now known as Champoux, as well as some of the best vineyards on Red Mountain. Corson also is a big fan of new oak and works hard to manage the aggressive tannins for which Washington Cabs and Merlots are known.

BEST BETS

Grâce $$ This Bordeaux-style blend of Cabernet Sauvignon, Merlot, and Cabernet Franc has enticing vanilla and black cherry aromas and rich blackberry, cedar, dark chocolate, and sweet spice flavors. This is a big, chewy wine that will match well with a marbled ribeye or will reward a few years in the cellar. (The name Grâce rhymes with "floss.")

Cabernet Sauvignon $$ Inviting black currant and sweet oak aromas lead to smooth, peppery, black fruit flavors. Brighter and more approachable in its youth than the Grâce, this Cab still has a lot of dense, chewy tannins backed by a ton of fruit and acidity.

Sauvignon Blanc $ With 25 percent Semillon, this is a classic white Bordeaux-style wine. The wine was fermented primarily in steel and shows off tropical fruit and apple aromas and flavors. Aging on the lees—the yeast sediment left over after fermentation—gives this wine a nice creaminess on the midpalate.

WHERE TO BUY: WINE SHOPS, WINERIES

334 Benson Road, Port Angeles, WA 98363; 360-417-3564; www.camaraderiecellars.com. Seasonal hours.

CANOE RIDGE VINEYARD

WALLA WALLA VALLEY   ESTABLISHED 1994

Canoe Ridge Vineyard represents the first investment in Washington by a California wine company. Chalone of Napa partnered with Walla Walla investors in the late '80s to plant a vineyard on a ridge named by Lewis and Clark as they made their way down the Columbia River to the Pacific. The winery is seventy miles to the east, where most of the original investors lived. Chalone has since bought all the shares of the vineyard and winery. Canoe Ridge Vineyard crafts great reds and has a big following for its Chardonnay and Gewürztraminer.

BEST BETS

Merlot $$ Canoe Ridge's signature wine is one of the better Merlots you'll find in Washington. It is a fruit-driven red with well-integrated oak and nicely managed tannins.

Cabernet Sauvignon $$$ A massive wine with appealing aromas and flavor that holds vanilla and sweet spice from oak aging. Essences of chocolate lead to a terrific finish.

Chardonnay $$ An annual favorite among Chardonnay lovers, this clean, fruit-driven white is loaded with telltale tropical fruit with vanilla and butter from oak treatment.

Gewürztraminer $ An Alsatian-style wine with floral, honey, and spice aromas and terrific varietal fruit flavors. This is the only Canoe Ridge wine not made from estate fruit.

WHERE TO BUY: WINERY, WINE SHOPS, GROCERY STORES

1102 W. Cherry St., Walla Walla, WA 99360. 509-527-0885; www.canoeridgevineyard.com. Open daily.

CAÑON DE SOL WINERY & VINEYARD

TRI-CITIES   ESTABLISHED 1999

Led by Victor Cruz, a group of friends launched this winery focused on tiny lots of high-quality red wines. The first efforts, Syrah and Merlot, showed extremely well and have caught the attention of discerning collectors, merchants, and wine stewards. The wines are crafted by the talented Charlie Hoppes.

BEST BETS

Merlot $$ Loaded with bright fruit including sweet plums and blackberries, with underlying mocha notes and ripe tannins. A versatile food wine worthy of a fine meal.

Syrah $$ Sweet French oak spices highlight the aromas, and plenty of fruit and round tannins make this a flavorful red. Match with lamb.

46415 E. Badger Road, Benton City, WA 99320; 509-588-6311; www.canondesol.com. Open by appointment.

CASCADE CLIFFS WINERY

COLUMBIA GORGE   ESTABLISHED 1985

With vineyards and winery sitting high above the spectacular Columbia Gorge, Cascade Cliffs must feel it's sitting on top of the world. Under the direction of winemaker Bob Lorkowski, Cascade Cliffs is successfully pioneering some unusual grapes (for the Northwest), including Barbera and Nebbiolo. The winery is gaining a cult following, so the wines can sell out quickly.

BEST BETS

Nebbiolo $$ Famous in Italy's Piedmont region, this red grape produces a delicious, sometimes spectacular wine showing aromas and flavors of oak spice, moist earth, and a medley of ripe berries. An excellent wine to match with veal.

Barbera $$ Another Italian variety, this is a delightful yet unpretentious red showing great depth of fruit with vanilla and chocolate undertones. Great with pasta in a putanesca sauce.

Goat Head Red $ If the name doesn't get you, the bright aromas and flavors of cranberries, spices, and raspberries will. A blend of several different grapes.

WHERE TO BUY: WINERY, WINE SHOPS

8866 Hwy. 14, Wishram, WA 98673; 509-767-1100; www.cascade cliffs.com. Seasonal hours.

CATERINA WINERY

SPOKANE   ESTABLISHED 1993

Using grapes from the vast Columbia Valley, Caterina has carefully built a reputation for producing consistently delicious to classic wines, with an emphasis on reds. Led by winemaker Mike Scott, the winery excels with Bordeaux varieties, especially Cabernet Sauvignon and Merlot.

BEST BETS

Willard Vineyard Merlot $$ A rare single-vineyard wine from Caterina, this is a rich, delicious beauty showing off ripe, bright fruit and oak aromas and a jammy, complex palate. A rare steak or pasta in a full-bodied red sauce would be great accompaniments.

Willard Vineyard Cabernet Sauvignon $$ An exhilarating red displaying complex fruit and spice nuances and supple tannins. A sure match for lamb.

Merlot $$ A lush, smoky red with ripe, bright fruit and spice flavors. A prototypical Washington Merlot.

WHERE TO BUY: WINERY, WINE SHOPS, GROCERY STORES

905 N. Washington St., Spokane, WA 99201; 509-328-5069; www.caterina.com. Open daily.

CAYUSE VINEYARDS

WALLA WALLA VALLEY   ESTABLISHED 1997

Christophe Baron is a native of France's Champagne region, but he isn't likely to make sparkling wine anytime soon. He's too busy making some of the most sought-after Syrah in the Pacific Northwest. Baron came to the Walla Walla Valley in 1993 as an intern at nearby Waterbrook Winery. From there, he spent time in Oregon, Australia, and Romania before returning and purchasing land south of Walla Walla on the Oregon side of the border. He planted three vineyards and now uses only estate-grown fruit. In addition to his highly regarded Syrah, he also makes a delicious Viognier and a Bordeaux-style red blend.

BEST BETS

Syrah $$–$$$ Baron realizes the importance of a wine's sense of place and, therefore, makes several Syrahs from his different vineyards, as well as blends from all of them. His Syrahs tend to be rich and jammy, with flavors of black cherries, plums, chocolate, licorice, cedar, and more. There's a reason his wine sells out nearly as quickly as it's released—it's some of the best wine available.

Viognier $$ Cayuse's Viognier differs in style from others. It is a bit less fruit-driven and tends to be creamier and rounder, more like a Chardonnay.

WHERE TO BUY: WINERY, WINE SHOPS

17 E. Main St., Walla Walla, WA 99362. 509-526-0686; www.cayuse vineyards.com. Open by appointment.

CHATEAU STE. MICHELLE

SEATTLE AREA   ESTABLISHED 1934

Washington's oldest winery also is its best. Its roots go back to the old National Wine Company and Pommerelle wineries, which opened their doors soon after Prohibition was repealed, later merged, and eventually became Ste. Michelle Vintners. In the early '70s, U.S. Tobacco of Connecticut purchased the winery, built a chateau in the Seattle suburb of Woodinville and propelled the fledgling Washington wine industry from obscurity. U.S. Tobacco formed Stimson Lane Vineyards and Estates, which now owns or controls more than half of Washington's vineyards and owns its largest wineries, as well as properties in California. Stimson Lane's leadership position in the industry comes with responsibility, which it fulfills with grace. In addition to promoting Washington wine across the continent and around the globe, Stimson Lane conducts a lot of viticultural research—then shares it with the rest of the industry.

Producing nearly thirty different wines, Ste. Michelle runs the gamut from Gewürztraminer, Riesling, and Chardonnay to Cabernet Sauvignon, Merlot, and Syrah.

BEST BETS

Columbia Valley wines $–$$ Ste. Michelle's standard wines are solid quality for value prices and include Riesling, Gewürztraminer, Pinot Gris, Sauvignon Blanc, Merlot, Cabernet Sauvignon, Semillon, and Chardonnay. From vintage to vintage, they're varietally pure, delicious, and built to drink relatively young.

Single-vineyard wines $$–$$$ Some of the country's best are among Ste. Michelle's single-vineyard bottlings. Cabernet Sauvignon and Merlot from Canoe Ridge and Chardonnay from Cold Creek should be keenly sought after, and don't overlook Indian Wells wines and the Horse Heaven Vineyard Sauvignon Blanc.

Reserve wines $$–$$$$ World-class handcrafted quality is the hallmark of Ste. Michelle's reserve wines. In addition to Cabernet Sauvignon, Merlot, Chardonnay, and Late Harvest Riesling, this line also includes Ste. Michelle's first Syrah and the nonvarietal bottling, its Meritage red blend.

International collaborations $$–$$$$$ Ste. Michelle makes several wines with European co-producers. Its first is Col Solare, a Bordeaux-style wine made with Antinori of Italy, one of Europe's oldest producers. It also crafts two Riesling-based wines with Ernst Loosen, the famed German Riesling winemaker. The first, called Eroica, is a highly acclaimed dry riesling. The second is Single Berry Select Riesling, an ultra-sweet, ultra-expensive, and ultra-rare dessert wine that earned *Wine Spectator*'s highest score ever for a Washington wine.

WHERE TO BUY: WINERY, WINE SHOPS, GROCERY STORES

14111 N.E. 145th Ave., Woodinville, WA 98072; 425-415-3636; www.ste-michelle.com. Open daily.

CHATTER CREEK WINERY

SEATTLE AREA   ESTABLISHED 1996

Longtime Columbia Winery cellarmaster Gordy Rawson started Alexia Sparkling Wine in 1996 so he could fulfill his passion for producing bubbly. Unfortunately, a New York vodka maker with a similar name meant he was soon forced to change the winery name to Chatter Creek. This worked out for the best for Rawson, because sparkling wine can make for a tough living as a company's sole product. He now focuses on still wines, though his love for bubbly remains.

BEST BETS

Syrah $$ Chatter Creek makes vineyard-designated Syrahs when their quality calls for it. Keep an eye out for the Lonesome Spring Ranch and Jack Jones Vineyard Syrahs, which show plenty of opulent plum and black fruit flavors and exceptional depth.

Cabernet Franc $$ A sultry, earthy wine with ripe raspberry and spice aromas and rich fruit flavors.

Cabernet Sauvignon $$ This is a big wine with telltale currants, coffee, chocolate, and other aromas and flavors. Serve with a marbled rib-eye or cellar it for a few years.

WHERE TO BUY: WINERY, WINE SHOPS

620 NE 55th St., Seattle, WA 98105; 206-985-2816; www.chatter creek.com. Open first and third Saturdays and by appointment.

CHINOOK WINES

YAKIMA VALLEY   ESTABLISHED 1983

Kay Simon and Clay Mackey own and operate one of Washington's finest boutique wineries. With Clay as viticulturist and Kay as winemaker, the pair craft world-class Merlot, Cabernet Sauvignon, and Cabernet Franc, and their Sauvignon Blanc and Semillon are consistently among the Northwest's best. With more than two decades in Washington wine country, these veterans can be expected to be among the top producers in each vintage. These wines should be highly sought after.

BEST BETS

Merlot $$ An elegant wine showing berry, vanilla, light oak, and spice aromas and flavors, a well-balanced mouth feel, and a long, rich finish. Pair with beef or chicken.

Cabernet Franc Rosé $ A superb rosé that is rapidly snapped up by aficionados each summer. It offers generous amounts of strawberry and pomegranate aromas and flavors with plenty of food-friendly structure. Cold fried chicken couldn't be a better match.

Cabernet Franc $$ Opening with exotic spice and black currant aromas, this is a luscious red showing plenty of berry flavors with pepper and olives. Try this with lamb.

Chardonnay $$ A superb wine showing fine balance between fruit and oak, this provides crispness and a long, rich finish. Enjoy with grilled halibut.

Corner of Wine Country Road and Wittkopf Loop, Prosser, WA 99350; 509-786-2725. Seasonal hours.

CLAAR CELLARS

YAKIMA AND COLUMBIA VALLEYS   ESTABLISHED 1997

With vineyards overlooking the beautiful Hanford Reach National Monument and a presence in the heart of the Yakima Valley, Claar Cellars is poised for success. Known early on for steely Rieslings, Claar now is developing a reputation for quality with its Cabernet Sauvignon, Merlot, Chardonnay, Sauvignon Blanc, Sangiovese, and others.

BEST BETS

Johannisberg Riesling $ A charming white with gorgeous orchard and citrus aromas and sweet spice and bright fruit flavors. Perfect balance of sugar and acidity gives this great mouth feel.

Sauvignon Blanc $ A dry, crisp, food-friendly wine with loads of apple and tropical fruit aromas and flavors. Pair this with chicken in a cream sauce, fresh pasta, or salmon.

Reserve Merlot $$ This luscious red is rich with ripe cherry and berry aromas and flavors and is laced with bittersweet chocolate. A chewy wine, this will pair well with a thick steak.

White Bluffs Cab–Merlot $ A complex blend that shows off the best of both varieties, this is a fruit-driven red with plenty of tannins that makes a good match for a ribeye.

WHERE TO BUY: WINERY, WINE SHOPS, GROCERY STORES

1001 Vintage Valley Parkway, Zillah, WA 98953; 509-829-6810; www.claarcellars.com. Open daily.

COL SOLARE

SEATTLE AREA   ESTABLISHED 1995

Two internationally regarded wineries have come together to create Col Solare. Chateau Ste. Michelle of Washington and Marchesi Antinori of Tuscany, Italy, collaborated to craft a Bordeaux-style red wine from Columbia Valley grapes. The winemakers for Ste. Michelle and Antinori select prime vineyards and agree on fermentation and cellar treatment, and the results often are spectacular.

BEST BETS

Col Solare red table wine $$$$$ This, the only wine produced by Col Solare, is a blend of Cabernet Sauvignon and Merlot, with a splash of Syrah in most vintages. It's a serious, age-worthy effort marked by ripe, black fruit and intense flavors that shows plenty of oak and rich, silky tannins. A class act.

P.O. Box 1976, Woodinville, WA 98072; 425-488-1133; www.stimson lane.com. There is no wine-tasting facility.

COLUMBIA CREST

COLUMBIA VALLEY   ESTABLISHED 1981

How can the Pacific Northwest's largest winery also be one of its best? Two words: Doug Gore. Columbia Crest's winemaker since 1984, Gore has perfected the art of making high-quality and high-value wines. With no wine priced at more than $30 (and most at $10 and under), Gore and his team are able to crank out millions of bottles of wine, each of which tastes handcrafted. In 2000, Columbia Crest had a great year, winning honors from consumers and critics alike. Just a year later, the giant had the agility to launch the Grand Estates series, superb wines at modest prices. And in addition to the wines' high quality, a visit to Columbia Crest is a delight, with beautiful grounds perfect for picnicking and one of the best tasting rooms and gift shops anywhere.

BEST BETS

Columbia Valley wines $ Columbia Crest offers no fewer than ten Columbia Valley wines, all generally under $11, and they are found in grocery stores nationwide. Their hallmark is the clean, consistent, varietally sound aromas and flavors. Be it Cabernet Sauvignon, Chardonnay, Semillon, or Riesling, these are just right for everyday quaffing, parties, or family meals.

Grand Estates wines $ Generally in the $10 range, Columbia Crest's Grand Estates Cabernet Sauvignon, Chardonnay, Merlot, and Syrah are among America's best and most accessible wines. Gore selects grapes from some of Washington's top vineyards for these wines, and they show remarkably well regardless of price.

Reserve wines $$ Taste any of Gore's Reserves, and you'll swear you're enjoying a wine two to three times more expensive. Especially fine are the Cabernet Sauvignon, Syrah, and Semillon Ice Wine, and don't overlook the Walter Clore Reserve, a Bordeaux-style blend named for the man who generally is credited with developing the Columbia Valley as a wine-growing region.

WHERE TO BUY: WINERY, WINE SHOPS, GROCERY STORES

Hwy. 221, Columbia Crest Drive, Paterson, WA 99345; 509-875-2061; www.columbia-crest.com. Open daily.

COLUMBIA GORGE WINERY

COLUMBIA GORGE   ESTABLISHED 1993

This small, family-run winery in the heart of the Columbia Gorge focuses on wines made from the grapes of famed Celilo Vineyards near Bingen. The winery makes many varieties, including Lemberger,

Chardonnay, Gewürztraminer, Sauvignon Blanc, Merlot, Syrah, and Pinot Noir. The winery also releases a line of value-minded wines under the Klickitat Canyon label.

BEST BETS

Celilo Vineyard Merlot $ Lovely raspberry and cherry aromas and flavors with sweet fruit and supple tannins. A tasty, enjoyable red to pair with pasta.

WHERE TO BUY: WINERY

6 Lyle-Snowden Road, Lyle, WA 98635; 509-365-2900; www.columbia gorgewinery.com. Open by appointment.

COLUMBIA WINERY

SEATTLE AREA   ESTABLISHED 1962

Touted as Washington's first premium winery, Columbia Winery began in the early '60s as Associated Vintners, a partnership of friends and University of Washington professors led by the venerable Lloyd Woodburne. Associated Vintners focused early on European grapes instead of the North American and hybrid grapes that were in style then. In 1979, AV hired David Lake, a Master of Wine who continues to shape the company. Lake pioneered single-vineyard bottlings in the early '80s, with perhaps his greatest achievement coming from the various wines he makes from Red Willow Vineyard in the western Yakima Valley. The collaboration between Lake and grower/owner Mike Sauer is legendary, as are the wines that result. In 2001, the winery was purchased by the giant Canandaigua Wine Company of New York.

BEST BETS

Red Willow Vineyard Syrah $$ Washington's red wine darling, Syrah, had humble beginnings at Red Willow Vineyard. The first release was in 1988, and today this continues to be one of the state's top Syrahs, showing depth of flavor amid bold, jammy fruit.

Red Willow Vineyard Sangiovese $$ A silky red with cherry fruit, layers of spice, and a smooth, supple mouth feel. Enjoy with lamb or pasta.

Milestone Merlot $$ Another Red Willow wine, a can't-miss Merlot that will reveal itself with a few years in the cellar. Typically rich in cherry aromas and black fruit with chocolate and spice flavors.

Wyckoff Vineyard Chardonnay $$ Lake began working with this vineyard in 1983, and that relationship has paid off with a wine rich in butterscotch, citrus, and tropical flavors and well-integrated oak.

Woodburne Cuvée Chardonnay $ An homage to the winery's roots, this consistently excellent white offers a complex array of fruit and herbal layers and bold flavors. A food-friendly wine to enjoy with seafood or chicken.

14030 N.E. 145th St., Woodinville, WA 98072; 206-488-2776; www.columbiawinery.com. Open daily.

COLVIN VINEYARDS

WALLA WALLA VALLEY   ESTABLISHED 1999

A college encounter with a 1978 Chateau Chevel Blanc sent Mark Colvin on a quest for wine knowledge. In the late '80s he learned about the Walla Walla Valley and in 1993 moved there to start a vineyard and winery. His early offerings, from the vaunted 1999 and 2000 vintages, have been well received. His focus on red wine varieties has led him to Carmenere, an obscure Bordeaux grape thought to have been extinct since the nineteenth century, which Colvin is reviving in Washington.

BEST BETS

Syrah $$ A bright, jammy red that shows off light herbal notes amid cedar, spice, and blackberry nuances. A silky, chocolate-laden finale makes this a good match for lamb or venison.

Cabernet Franc $$ A smooth, approachable red with yummy vanilla, oak, and currant aromas and full, jammy flavors with hints of bittersweet chocolate. A good match with ribeye steaks, tortellini, dark chocolates, or casseroles.

Walla Walla Red $$ A blend of Cabernet Sauvignon, Merlot, and Cabernet Franc, this is a nicely priced red with a delicious balance of toasty oak, vanilla, concentrated blackberries, cherries and plums, and big tannins. Enjoy this with rich, Italian-inspired dishes, thick cuts of beef, or even gourmet pizza.

4122 Powerline Road, Walla Walla, WA 99362; 509-527-9463; www.colvinvineyards.com. Open Saturdays.

COUGAR CREST WINERY

WALLA WALLA VALLEY   ESTABLISHED 2001

This young winery in the Walla Walla Airport industrial area is focusing on Bordeaux- and Rhône-style reds from estate vineyards. The first release, a Syrah, shows great promise. This is a winery to keep an eye on.

BEST BETS

Syrah $$ Tasted in its youth, this wine shows tremendous potential, with intense fruit, desirable acidity, and great length. It should be a blockbuster wine that will pair well with beef or lamb.

202 A St., Walla Walla, WA 99362; 509-938-3172. Open by appointment.

COVEY RUN VINTNERS

YAKIMA VALLEY   ESTABLISHED 1982

One of the Yakima Valley's modern-day pioneer wineries, Covey Run started life as Quail Run, a name it changed after a legal battle with a California winery. It became part of Associated Vintners, which in 2001 was sold to the giant Canandaigua Wine Company of New York. It produces delicious, value-priced wines as well as higher-end dry and dessert wines.

BEST BETS

Cabernet Sauvignon $ This consistently delicious red is a big wine with bold fruit, integrated oak, and rich tannins. Priced for everyday enjoyment.

Chardonnay $ With kisses of toasty oak, this wine's citrus and tropical fruit flavors shine through. Pair with seafood, pasta in a cream sauce, or chicken.

Morio Muskat $ Not a true Muscat, this is a cross of Pinot Blanc and Sylvaner, of which little is planted in North America. It's an outrageously aromatic wine with fresh, crisp flavors and well-balanced sugar. Perfect with cold chicken on a summer picnic.

Riesling Ice Wine $$ Incredibly sweet (20 percent residual sugar) but not cloying thanks to the grape's naturally high acidity. Orange and peach flavors with nectarine and honey undertones. A rare treat.

WHERE TO BUY: GROCERY STORES

14030 N.E. 145th St., Woodinville, WA 98072-1248; 888-659-7900; www.coveyrun.com. No tasting facility.

C. R. SANDIDGE WINES

YAKIMA VALLEY   ESTABLISHED 2000

Washington native Ray Sandidge honed his winemaking skills in New York and Germany before coming home to lead the efforts of Kestrel Vintners. In 2000 he began to make small amounts of high-quality wines under his own label. His focus is on single-vineyard Syrah, a Bordeaux-style blend, and Viognier. His early efforts are first rate, so expect more excellent wines from Ray Sandidge.

BEST BETS

Minick Vineyard Syrah $$ A tremendous first release, this is a rich red with dark chocolate and dusty cherry aromas with complex layers of jammy black cherry fruit, sweet spice, and good acidity. A delicious wine to pair with lamb or sweetbreads.

107 Sunset Way, Zillah, WA 98953; 509-829-5753; www.crsandidge wines.com. Not open to the public.

DELILLE CELLARS

SEATTLE AREA   ESTABLISHED 1992

Certainly one of Washington's finest wineries, DeLille focuses primarily on Bordeaux-style blends of great depth, breadth, and finesse. Led by winemaker Chris Upchurch, DeLille quickly gained a following among consumers interested in superior wines. DeLille's approach is to find excellent vineyard sources and expertly blend Cabernet Sauvignon, Merlot, and Cabernet Franc for the reds and Sauvignon Blanc and Semillon for its white. It also crafts a beautiful Syrah. The wines will age elegantly for several years, though few consumers will be willing to wait that long.

BEST BETS

Chaleur Estate $$$ A powerful red with complex black fruit, smoky oak, velvety tannins, and incredible depth for a long finish. A great wine to be served with a great meal.

Harrison Hill $$$ From a tiny Yakima Valley vineyard comes this elegant and graceful red with complex black fruit, pepper, spice, oak, and more. Wow your wine-drinking friends with this and a cut of prime rib.

D2 $$ A second wine, if you will, but it is no slouch. This red blend is rich in fruit, oak, and tannins and will hold its own among the world's best.

Chaleur Estate Blanc $$ This white Bordeaux blend will make you forget about Chardonnay. Oak-aged Semillon is the dominant component, with rich texture and fig and tropical flavors.

Doyenne $$$ DeLille's only 100 percent varietal wine, this Syrah is a hedonistic pleasure with its opulent fruit flavors and a peppery backbone. A grand match with lamb dishes.

WHERE TO BUY: WINERY, WINE SHOPS, GROCERY STORES

14208 Woodinville-Redmond Road, Woodinville, WA 98052; 425-489-0544; www.delillecellars.com. Seasonal hours.

DISTEFANO WINES

SEATTLE AREA   ESTABLISHED 1984

Led by owner/winemaker Mark Newton, DiStefano Wines focuses on high-quality Bordeaux-style wines. The former nuclear engineer began his career with an enthusiasm for sparkling wines, though he changed his focus in the early '90s. A Syrah and Meritage also have been added to the mix.

BEST BETS

Sauvignon Blanc $ Blended with the other great white grape of Bordeaux, Semillon, this crisp, delicious wine is loaded with tropical and apple aromas and flavors with underlying orange notes.

Sogno $$ This could be called DiStefano's signature wine, as this Cabernet Franc–based wine is elegant yet powerful, with rich berry and chocolate flavors and telltale smooth tannins. Enjoy with sirloin or pasta. Also check out the Cabernet Franc Rosé.

Cabernet Sauvignon $$ A big, sophisticated red with dreamy violet and black currant aromas, penetrating depth, and tremendous balance of fruit, tannin, and acidity.

Merlot $$ Just what you might hope for from a Washington Merlot, this offers bright fruit, supple tannins, and a smooth finish.

WHERE TO BUY: WINERY, WINE SHOPS

12280 Woodinville Dr. N.E., Woodinville, WA 98072; 425-487-1648; www.distefanowinery.com. Open weekends or by appointment.

DOMAINE STE. MICHELLE

COLUMBIA VALLEY   ESTABLISHED 1978

Making sparkling wine is more than just a hobby for Stimson Lane, the parent company for Domaine Ste. Michelle, Columbia Crest, Chateau Ste. Michelle, and others. With its production of more than a quarter-million cases per year, Domaine Ste. Michelle is one of Washington's largest wineries. Under the watchful and talented eyes of winemaker Rick Casqueiro, Domaine Ste. Michelle has won dozens of awards for its good quality, value-priced Methode Champenoise bubbly.

BEST BETS

Blanc de Noir $ With its beautiful cherry hue and delicate strawberry and raspberry flavors, this is a crowd pleaser made from Pinot Noir. A hint of residual sugar rounds out this delicious wine.

Cuvée Brut $ Little residual sugar (about 1 percent) is evident in this smoky, citrusy sparkler with approachable tropical and cake aromas and flavors.

Blanc de Blanc $ A classic bubbly with light yeast and cake aromas accompanied by flavors of fresh apples and citrus. Crisp bubbles give it a dynamite finish.

Extra Dry $ In Champagne (and the New World) "extra dry" means just the opposite. Hence, this is Domaine Ste. Michelle's sweetest sparkler, with more than 2 percent residual sugar backing up the tropical fruit aromas and flavors.

Hwy. 221, Columbia Crest Drive, Paterson, WA 99345; 509-875-2061. No tasting facility.

DUNHAM CELLARS / TREY MARIE

WALLA WALLA VALLEY   ESTABLISHED 1995

Eric Dunham began his winemaking career at L'Ecole No. 41, learning his craft from Marty Clubb. He made minuscule amounts beginning in 1995 to strong acclaim and left L'Ecole in 1998 to focus on his own label, which has received rave reviews and industry accolades. In 2000 he and his parents began a second winery with different partners, called Trey Marie, which met with immediate success. The two operations were treated separately until they merged in early 2003.

BEST BETS

Cabernet Sauvignon $$$ Typically huge and dense, this Cab annually wins medals internationally and sells out quickly. It's packed with black fruit and has tons of acidity and tannins to back it up. An age-worthy and classy wine.

Syrah $$$ A sensual and seductive red that opens with light oak and dark berry aromas and gives way to supple, jammy flavors including those of ripe plums, blackberries, and vanilla. A sure bet with lamb or sweetbreads.

Trutina $$$ This Bordeaux-style blend of Merlot, Cabernet Sauvignon, and Cabernet Franc is loaded with toasty oak and rich fruit aromas and flavors. It is layered with fruit, cedar, chocolate, spice, and more

WHERE TO BUY: WINERY, WINE SHOPS

105 E. Boeing Ave., Walla Walla, WA 99360; Dunham, 509-529-4685; Trey Marie, 509-529-1371; www.dunhamcellars.com. Open daily.

E. B. FOOTE WINERY

SEATTLE AREA   ESTABLISHED 1978

One of Washington's older wineries, E. B. Foote was purchased from Gene Foote in the early '90s by Sherill Miller and Rick Higgenbotham. The winery is respected especially for its reds. Tucked away in the Seattle suburb of Burien, the winery uses grapes from the Columbia Valley. The Merlot has won accolades in recent vintages, and the Cabernet Sauvignon, Syrah, Chardonnay, and Cab–Merlot also come highly recommended. And keep an eye out for a tasty white sipper called Sweet Sherill.

BEST BETS

Merlot $$ Consistently high quality makes this a top pick vintage after vintage, thanks to its opulent, approachable fruit, jammy flavors, and robust tannins. Serve with ribs, duck, pork, or vegetable stews.

Cellar Reserve Cabernet Sauvignon $$$ This enchanting wine opens with spice, oak and blackberry aromas that lead to succulent jammy fruit with tons of complex nuances. A huge wine that will pair well with a T-bone.

Syrah $$ A hedonistic and satisfying wine with delicious spice and vanilla from oak aging, dark fruit, and a mellow finish. A great match for lamb.

WHERE TO BUY: WINERY, WINE SHOPS, GROCERY STORES

127B S.W. 153rd St., Burien, WA 98166; 206-242-3852. Open Tuesdays, Thursdays, and Saturdays.

EATON HILL WINERY

YAKIMA VALLEY   ESTABLISHED 1988

Set in a turn-of-the-century farmhouse and outbuilding, Eaton Hill Winery typifies Yakima Valley wineries with its crisp, delicious whites and ripe, elegant reds. Eaton Hill crafts a wide range of wines, including classic varieties and some Ports.

BEST BETS

Konnowac Vineyard Cabernet Sauvignon $$ A superb example of the king of red wines, this provides rich aromas and flavors including those of black currants, cherries, blackberries, dark chocolate, spice, and vanilla. A massive wine that's well worth seeking out.

Semillon $ Showing classic varietal tendencies, including fresh fig and herbal notes and a creamy mouth feel, this should pair well with scallops or crab in a butter sauce.

Konnowac Vineyard Cabernet Franc $ A great wine at a great price, this opens with aromas of freshly split cedar with underlying notes of mint. The palate explodes with dark fruit flavors. Pair with lamb, beef, or chicken in a heavy sauce.

Sunglow $ An unusual blend of Riesling and nectarine juice, this is a tasty brunch wine that will be a hit with beginning wine drinkers.

WHERE TO BUY: WINERY, WINE SHOPS, GROCERY STORES

530 Gurley Road, Granger, WA 98932; 509-854-2220.
Seasonal hours.

ENGLISH ESTATE

SOUTHWEST WASHINGTON   ESTABLISHED 2001

This young winery is producing Pinot Noir from its twenty-acre estate vineyards that were planted beginning in 1983. The winery's early efforts include standard Pinot Noirs, as well as a spritzy nouveau-style red and a sweet wine.

BEST BETS

Gravel Mine Vineyard Pinot Noir $$ A bright, tasty wine showing off berry and cherry aromas and flavors, refreshing acidity, and a medium finish. Enjoy with beef or chicken.

Gravel Mine Vineyard Pinot Noir Nectar $$ A sweet wine that offers strawberry and cherry aromas and flavors. A tasty after-dinner sipper.

WHERE TO BUY: WINERY, WINE SHOPS

17908 S.E. 1st St., Vancouver, WA 98684; 360-260-4170; www.english estatewinery.com. Open weekends.

FACELLI WINERY

SEATTLE AREA   ESTABLISHED 1988

Lou Facelli began working with Washington grapes in the early '80s when he opened his first winery in Idaho. In the late '80s he relocated to the Seattle area, where he makes pleasing and popular wines in a business park down the road from Chateau Ste. Michelle. Facelli works with some of the state's top vineyards, including Red Willow, Bacchus, and Dionysus.

BEST BETS

Sangiovese $$ A spectacular, Italian-style red with grapes from vaunted Red Willow Vineyard. This is a deep, jammy wine with dusty cherry aromas and penetrating flavors. Highly recommended.

Cabernet Franc $$ From the Bacchus Vineyard block of famed Sagemoor Vineyards in the Columbia Basin comes this elegant Cab Franc. It's a smooth, layered wine with violet and blueberry aromas and rich berry and sweet spice flavors.

Lemberger $ This much-maligned grape is underappreciated, primarily because its name sounds like that of a stinky cheese. In fact it produces delicious wines like this one: a round, rich, fruit-driven red that pairs well with many dishes, including pasta, steak, and meatloaf.

Late Harvest Syrah $ A rare, perhaps unique, wine for the Northwest, this sweet red opens with plum jam aromas and a rich midpalate. Despite the more than 4 percent residual sugar, this doesn't come across as overly sweet. Try it as an after-dinner treat with dark chocolate.

16120 Woodinville-Redmond Road N.E., Woodinville, WA 98072;
206-488-1020; www.facelliwinery.com. Open weekends.

FAIRWINDS WINERY

OLYMPIC PENINSULA   ESTABLISHED 1995

Two retired Coast Guard buddies and their spouses launched Fair-
Winds Winery, just outside the historic maritime town of Port
Townsend. Michael and Judy Cavett and Harry and Zo Ann Dudley
started their tiny operation with a few used barrels, small tanks, con-
verted household appliances, and a lot of hard work. With grapes from
Eastern Washington, FairWinds makes small lots of reds and whites,
bottling and labeling by hand in a humble barn-turned-winery. In
2002, the Cavetts took full ownership of FairWinds.

BEST BETS

Lemberger $ Bright cherry and cranberry aromas and flavors make
this a flavorful wine that will match well with everyday meals, such
as casseroles, pizza, or grilled chicken.

Gewürztraminer $ Classic grapefruit aromas and crisp, delicious fla-
vors make this a favorite, especially with Thai or Indian cuisine.

Aligoté $ A rare variety, and FairWinds is one of a handful of wineri-
es in the Northwest to make this fruit-driven wine. Enjoy with picnic fare or shellfish.

WHERE TO BUY: WINERY, WINE SHOPS

1984 Hastings Ave. W., Port Townsend, WA 98368; 360-385-6899;
www.fairwindswinery.com. Open weekends.

FIDELITAS

COLUMBIA VALLEY   ESTABLISHED 2000

Charlie Hoppes is one of Washington's most talented and respected
winemakers. After several years as red winemaker for Chateau Ste.
Michelle and head winemaker for Three Rivers Winery, Hoppes ven-
tured out on his own, making tiny amounts of high-quality blends.
Like anything made by Hoppes, this wine should be highly sought after.

BEST BETS

Meritage $$ A classic blend with Cabernet Sauvignon, Merlot,
and Cabernet Franc, this is rich in complex aromas and flavors
of chocolate, spice, espresso, and dark fruit, all backed by great
balance and huge structure. Serve with your best cut of beef.

WHERE TO BUY: WINERY, WINE SHOPS

At Cañon de Sol Winery, 46415 E. Badger Road, Benton City, WA
99320; 509-588-6311. By appointment.

FIELDING HILLS WINERY

NORTH-CENTRAL WASHINGTON   ESTABLISHED 2000

This small winery gained recognition quickly. The rich, succulent reds of Fielding Hills might remind you of a big Walla Walla wine. In fact, winemaker/owner Mike Wade was inspired by some of Walla Walla's boutique wineries before he launched his own operation. If early success is any indication, Fielding Hills is a winery to watch.

BEST BETS

Red Table Wine $$ A fabulous blend of Cabernet Sauvignon and Merlot, this is loaded with big aromas and flavors of chocolate, plum, blackberry, coffee, vanilla, and charred oak. Pair this wine with a thick, rare steak.

Cabernet Sauvignon $$ This graceful red provides aromas of black pepper, pencil shavings, vanilla, and espresso with flavors of sweet, jammy fruit and rich tannins. Age for a half decade or more.

Merlot $$ A ripe, lush red showing blackberry and vanilla aromas and cherry and spice flavors. Supple tannins back this up and make it a good match for pasta or veal.

WHERE TO BUY: WINERY, WINE SHOPS

1150 N. Jackson St., East Wenatchee, WA 98802; 509-662-7153; www.fieldinghills.com. Open by appointment.

FIRESTEED CELLARS

SEATTLE AREA   ESTABLISHED 1992

Howard Rossbach has hit on a pretty successful idea: He owns a "virtual winery." He doesn't grow grapes, and he doesn't make wine. Rather, he contracts with growers and wineries to make his good-quality, great-value wines to his specification. Purists may not care for the practice, but consumers love the consistently good wines and the prices, usually around $10. Most of Firesteed's wines are from Oregon grapes, though it also bottles a Barbera with juice from Italy's Piedmont region.

BEST BETS

Pinot Gris $ Crisp, minerally, and loaded with orchard fruit aromas and flavors, this is a delicious everyday wine built to match with shellfish, chicken, and pasta in a cream sauce.

Pinot Noir $ Lighter and less powerful than its contemporaries, this is an affordable and approachable red with plenty of bright varietal characteristics and an underlying elegance that makes it a delicious match with pork, chicken, and turkey.

WHERE TO BUY: WINE SHOPS, GROCERY STORES

1809 Seventh Ave., Suite 1108, Seattle, WA 98101; 206-233-0683; www.firesteed.com. Not open to the public.

FORGERON CELLARS

WALLA WALLA VALLEY   ESTABLISHED 2001

This young winery in downtown Walla Walla made its first inspired move when it hired Marie-Eve Gilla from Gordon Brothers Cellars in Pasco, Washington. Gilla, a French-trained winemaker, is talented with Bordeaux-style reds as well as award-winning Chardonnays, and serves this new venture well. In addition to the Chardonnay reviewed here, look for future releases of Merlot, Cabernet Sauvignon, Syrah, and Zinfandel.

BEST BETS

Chardonnay $$ A bold white tasted from the barrel, this shows off butter and vanilla aromas melding with ripe apples, lemons, and pineapples. It's a big wine that will pair well with such appetizers as shrimp and oysters.

WHERE TO BUY: WINERY

33 W. Birch St., Walla Walla, WA 99362; 509-522-9463; www.forgeron cellars.com. Open by appointment.

FOX ESTATE WINERY

COLUMBIA VALLEY   ESTABLISHED 1999

A longtime Columbia Basin farming family planted wine grapes in the early '80s and opened its winery in the late '90s. Its first efforts were well received, and more good things can be expected from Fox in the future.

BEST BETS

Riesling $ A delicious white with sweet tropical fruit aromas and flavors of pears, apples, and oranges. The ample sugar is well balanced with good acidity that makes this a delightful sipper.

Cabernet Sauvignon $$ Classic oak, vanilla, and berry aromas and flavors with rich tannins and a lengthy finish. Serve with beef.

WHERE TO BUY: WINERY, WINE SHOPS

24962 Hwy. 243 S., Mattawa, WA 99349; 509-932-5818; www.fox estatewinery.com. Open weekdays and by appointment.

GIBBONS LANE WINERY / DONEDÉI

SEATTLE AREA   ESTABLISHED 1999

Owner/winemaker Carolyn Lakewold learned the craft under the tutelage of Doug McCrea, one of Washington's most talented wine-makers, and Bob Andrake, a nearby winemaker. The early efforts are nothing short of spectacular, with a huge Merlot and Cabernet Sauvignon made in minuscule amounts.

BEST BETS

Merlot $$$ A big, classy red showing off aromas of black olives, oak, and cherry and rich, plummy flavors with a lingering finish. This would be perfect with veal or lamb.

Cabernet Sauvignon $$$ A deep, elegant wine that opens with aromas of mint, chocolate, plums, and black currants and follows with thick, jammy, and explosive fruit flavors with complex nuances of chocolate, spice and Turkish coffee. A wine worth aging or pairing with a rare ribeye.

WHERE TO BUY: WINERY, WINE SHOPS

P.O. Box 7735, Olympia, WA 98507; 360-956-0821; www.donedei.com. Not open to the public.

GLEN FIONA

WALLA WALLA VALLEY   ESTABLISHED 1995

Glen Fiona, a Gaelic phrase that means "Valley of the Vine," launched with great success, its first vintage winning best of show in a prestigious Seattle wine judging. The winery focuses on Syrah, offering no fewer than four styles of the classic Rhône Valley variety. In 2002, co-founder and winemaker Rusty Figgins left Glen Fiona to make wine for nearby Northstar, a high-end Merlot producer.

BEST BETS

Bacchus Vineyard Syrah $$ Usually released within eight months of harvest, this fruit-driven Syrah is approachable in its youth and crafted to be enjoyed in its first five years.

Puncheon Aged Syrah $$$ This traditionally made red often is co-fermented with Viognier, a white wine grape from the Rhône. When fermented together after harvest, no color is lost. The Viognier adds complexity to an already richly layered wine that will age nicely for up to a decade.

Basket Press Reserve Syrah $$$$ Typically blended with Cinsault, a popular red grape in France, this is rich with aromas and flavors of cedar, blackberries, plums, and jam. This is crafted with patience in mind, so wait at least five years after vintage to consume.

WHERE TO BUY: WINERY, WINE SHOPS

1249 Lyday Lane, Walla Walla, WA 99360; 509-522-2566; www.glen fiona.com. Open Saturdays and by appointment.

GOLD DIGGER CELLARS

NORTH-CENTRAL WASHINGTON   ESTABLISHED 2000

During visits to British Columbia's Okanagan Valley, one must wonder why a few wineries haven't popped up just south of the border in Washington. The climate, soil, and benchlands are identical. In fact, the only difference is the spelling of Okanagan (vs. Okanogan). The towns of Oroville and Tonasket are in apple country, and one apple cooperative, Gold Digger, has launched a vineyard and winemaking venture with Gold Digger Cellars. Its early efforts have shown promise, and as its young vines mature, we expect good things.

BEST BETS

Pinot Noir $$ A red rich in tart cherry and cranberry flavors and oak and fruit aromas with lovely herbal nuances.

Chardonnay $ A fruit-driven wine with light oak treatment and orchard fruit and citrus flavors.

Gewürztraminer $ Classic grapefruit and perfumy characteristics and an approachable mouth feel make this perfect for lightly spicy dishes.

WHERE TO BUY: WINERY, WINE SHOPS, GROCERY STORES

1205 Main St., Oroville, WA 98844; 509-476-4887; www.golddigger cellars.com. Open Monday-Saturday.

GOOSE RIDGE VINEYARD

COLUMBIA VALLEY   ESTABLISHED 2000

The Monson family planted more than a thousand acres of vineyards in the Columbia Valley across the freeway from Red Mountain. Most of the grapes go to Chateau Ste. Michelle and its fellow Stimson Lane wineries, but the Monsons also launched their own small winery under the direction of winemaker Charlie Hoppes. The early efforts show depth and classic varietal tendencies, making Goose Ridge a winery to watch.

BEST BETS

Meritage $$$ An intense blend of Cabernet Sauvignon and Merlot, this is a bold, dark wine showing off toasty oak, black olives, and dark fruit. A good wine to pair with steak.

Chardonnay $$ A toasty and herbal wine that is backed up with bright fruit, cleansing acidity, and a creamy mouth feel. Enjoy with seafood or chicken.

WHERE TO BUY: WINERY, WINE SHOPS

16304 N. Dallas Road, Richland, WA 99352; 509-837-4424. Open by appointment.

GORDON BROTHERS CELLARS

COLUMBIA VALLEY   ESTABLISHED 1982

Gordon Brothers started as a grape grower and eventually began making its own wine. With nearly 100 acres of wine grapes on its beautiful estate vineyard overlooking the Snake River, Gordon Brothers uses estate grapes for all of its wine and sells the rest to other wineries. This gives Gordon Brothers total control of its product from bud break through bottling. Since recovering from the 1996 winter freeze that devastated vineyards throughout the Columbia Valley, Gordon Brothers has been on a roll, crafting stunning reds and award-winning whites with great consumer appeal. In 2002, Gordon Brothers was purchased by the owners of Freemark Abbey of California.

BEST BETS

Chardonnay $$ A well made, food-friendly white with enough oak aging to satisfy California Chardonnay fans, yet with ample fruit and acidity to make an enjoyable match with seafood, chicken, and shellfish. Great balance throughout.

Tradition $$$ This Bordeaux-style red blend is a deeply rich wine that shows off the Columbia Valley's best attributes. A blend of Cabernet Sauvignon, Merlot, and Cabernet Franc, Tradition can stand up to some of the region's best reds.

Merlot $$ In a region known for its Merlots, this stands out. With its cherry and pepper aromas and smooth, fruit-laden flavors, this Merlot has enough fruit and acidity to age nicely for five or more years after vintage.

WHERE TO BUY: WINERY, WINE SHOPS, GROCERY STORES

5960 Burden Blvd., Pasco, WA 99301; 509-547-6331; www.gordon wines.com. Open daily.

GREENBANK CELLARS

PUGET SOUND   ESTABLISHED 1998

Owner/winemaker Frank Rayle produces small amounts of wine with grapes from throughout the Northwest. His first wines include Riesling and Cabernet Sauvignon from the Yakima Valley and Sauvignon Blanc and loganberry from the Willamette Valley. His own vineyard includes Madeleine Angevine, Müller-Thurgau, and Sieggerebe.

BEST BETS

Cabernet Sauvignon $$ Smooth and delicious with classic blackberry, blueberry, and black currant nuances. A lovely wine.

Riesling $ Alsatian in style, this crisp, clean white opens with orchard and citrus aromas and lovely fruit flavors. Wonderfully balanced, this will match well with seafood or Asian-inspired cuisine.

Loganberry $ Richly structured aromas lead to deliciously tart fruit flavors. Try with turkey or barbecued chicken.

WHERE TO BUY: WINERY

3112 Day Road, Greenbank, WA 98253; 360-678-3964; www. whidbey.com/wine. Open seasonally or by appointment.

HARLEQUIN WINE CELLARS

SEATTLE AREA   ESTABLISHED 1999

Robert Goodfriend is a bit unusual among Washington winemakers because he also embraces Oregon grapes. The co-owner/winemaker for Harlequin, a small suburban winery south of Seattle, worked at Silvan Ridge Winery in Oregon before moving to Seattle, and he has a great love for Pinot Noir. His style with this wine also shows through on his Washington offerings—Syrah and Cabernet Sauvignon—with smooth, sultry wines that will win you over with their subtleties rather than their brashness.

BEST BETS

Syrah $$ From Sundance Vineyard on the Wahluke Slope, this is a sexy wine that shows off supple black, jammy fruit with hints of mint in the background plus blueberries and mocha through the palate. A sure bet for lamb.

Cabernet Sauvignon $$ A gentlemanly red that opens with aromas of pencil shavings and subtle black fruit, with rich black currants and blackberries on the palate. Enjoy this with prime rib.

Pinot Noir $$ From the Willamette Valley's Hoodview Vineyard, this offers earthy, cherry, floral aromas and berry, vanilla, peppercorn flavors, all backed up with a velvety midpalate. Try this with delicate meats or grilled vegetables.

WHERE TO BUY: WINERY, WINE SHOPS

19264 208th Ave. S.E., Renton, WA 98058; 425-413-4633; www. harlequinwine.com. Open by appointment.

HEDGES CELLARS

RED MOUNTAIN AND SEATTLE AREA   ESTABLISHED 1987

The French term terroir *(tear-WAHR) is an important one for the Hedges family. Terroir refers to the soil and weather conditions that make a particular area good for growing a specific grape. Tom Hedges believes the conditions on Red Mountain in the lower Yakima Valley are perfect for Cabernet Sauvignon and Merlot. The three dozen wineries that buy grapes from Red Mountain would agree. In its chateau on Red Mountain, Hedges specializes in Bordeaux-style blends. It also has a tasting room in Issaquah, east of Seattle.*

BEST BETS

Three Vineyards $$ The Hedges signature wine is primarily Cabernet Sauvignon and Merlot, with a splash of Cabernet Franc. It's a big wine with great balance of dark fruit flavors, oak, and acidity that give it aging potential for a decade or more, though it's also approachable in its youth.

Red Mountain Reserve $$$ Mostly Cabernet Sauvignon with some Merlot, the top Hedges wine is deep with blackberry and black cherry flavors and rich with complexity, including cedar, cassis, chocolate, and spices. This is a wine to hold onto for at least five years.

Fumé-Chardonnay $ This is the only Hedges white wine, a delicious blend of Sauvignon Blanc and Chardonnay. It's a fruit-driven wine that should be enjoyed within a year or two of the vintage date.

WHERE TO BUY: WINERY, WINE SHOPS, GROCERY STORES

195 N.E. Gilman Blvd., Issaquah, WA 98027, 425-391-6056; www.hedgescellars.com. The tasting room in Issaquah is open Monday–Saturday. The winery on Red Mountain is open by appointment.

HIGHTOWER CELLARS

RED MOUNTAIN   ESTABLISHED 1997

Tim and Kelly Hightower make small amounts of high-quality, handcrafted Cabernet Sauvignon. They focus on grapes from such fine vineyards as Boushey, Artz, Pepper Bridge, and Alder Ridge as they produce the wines from vine to bottle.

BEST BETS

Cabernet Sauvignon $$ Hightower's first wine is a Cab with small amounts of Merlot blended in. The result is a red wine of distinction with wonderful depth, power, and grace.

WHERE TO BUY: WINERY, WINE SHOPS

19418 E. 583 PR N.E., Benton City, WA 99320; 509-588-2867; www.hightowercellars.com. Open by appointment.

HINZERLING WINERY

YAKIMA VALLEY   ESTABLISHED 1976

One of the Yakima Valley's true pioneers, Mike Wallace moved east of the Cascades in the early '70s to grow grapes. He started his winery a few years later and has established a reputation for making noteworthy Ports in the traditional style, and now makes no fewer than five Ports, both white and red. Also keep an eye out for his traditional dry wines, including Cabernet Sauvignon. Wallace also has a bed-and-breakfast at the winery.

BEST BETS

Three Muses Ruby Port $$ A blend of Lemberger, Cabernet Sauvignon, and Merlot, this is a satisfying Port with aromas and flavors of dark chocolate and deep, rich fruit. Excellent for sipping or with biscotti.

Wallace Vintage Port $$ Made from Cabernet Sauvignon, this is one of the finest ports you'll find in the Pacific Northwest, with its penetrating aromas and flavors of plums, chocolate, and black cherries. Enjoy with Stilton.

Rainy Day Fine Tawny Port $$ A smooth, concentrated wine revealing dried fruit aromas and nutty, caramel-like flavors. A delicious style that would pair well with a fine cigar.

Collage $$ A Port-like white wine made from Muscat Canelli, range Muscat, and Early Muscat, this is a full-bodied dessert wine showing floral and orange oil aspects with flavors of ripe peaches with honey drizzled on them. A luscious wine.

WHERE TO BUY: WINERY, WINE SHOPS

1520 Sheridan Ave., Prosser, WA 99350; 509-786-2163; www. hinzerling.com. Open daily.

HOGUE CELLARS

YAKIMA VALLEY   ESTABLISHED 1982

When Mike and Gary Hogue launched their winery in the early '80s, little did they realize it would grow into one of the Northwest's largest operations. Under the guidance of Rob Griffin, Hogue became a top winery. After Griffin left in 1990, David Forsyth took over the wine-making duties. In the mid-'90s, extensive vineyard work and selection made Hogue's red wine program a high-end force on the national scene. Coupled with its always-strong whites, Hogue is one of the Northwest's best. In 2001 the Hogues sold the winery to Vincor, a Canadian-based company that owns some of British Columbia's top wineries (Jackson-Triggs, Inniskillin Okanagan, Sumac Ridge, and Hawthorne Mountain).

BEST BETS

Reserve Chardonnay $$ This powerfully rich and creamy wine offers incredible balance of oak and tropical fruit with plenty of nooks and crannies to explore. A safe bet with seafood.

Genesis Syrah $$ A classy and complex red with layers of black fruit and jammy tannins, this is the perfect foil for lamb.

Cab–Merlot $ Hogue didn't invent this blend, but it has certainly perfected it. A great wine at a bargain price, this is rich in cherry and berry fruit with vanilla and oak nuances. Enjoy any night of the week.

Blue Franc $ With its name derived from the Austrian name for the Lemberger grape, this is a fruity and approachable red that shows refinement and class.

Gewürztraminer $ Full of grapefruit aromas and fresh citrus and orchard flavors, this is a joyous wine that will match with curries or pasta.

Riesling $ Hogue makes off-dry and late-harvest versions of this classic Washington grape, often with outstanding results. A great match with shellfish, pasta in a clam sauce, or chicken.

2800 Lee Road, Prosser, WA 99350; 509-786-4557; www.hoguecellars. com. Open daily.

HOODSPORT WINERY

OLYMPIC PENINSULA   ESTABLISHED 1979

Located on the southern end of Hood Canal, Hoodsport Winery has built its reputation over the years on delicious, accessible wines. It gets grapes from Eastern Washington and makes fruit wines from raspberries, cranberries, rhubarb, and loganberries. Hoodsport also specializes in a red wine made with a grape called Island Belle, grown on a nearby vineyard. The grape is believed to be a North American variety also called Campbell's Early. Though some controversy surrounds the grape's origins, there's no doubt it's a favorite of the winery as well as of its customers. In addition to the winery, Hoodsport has a tasting room in Tacoma.

BEST BETS

Raspberry $ This reveals an explosion of raspberries from first whiff through the long finish. This wine tastes more like raspberries than raspberries do. Try this poured over vanilla ice cream.

Cabernet Sauvignon $$ From Yakima Valley grapes, this Cab shows off smoky oak and bright cherry and berry aromas with approachable tannins. A food-friendly wine that would match well with pasta, beef, or hearty stews.

Cabernet Franc $$ An outstanding wine loaded with espresso, vanilla, and raspberry flavors. This is a surpassing effort worthy of a fine steak.

Chardonnay $$ A well-balanced white with ample fruit that melds with modest oak aging. The crisp, fruit-driven palate makes this a good match with halibut, scallops, or baked chicken.

WHERE TO BUY: WINERY, WINE SHOPS, GROCERY STORES

Winery: N. 23501 Hwy. 101, Hoodsport, WA 98548; 800-580-9894; www.hoodsport.com. Open daily. Tacoma tasting room: 1948 Pacific Ave., Tacoma, WA 98402; 253-396-9463. Open Monday–Saturday.

HORIZON'S EDGE WINERY

YAKIMA VALLEY   ESTABLISHED 1984

Perhaps as well known for its distinctive and colorful labels as for the wines inside, Horizon's Edge produces a wide variety of dry and sweet wines. The winery has been renowned for its two styles of Muscat Canelli, as well as its big, buttery Monster Chardonnay. Also check out its Cream Sherry, a rarity in Washington.

BEST BETS

Muscat Canelli $ A classic example of an underappreciated variety, this provides wonderful aromatics of white flowers, rose water, and honeysuckle. Its flavors are off-dry with just under 2 percent residual sugar, and it has plenty of structure to back up the lovely citrus flavors. A perfect brunch or picnic wine.

Nouveaux-Riche $ A sweet dessert wine made from Muscat Canelli, this is ripe with floral, melon, and honey aromas and flavors. A delicious after-dinner sipper.

Butterfly Ice Wine $$ Made from Chardonnay, this offers honey, apricot, and orange peel aromas and flavors and a smooth, delicious palate.

Monster Chardonnay $$ For those who crave big, buttery styles, this is it. Amid all the oak and butter are plenty of underlying pear and apple flavors.

WHERE TO BUY: WINERY, WINE SHOPS

4530 E. Zillah Drive, Zillah, WA 98953; 509-829-6401. Open Friday–Monday.

HYATT VINEYARDS

YAKIMA VALLEY   ESTABLISHED 1987

Since its start in the mid-'80s, Hyatt Vineyards has been one of the Yakima Valley's best producers. It makes a good variety of classic wines, including Cabernet Sauvignon, Merlot, Sangiovese, Chardonnay, and blends. Of special interest are two Black Muscats, a rosé, and a natural ice wine.

BEST BETS

Merlot $ A consistently top-rated red, this Merlot is loaded with berries, chocolate, cedar, and more. It's a big, rich wine with moderate tannins that should pair well with beef, pasta, turkey, or hearty stews.

Black Muscat Ice Wine $$ This wine is only produced if conditions allow the grapes to freeze on the vine. When this happens, you'll be treated to an outstanding dessert wine with luscious citrus and stone fruit aromas and spicy orange and honey flavors, and with plenty of acidity to back up the ample sugar. Try this with poached pears stuffed with gorgonzola.

Cab–Merlot $ A delicious wine at a great value, this red blend offers tasty up-front fruit as well as underlying complexities of cedar, spice, and chocolate.

Chardonnay $ A steely Chardonnay that shows off plenty of fruit as well as light oak aging. The long, crisp finish will pair nicely with oysters, chicken, or pasta.

2020 Gilbert Road, Zillah, WA 98953; 509-829-6333; www.hyattvineyards.com. Open daily.

ISENHOWER CELLARS

WALLA WALLA VALLEY   ESTABLISHED 1999

This boutique winery is lovingly run by Brett and Denise Isenhower, who get their grapes from all four Eastern Washington wine-producing areas and are making red wines that show plenty of character and promise

BEST BETS

Syrah $$ A mouth-filling red showing rich, lush flavors of plums, blackberries, and vanilla spice; it has refreshing acidity, and drink-now mouth weight. Pair with lamb or sweetbreads.

Red Paintbrush $$ A blend of Cabernet Sauvignon, Merlot, and Syrah, this is a finely structured wine that exhibits blackberry and black cherry aromas and flavors with hints of vanilla bean and sweet oak spice. A lush midpalate leads to approachable tannins. An enjoyable wine to match with pasta, beef, or venison.

WHERE TO BUY: WINERY, WINE SHOPS

3471 Pranger Road, Walla Walla, WA 99362; 509-526-7896; www.isenhowercellars.com. Open for Walla Walla Valley wine events and by appointment.

JANUIK WINERY

SEATTLE AREA   ESTABLISHED 1999

Nearly two decades as one of Washington's top winemakers have given Mike Januik an advantage now that he has started out on his own. The former Chateau Ste. Michelle winemaker launched his own project at just the right time, as the 1999 and 2000 vintages are two of the most heralded in the state's short winemaking history. Januik secures grapes from such top vineyards as Klipsun, Cold Creek, Seven Hills, Conner Lee, Champoux, and Ciel du Cheval. The results are some of the most highly sought-after wines in the Northwest. Serious collectors will get on his mailing list now.

BEST BETS

Cold Creek Vineyard Chardonnay $$ From perhaps the finest vineyard in the state, this Chardonnay is everything you'd expect, with great structure, depth of flavor, and just the right balance of oak and fruit.

Merlot $$ A smooth, supple wine with wonderful cherry and vanilla extract aromas and rich, jammy flavors. A warm and inviting Merlot.

Cabernet Sauvignon $$ A classy Cab with great aging potential, this is loaded with black currant, oak, and spice aromas and deep, penetrating black fruit flavors. Tannins are perfectly balanced with the fruit and acidity. Serve with your finest cut of beef.

WHERE TO BUY: WINERY, WINE SHOPS

19730 144th Ave. N.E., Woodinville, WA 98072; 425-481-5502; www.januikwinery.com. Open by appointment.

JARDIN WINES

SEATTLE AREA   ESTABLISHED 2000

Craig and Bree Friedl launched their tiny winery in the suburbs of Seattle in 2000 and released their first wines a year later. Using fruit from Carter Vineyard in the Yakima Valley, Jardin's first wines are Chardonnay and Merlot. In future releases, look for Cabernet Sauvignon and a blend called Scandalous Red to be added to the portfolio.

BEST BETS

Chardonnay $$ This toasty, buttery white offers plenty of oak without hiding the tasty citrus and dried tropical fruit. A big, long, creamy wine that would serve well as an aperitif with chilled shrimp.

Merlot $$ A bright, smooth, luscious wine, this red offers cherry and mocha aromas and flavors and a long, soft landing. Pair this with lamb chops, turkey, or Cougar Gold cheese.

WHERE TO BUY: WINERY, WINE SHOPS

22309 Seventh Ave. S., #2A, Des Moines, WA 98198; 206-931-4453; www.jardinwines.com. Open by appointment.

JM CELLARS

SEATTLE AREA   ESTABLISHED 1999

John and Peggy Bigelow launched JM Cellars with the 1999 vintage. Their first two wines, a red blend called Tre Fanciulli and a Sauvignon Blanc, were well received. In future releases, look for more blends as well as varietal bottlings, including Cabernet Sauvignon, Merlot, and Cabernet Franc. Their focus is on grapes from the Red Mountain appellation, though they also buy fruit from the Yakima and Columbia Valleys.

BEST BETS

Tre Fanciulli $$ A blend of Cabernet Sauvignon, Merlot, and Syrah, this is a superior red loaded with rich berry and cherry flavors and laced with licorice and coffee. It's a big, chewy wine with a memorable finish.

Klipsun Vineyards Sauvignon Blanc $ This is a fine example of one of Washington's most food-friendly varieties. It offers complex orchard, citrus, and tropical fruit aromas and flavors with hints of light oak. Pair this with salmon, chicken, or pasta tossed with extra virgin olive oil and freshly grated Parmesan.

WHERE TO BUY: WINERY, WINE SHOPS

14404 137th Place N.E., Woodinville, WA 98072; 206-321-0052; www.jmcellars.com. Open by appointment.

K VINTNERS

WALLA WALLA VALLEY   ESTABLISHED 1999

Meet Charles Smith and you'll get the distinct impression he's a guy wanting to have some fun. He looks like he'd fit in better with a rock band than with a winery in one of America's hottest wine regions. He has come up with a wine name that will make you laugh (K Syrah). But taste his wines, and you'll realize he's dead serious about making high-quality Syrah, and the moderate price will help you appreciate his work even more.

BEST BETS

Syrah $$ A bold, deep red with focused plum and blackberry aromas and flavors with excellent balance of fruit, acidity, and tannin for matching with lamb, prime rib, or mild cheeses.

End of the Road Ranch Syrah $$ From famed Red Mountain comes a more hedonistic red with in-your-face jammy aromas and flavors. It's a sexy wine that would pair well with beef or turkey.

WHERE TO BUY: WINERY, WINE SHOPS

820 Mill Creek Road, Walla Walla, WA 99362; 509-526-5230; www.kvintners.com. Open by appointment.

KALAMAR WINERY

SEATTLE AREA   ESTABLISHED 1999

A boutique winery south of Seattle, Kalamar is dedicated to creating small amounts of handcrafted reds with a focus on Yakima Valley Merlot. The operation is a family affair, with Mark and Lisa Kalamar making the wine, while brother Greg's painting of the winemakers' wedding reception provides the label art.

BEST BETS

Merlot $$ A rich, dark wine with aromas and flavors of freshly split cedar, espresso, chocolate, and black fruit that explodes on the palate. A deep, penetrating wine to pair with your rarest, thickest steak.

WHERE TO BUY: WINERY, WINE SHOPS

5906 218th Ave. E., Sumner, WA 98390; 253-862-9844; www.kalamar winery.com. Open by appointment.

KESTREL VINTNERS

YAKIMA VALLEY   ESTABLISHED 1995

Positioning itself as a winery with a "Grand Cru mentality," Kestrel opened in the heart of the Yakima Valley with a bang. Its wines garnered quick praise, and under the guidance of winemaker Ray Sandidge, Kestrel's wines continue to develop into some of the finest in the valley. Though it makes a smattering of white wines, primarily two Chardonnays (standard and a rare ice wine), Kestrel excels at reds, particularly those from three-decade-old vines, which it uses for its Old Vines series.

BEST BETS

Syrah $$ Kestrel makes at least two styles. This, the lower-priced of the two, is a sophisticated red with rich, jammy flavors and plenty of backbone. It offers layers of flavors and has enough acidity to give it cellar potential. But who would want to wait?

Old Vines Merlot $$$$ A big, complex wine showing dark, bold aromas and equally rich flavors. Ample tannins and acidity give this aging potential.

Old Vines Cabernet Sauvignon $$$$ A brooding, dark wine with a cauldron of complexity in the aromas and flavors. The charming mouth feel and long finish make this an elegant wine.

Raptor Red $$$$ A blend of Merlot and Cabernet Sauvignon, this is an opulent wine with savory aromas and mouth-filling flavors. The supple, appealing finish gives this great steak- or venison-matching potential.

WHERE TO BUY: WINERY, WINE SHOPS, GROCERY STORES

2890 Lee Road, Prosser, WA 99350; 509-786-2675; www.kestrel wines.com. Open daily.

KIONA VINEYARDS WINERY

RED MOUNTAIN   ESTABLISHED 1980

When wine lovers talk about consistently high-quality Washington wines, the name Kiona inevitably enters into the conversation. Liter for liter, no winery wins more accolades than Kiona, and for good reason: The large number of wines produced—from Lemberger and Merlot to a spectacular Chenin Blanc Ice Wine—are consistently good to great. For this, Kiona deserves to be on the same list as Chateau Ste. Michelle, Washington Hills Cellars, and Hogue Cellars, among those wineries that produce top-quality and widely available Washington wines.

BEST BETS

Cabernet Sauvignon $$ Kiona makes two Cabs: one from estate grapes and one from various vineyards. Both are of outstanding quality with classic black fruit and spice aromas, rich flavors, bold tannins, and lengthy finishes.

Lemberger $ Kiona is perhaps the state's best producer of this rare Austrian variety. This is a lush wine with fruit-driven aromas and rich, spicy flavors. An appealling match for just about anything, including meatloaf.

Dry Riesling $ A crisp, flinty wine with floral and bright fruit aromas and flavors, and classic underlying apple nuances. Serve with chicken or spicy chorizo dishes.

Chenin Blanc Ice Wine $$ It's rare to find an ice wine this good south of the Canadian border. Kiona's is a natural (frozen on the vine) ice wine with attractive honeysuckle and orchard fruit aromas and flavors. Not as thick as typical British Columbia ice wines, this is a wonderful and approachable treat.

WHERE TO BUY: WINERY, WINE SHOPS, GROCERY STORES

44612 N. Sunset Road, Benton City, WA 99320; 509-588-6716. Open daily.

KNIPPRATH CELLARS

SPOKANE   ESTABLISHED 1991

Henning Knipprath is a talented winemaker who excels at Germanic and Port-style wines. The winery is truly a family affair, with Henning's wife, children, and mother all pitching in to make the operation a success. The winery is in a historic schoolhouse in the center of Spokane.

BEST BETS

Gewürztraminer $ One of the tastiest Gewürztraminers you'll likely find in the Northwest, this is an aromatic white loaded with grapefruit and sweet spice aromas and flavors. A classic match for Asian-inspired cuisine, as well as pork or pasta tossed with pesto.

Positron Port $$ Often blended with various red grapes, this is a wonderful winter sipper with smooth, rich flavors and a sweet, delicious finish. Enjoy with Stilton.

Au Chocolat! $$ This is the Positron Port infused with chocolate, and it's a hedonistic delight. Purists might not like the addition of chocolate, but this will please a lot of palates.

Lagrima $$ A rare white Port, this is loaded with pear, orange peel, cinnamon, and golden raisin flavors. Sip this on its own or with biscotti.

WHERE TO BUY: WINERY, WINE SHOPS, GROCERY STORES

5634 E. Commerce Ave., Spokane, WA 99212; 509-534-5121; www.knipprath-cellars.com. Open Wednesday–Sunday.

L'ECOLE NO. 41

The winery with the distinctive label featuring a child's drawing of a schoolhouse is one of Washington's highest-quality producers. Led by owner/winemaker Marty Clubb, L'Ecole is one of the few wineries in the Walla Walla Valley that excels with white wines. Clubb loves Semillon, a grape most closely associated with France's Bordeaux region, and makes no fewer than three kinds of Semillon wine. But that doesn't mean L'Ecole is a slouch at reds. In fact, its greatest strength is with Cabernet Sauvignon, Merlot, and blends of the two.

L'Ecole gets grapes from throughout the huge Columbia Valley appellation, but in recent years Clubb has been dedicated to increasing the amount of fruit he obtains from the Walla Walla Valley. He has reinforced this with his ownership (with Leonetti Cellar and Pepper Bridge Winery) in Seven Hills Vineyard, one of the top vineyards in the Northwest for Bordeaux varieties. The vineyard is in Oregon, about fifteen minutes south of Walla Walla. If you want Marty Clubb's best wine, plan to buy a mixed case. He doesn't make any bad wines— or even any that are average or mediocre.

BEST BETS

Wahluke Slope Semillon $$ A sophisticated dry white wine that is a great alternative to Chardonnay. Aged in oak, this Semillon offers incredible depth of flavor and matches well with seafood, poultry, and pasta.

Walla Walla Valley Cabernet Sauvignon $$$ L'Ecole's place in the industry gives Clubb access to some of the best fruit in the valley, so his Cabernet Sauvignon consistently has tremendous flavors and a distinctive jamminess in the midpalate. It's approachable in its youth, yet capable of aging gracefully for a decade or more.

Apogee $$$ This Bordeaux-style blend simply is one of the best wines in Washington and can hold its own against wines from the top producers in California and France. Sweet French oak aromas and flavors meld with black fruit, supple tannins, mocha, peppercorns, and cardamom. Apogee is a symphony for the palate.

Syrah $$$ A consistently great red, this is a sensual Syrah that is outstanding from first whiff through the lengthy finish. It provides bold, rich aromas and flavors led by spice, oak, blackberry, plum, and vanilla. It embodies everything great about Washington Syrah.

WHERE TO BUY: WINERY, WINE SHOPS, GROCERY STORES

41 Lowden School Road, Lowden, WA 99360; 509-525-0940; www.lecole.com. Open daily.

LA TOSCANA WINERY

NORTH-CENTRAL WASHINGTON   ESTABLISHED 1999

Tucked in the hills between Leavenworth and Cashmere is a small winery that is ready to make a lot of noise. La Toscana is the work of Warren and Julie Moyles, who are crafting some giant red wines from their estate vineyards as well as with grapes purchased from Red Mountain. The winery also features a bed-and-breakfast with a decidedly Italian feel to it.

BEST BETS

Cabernet Sauvignon $$ A big, jammy wine with lush blackberry and huckleberry aromas and flavors, and with plenty of structure and balance. Try this with lamb or venison.

Merlot $$ A complex red offering aromas and flavors of plums, blackberries, tobacco leaf, and cigar box. A concentrated wine with a smooth, wonderful mouth feel. Enjoy with pasta or beef.

Cabernet Sauvignon—Cabernet Franc $$ A spicy, inky blend with aromas of vanilla, espresso, and vanilla and huge dark fruit flavors and chalky tannins. Try this with a rare ribeye steak.

WHERE TO BUY: WINERY, WINE SHOPS

9020 Foster Road, Cashmere, WA 98815; 509-548-5448. Open by appointment.

LATAH CREEK WINE CELLARS

SPOKANE   ESTABLISHED 1982

Owner/winemaker Mike Conway got his start in the '70s in the heady days of the California wine industry. In the early '80s he moved to Washington to help start Hogue Cellars in the Yakima Valley and Latah Creek in Spokane. Today, Conway makes a wide variety of good-quality, popular wines. In addition to the wines reviewed here, check out Latah's wonderfully refreshing Huckleberry Riesling.

BEST BETS

Chardonnay $ A delicious example of balance between fruit and oak, this white shows off bright citrus and orchard fruits with a creamy backdrop of butter and oak. A good match for shellfish or grilled chicken.

Moscato d'Latah $ Styled after a popular Italian wine, this sweet, refreshing, and slightly effervescent wine is a real crowd pleaser. It's rich with ripe flavors of apricots, nectarines, peaches, and honey and is a perfect brunch or picnic sipper.

Muscat Canelli $ Muscat is one of the most beautifully aromatic white wines in Washington, and Latah's version is a choice example with its tropical aromas and crisp, refreshing flavors. Enjoy this with stir-fry dishes or cold chicken.

Merlot $ A bright, smooth wine showing off cherry and vanilla a
romas and jammy, enjoyable flavors, this versatile wine will pair
well with pasta, flank steak, or pizza.

E. 13030 Indiana Ave., Spokane, WA 99216; 509-926-0164;
www.latahcreek.com. Open daily.

LEONETTI CELLAR

WALLA WALLA VALLEY   ESTABLISHED 1978

Easily the most sought-after wines in the Pacific Northwest, those of
Leonetti Cellar set the bar high early, starting with the winery's 1978
Cabernet Sauvignon that won award after award. Owner and wine-
maker Gary Figgins is one of the kindest, most down-to-earth folks
you'll ever meet. His wines are highly allocated—available only to
those on "the list," and only once a year at that. The first weekend in
May—dubbed Leonetti Weekend by most, but officially called Spring
Release Weekend by the other Walla Walla wineries open that week-
end—is when Leonetti's customers can come to the winery, taste the
new releases, and pick up their wine. While others in the business might
begrudge Leonetti's success, they also benefit: Leonetti Weekend is the
largest for retail sales throughout the Columbia Valley because wine-
loving Puget Sounders purchase large quantities of wine along the way
as they make their annual pilgrimage to Walla Walla.

From the beginning, Figgins's philosophy has been to surround
himself with quality and to make the best wine possible. His son Chris
continues that tradition as he works side by side with Gary. In 2001,
Leonetti finished construction of a new winery, complete with under-
ground caves and a private fishing pond. Leonetti is a true cult winery,
and its name is whispered with reverence by knowledgeable wine lovers,
even those who have never had the opportunity to taste its wines.

Leonetti makes red wine only, and all of it is exceptional. Is it the
best in the Northwest? That's debatable (and not everyone will want
to pay the steep price of owning a bottle), but it's unlikely to disappoint
anyone's palate and will make any special occasion that much better.

BEST BETS

Reserve Cabernet Sauvignon $$$$$$ If you can ever get a taste of this
rare wine, you'll be enjoying one of the finest Cabs in the world.
Leonetti produces its Reserve Cab only a few times a decade—and
in small amounts at high prices. It's Leonetti's most age-worthy
wine, a gem that likely will taste incredible for a decade.

Cabernet Sauvignon $$$$ Leonetti is able to obtain the best fruit from
throughout the Columbia Valley, so its regular Cab always has
extravagantly delicious cassis, black fruit, cedar, chocolate, vanilla,
and tobacco and provides great complexity. It is generally aged in
new French oak that also imparts a delicious smoothness. Rule of

thumb for aging is to wait at least five years after vintage to open, but wait no more than twenty years to drink it up.

Merlot $$$$ Smooth and rich from start to finish, this is one of the finest Merlots you're likely to taste. Again, plenty of new oak aging, though less than the Cab (and released a year earlier). Optimal drinking age will be four to ten years after vintage.

Sangiovese $$$$ This wine is a nod to Gary's Italian heritage, and he makes one of the richest around. This is no straw-covered jug of Chianti, but rather a serious, oak-aged, Cabernet-infused big red wine that imparts Sangiovese's trademark bright cherry aromas and flavors, earthiness, and sweet spices.

WHERE TO BUY: WINERY, WINE SHOPS

1875 Foothills Lane, Walla Walla, WA 99362; 509-525-1428; www.leonetticellar.com. Open annually to mailing list customers only.

LOPEZ ISLAND VINEYARDS

PUGET SOUND   ESTABLISHED 1990

Led by owner/winemaker Brent Charnley, Lopez Island produces wines of distinction from its estate organic vineyards in the San Juan Islands, as well as from grapes grown in the Yakima Valley. Of particular interest are the Madeleine Angevine and Siegerrebe from the estate vineyards and the Cab–Merlot blend from Crawford Vineyard.

BEST BETS

Madeleine Angevine $ A delightful up-front white that reveals Riesling-like fruit and delicious depth. Made bone dry, it gives the impression of sweetness because of all the fruit. Perfect with fiery Asian-inspired shrimp.

Siegerrebe $ A somewhat rare white variety from Austria, this is a naturally sweeter wine that shows off gorgeous aromas and flavors of pears, mangoes, and kiwis and great balance of flavor, sugar, and acidity. Enjoy with a cheese plate or brunch fare.

Cab–Merlot $$ A complex red showing anise and sweet herbal notes amid dark berry aromas and ripe fruit with subtle spice characteristics. Approachable tannins make this a food-friendly wine.

Chardonnay $ A fruit-driven wine showing apple and pineapple characteristics with hints of toasty oak and creaminess that reveal barrel fermentation. Try this with halibut, scallops, or grilled chicken.

WHERE TO BUY: WINERY, WINE SHOPS

724B Fisherman Bay Road, Lopez Island, WA 98261; 360-468-3644; www.lopezislandvineyards.com. Seasonal hours.

LOST MOUNTAIN WINERY

OLYMPIC PENINSULA   ESTABLISHED 1982

Lost Mountain Winery is a tribute to Romeo Conca, who ran the winery until his death in 1997. He was affectionately known for making rich, tasty wines in the tradition of Italian home winemaking. Son and daughter-in-law Steve and Sue Conca now operate the winery nestled high in the foothills of the Olympic Mountains, and they're taking the wines to new heights with some of the best reds produced in the state. Using grapes primarily from the Columbia Valley, Lost Mountain is making a new name for itself with high-end Syrah, Merlot, Cabernet Franc, and Cabernet Sauvignon. Additionally, the Concas bring in a bit of California Zinfandel, just as Romeo did.

BEST BETS

Syrah $$ With grapes from famed Bacchus Vineyard north of Pasco, Washington, this is one of the best Syrahs you'll come across. Richly structured with gobs of black, jammy fruit, this offers layers of complexity that show how great this grape can be.

Cabernet Franc $$ An elegant wine with vanilla, cedar, and black cherry aromas and flavors, with a smooth, dark chocolate finish. One of the best you'll find in the Pacific Northwest.

Lost Mountain Red $$ Typically from California Zinfandel and Petite Sirah, this is a nouveau-style red with yummy up-front raspberry flavors. Enjoy with a big plate of pasta.

WHERE TO BUY: WINERY, WINE SHOPS

3174 Lost Mountain Road, Sequim, WA 98382; 360-683-5229; www.lostmountain.com. Seasonal hours.

MARCHETTI WINES

SEATTLE AREA   ESTABLISHED 2000

Marchetti is a small producer specializing in Old World–style red wines using no additional sulfites or chemicals. The winemaker grew up in an Italian family and has made wine for more than thirty years using Washington and California grapes.

BEST BETS

Cabernet Franc $$ A smooth, jammy red from Washington grapes with rich cherry flavors and bright, approachable fruit.

Cabernet Sauvignon $$ Ripe, tasty black fruit from Washington's Columbia Valley. Hints of herbs and black olives highlight this delicious red wine.

WHERE TO BUY: WINERY, WINE SHOPS

3709 Fuller Lane S.E., Olympia, WA 98501; 360-456-5409. Not open to the public.

MARKET CELLAR WINERY

SEATTLE AREA   ESTABLISHED 1996

John Farias has been helping others make wine and brew beer for a long time—since 1965, in fact. The longtime owner of Seattle's Liberty Malt Supply launched his own modest winery in the mid-'90s on the street below the Pike Place Market. There, he and partner Tom Weishamtel craft a few hundred cases of unpretentious wines. All are from Yakima Valley grapes, and no bottle costs more than about $10.

BEST BETS

Cabernet Sauvignon $ A tasty, straightforward Cab meant to enjoy with everyday meals, this offers solid fruit and moderate tannins.

Merlot $ A medium-bodied Merlot with bright fruit, soft tannins, and a medium finish.

WHERE TO BUY: WINERY, WINE SHOPS

1432 Western Ave., Seattle, WA 98101; 206-622-1880; www.market cellarwinery.com. Open Monday–Saturday.

MARSHAL'S WINERY

COLUMBIA GORGE   ESTABLISHED 2000

Ron Johnson, affectionately known as RonJohn, has his own ideas about winemaking in this small family-run winery. In addition to a delicious Cabernet Sauvignon and a Syrah (which he calls Sharaz), RonJohn makes a delightful red wine from Black Homburg grapes, as well as a red dessert wine called Sweet Ana Marie. The winery is named after his son, and a couple of his eight wines are named for family members.

BEST BETS

Cabernet Sauvignon $$ A rich, deep red showing cola and spice aromas and deep, penetrating fruit. A well-balanced and elegant wine. Serve with beef dishes or lasagna.

Sharaz $$ A luscious red with mouth-filling flavors of oak spice, vanilla, blackberry, and strawberry jam and a backbone of tannin and acidity. Enjoy with lamb or sweetbreads.

Merlot $$ Showing off oak that mingles with plenty of bright, rich fruit, this is a tasty and fruit-forward wine to enjoy with chicken, pizza, or meatloaf.

Sweet Ana Marie $ One of the winery's best-sellers, this sweet red might remind you of Dr Pepper with hints of black fruit. Serve this a bit chilled.

WHERE TO BUY: WINERY

150 Oak Creek Road, Dallesport, WA 98617; 509-767-4633. Open daily.

MARYHILL WINERY

COLUMBIA GORGE   ESTABLISHED 1999

With sweeping views of the Columbia Gorge and Mount Hood and a beautiful tasting room, the Gorge's destination winery is an instant favorite with wine tourists. The winery, just west of the Maryhill Museum, opened in spring 2001 with seven wines from Columbia Valley grapes.

BEST BETS

Sangiovese $$ This Italian variety is most famous for being the key ingredient for Chianti. It is rich and fruity with cherry and raspberry aromas and smoky flavors backed up by robust tannins. Perfect for thick slabs of lasagna.

Merlot $$ Bright and approachable, this is everything you could hope for in a drink-now Washington Merlot. Plenty of ripe, bright fruit and oak spice.

Chardonnay $ Fruit-forward in style and very affordable, this has terrific balance between apples, citrus, and light oak. Match with shellfish, fettuccine in a clam sauce, or grilled salmon.

Zinfandel $$ Huge aromatics invite further exploration of this luscious red wine. A mouthful provides delicious, juicy flavors of ripe blackberries, bittersweet chocolate, and great depth of flavor.

WHERE TO BUY: WINERY, WINE SHOPS, GROCERY STORES

9774 Hwy. 14, Goldendale, WA 98620; 877-627-9445; www.mary hillwinery.com. Open daily.

MATTHEWS CELLARS

SEATTLE AREA   ESTABLISHED 1993

Matt Loso has dedicated himself to producing world-class Bordeaux-style wines. To achieve this, he seeks out Washington's finest grapes, uses the best equipment—including only French oak barrels—and exercises patience as the wines develop and mature. The results: exceptional age-worthy wines highly sought by discerning connoisseurs.

BEST BETS

Red Wine $$$ This wine is a blend of fruits from several top Columbia Valley vineyards, but don't let its simple title fool you. It's a juicy mouthful with long plum, cherry, and blackberry fruit with complex nuances of oak spice, dried herbs, and chocolate—all backed up with well-balanced and -managed acidity and tannins. Save it for the finest occasions.

Claret $$ A red blend that is an elegant and complex wine with supple notes of cherry, blackberry, sweet spice, bittersweet chocolate, and espresso. In the Old World, a Claret is a "second" wine from barrels not deemed worthy of the primary blend. Even if this were the case here, this is an outstanding effort and a substantial wine.

Sauvignon Blanc $$ From famed Klipsun Vineyard on Red Mountain, this luscious white offers the best of this variety, from floral, apple, and citrus notes to mint, gooseberries, and a flinty, smoky edge. A wine to pair with the best of Northwest seafood.

White Wine $$ A white Bordeaux blend of Semillon with Sauvignon Blanc, this is a rich, silky wine with fresh fig and tropical notes, a creamy midpalate, and a long finish. Imagine this with scallops sautéed in butter.

WHERE TO BUY: WINERY, WINE SHOPS

16116 140th Place N.E., Woodinville, WA 98072; 425-487-9810; www.matthewscellars.com. Open by appointment.

MCCREA CELLARS

PUGET SOUND   ESTABLISHED 1988

Doug McCrea's achievements are proof that care, focus, and hard work can result in greatness. The New Orleans native's passion for Rhône varieties—primarily Syrah and Viognier—makes him one of Washington's top winemakers. He makes no fewer than five different Syrahs each year, and consistently they are some of the nation's best. His work with Viognier shows just how well this white grape can perform in Washington, and his Chardonnay is consistently outstanding.

BEST BETS

Cuvée Orleans Syrah $$$$ This blend from two of the Yakima Valley's top Syrah vineyards (Boushey Grand Côte and Ciel du Cheval) is a thick, dense wine loaded with layer after layer of complex fruit, spice, and other components. It'll make you cry "Uncle!" Also look for the vineyard-designated Syrahs from these two vineyards.

Syrah $$$ McCrea's "standard" Yakima Valley Syrah is no slouch with its jammy midpalate and creamy chocolate finish. A consistently outstanding effort.

Chardonnay $$$ Typically aged in 100 percent French oak, this shows the big, buttery side of Chardonnay, yet it is well balanced with expressive tropical fruit and intriguing depth.

La Mer $$ A blend of Chardonnay and Viognier that opens with floral and fruit aromas and arouses the taste buds with supple, concentrated fruit flavors and terrific mouth weight.

Viognier $$ A charming white with complex citrus and tropical nuances. Match this with duck or Asian-inspired dishes.

WHERE TO BUY: WINERY, WINE SHOPS

13443 118th Ave. S.E., Rainier, WA 98576; 360-458-9463; www.mccreacellars.com. Open twice annually to mailing list members.

MOONLIGHT SPARKLING WINE CELLARS

TRI-CITIES   ESTABLISHED 2001

Allan Pangborn knows sparkling wine about as well as anyone in the Pacific Northwest. Bubbly has been the specialty of the Sonoma Valley native for more than two decades, and he was the first winemaker for Domaine Ste. Michelle, Stimson Lane's sparkling wine house. Pangborn studied winemaking in California, France, and Austria and now makes small lots of Chardonnay-based bubbly in Washington wine country.

BEST BETS

Blanc de Blanc $$ A splendid French-style sparkler that shows off aromas of apples and light berries, great bubbles, a hint of sweetness, and terrific balance. This would pair well with oysters or ahi tartar.

WHERE TO BUY: WINERY, WINE SHOPS

4704 W. 12th Ave., Kennewick, WA 99338; 509-735-7237; www.moonlightcellars.com. Open by appointment.

MOUNT BAKER VINEYARDS

NORTHWEST WASHINGTON   ESTABLISHED 1982

In the lush Nooksack Valley north of Bellingham, Mount Baker Vineyards quietly goes about making wines from estate fruit as well as from grapes grown east of the Cascades. The winery, a joy to visit, is situated about as close as you can get to Canada without having to learn the metric system. Mount Baker Vineyards makes wines for every palate, from delicious fruit wines to world-class Merlots and Syrahs.

BEST BETS

Barrel Select Merlot $ A superior wine at a great price, this is a big, juicy red with wonderful aromas of berries and vanilla and flavors that include those of cherries, black fruit, spices, and cedar. A jammy midpalate and plenty of length make this a favorite.

Barrel Select Syrah $$ A jammy and richly structured wine with hedonistic aromas and ripe plum flavors. This would go perfectly with grilled lamb.

Barrel Select Pinot Gris $ Showing a bit of toastiness on the aromas, this food-friendly white reveals loads of citrus and orchard fruits with crisp acidity. Salmon, mussels, or baked chicken will work well with it.

Rosetta Rosé $ This blend of Merlot, Syrah, Lemberger, and Siegerrebe is a delicate and serious rosé with aromas and flavors of strawberries, cranberries, and cherries. A clean, dry wine, this pairs well with a ham or egg salad sandwich.

4298 Mount Baker Hwy., Everson, WA 98247; 360-592-2300. Open daily.

MOUNTAIN DOME WINERY / GRANDE RONDE CELLARS

SPOKANE   ESTABLISHED 1984

Michael Manz and his family produce sparkling wines under the Mountain Dome label using classic Champagne methods. Made from Chardonnay, Pinot Noir, and Pinot Meunier, the sparklers show the care and quality that go into them. In the late '90s, Manz launched the Grande Ronde Cellars label to produce rich Bordeaux-style wines.

BEST BETS

Mountain Dome Brut $$ A crisp bubbly that shows delicious orchard fruit aromas and flavors with good hints of cake and nuttiness. A great match for shellfish or chicken.

Pleasant Prairie Pinot Noir $$ A rare still wine for Mountain Dome, this is a fine Pinot Noir from a cooler area in the Columbia Gorge. An elegant wine showing depth of fruit amid exotic spices and hints of vanilla.

Grande Ronde Cellars Cabernet Sauvignon $$$ A tasty Cab with aromas of violets and berries and flavors of big, juicy blueberries and blackberries. Try this with barbecued ribs.

Grande Ronde Cellars Merlot $$$ Aromas of pipe tobacco, vanilla, and black cherries lead to bright, approachable fruit on the palate. A delicious steak wine.

WHERE TO BUY: WINERY, WINE SHOPS, GROCERY STORES

16315 E. Temple Road, Spokane, WA 99217; 509-928-2788; www.mountaindome.com. Open by appointment.

NORTHSTAR

WALLA WALLA VALLEY   ESTABLISHED 1994

Northstar is a high-end, small-production winery for Stimson Lane, which owns Columbia Crest, Chateau Ste. Michelle, and others. Its focus is exclusively Merlot, from grapes grown in some of the Columbia Valley's best vineyards, including Indian Wells, Cold Creek, and Conner Lee. In 2002 a new production facility and tasting room opened in Walla Walla.

BEST BETS

Merlot $$$$ Northstar's focus is on Washington's most famous grape. This is a Bordeaux-style wine blended with a small amount of Cabernet Sauvignon and aged in a large amount (sometimes 100 percent) of new French oak. The results are a big wine showing off the dark richness and the fruity approachability of the variety. It's a wine for a special meal and should age well for a decade or more.

WHERE TO BUY: WINERY, WINE SHOPS

1736 J. B. George Road, Walla Walla, WA 99362; 509-525-6100; www.northstarmerlot.com. Open by appointment.

NOVELTY HILL WINERY

SEATTLE AREA   ESTABLISHED 2000

This young winery is off to a strong start, with master winemaker Mike Januik crafting the product. There are plans to build a grand winery in the foothills of the Cascades east of Seattle and to establish a vineyard on the Royal Slope in the Columbia Valley.

BEST BETS

Sauvignon Blanc $$ A rich, ripe, fruit-driven white with tropical and citrus aromas and flavors. It's easy to imagine drinking this with a plate filled with spicy barbecued prawns.

WHERE TO BUY: WINERY, WINE SHOPS

19730 144th Ave. N.E., Woodinville, WA 98072; 425-481-8317; www.noveltyhillwines.com. Open by appointment.

OAKWOOD CELLARS

RED MOUNTAIN   ESTABLISHED 1986

Eppie Skelton is a Red Mountain pioneer who started her winery in the mid-'80s. While she makes a number of delicious red and white wines, she has gained a following for Lemberger, a wonderful yet misunderstood grape (mostly because its name sounds similar to that of a strong cheese). Oakwood makes two styles of Lemberger, a luscious red and a rosé.

BEST BETS

Lemberger $ A delicious wine at a great price, this lovely red shows off light oak aging with aromas and flavors that burst with fresh cherries, plums, blackberries, and more. Enjoy with barbecue fare.

Lemberger Blanc $ An off-dry rosé that provides aromas and flavors of fresh strawberries, cranberries, and cherries and a smooth, crisp mouth feel. Goes well with turkey.

Cabernet Sauvignon $$ A refined red showing off aromas and flavors of black currants, blackberries, vanilla, and oak. A fresh, rich, flavorful wine with right-on structure. A good wine to serve with lamb or beef.

Muscat Canelli $ Few wines are as aromatic as Muscat Canelli, and Oakwood's is loaded with inspiring grapefruit and white floral aromas and exotic fruit flavors. Even with a bit of residual sugar, this isn't just a sweet wine but a long, smooth sipper.

40504 N. Demoss Road, Benton City, WA 99320; 509-588-5332.
Open weekends or by appointment.

OLYMPIC CELLARS

OLYMPIC PENINSULA   ESTABLISHED 1979

This winery in a historic barn on Highway 101 west of Sequim produces
a wide array of good-quality wines using grapes from the Columbia
Valley. In addition to Riesling, Chardonnay, Merlot, Lemberger, and
Cabernet Sauvignon, Olympic offers two delicious, unpretentious
blends called Dungeness Red and Dungeness White, named after the
succulent crab and nearby landmark.

BEST BETS

Dungeness Red $ A blend that includes Lemberger, this bright, fruit-driven red enjoys good depth of flavor. A fresh wine to enjoy any day of the week.

Dungeness White $ Primarily Riesling, this has hints of sugar expertly backed up with plenty of crispness and loaded with orchard and citrus flavors. Enjoy with its namesake crab.

Cabernet Sauvignon $$ Opening with classic black currant and sweet spiciness from oak aging, this is a serious wine with brooding black fruit that is smooth and flavorful throughout.

WHERE TO BUY, WINERY, WINE SHOPS

255410 Hwy. 101, Port Angeles, WA 98362; 360-452-0160;
www.olympiccellars.com. Open daily.

OWEN-SULLIVAN WINERY

SEATTLE AREA   ESTABLISHED 1997

This collaboration between Bill Owen and Rob Sullivan is resulting in
wines of depth and power. The suburban winery south of Seattle pro-
duces primarily red wines from some of Washington's top vineyards,
including Klipsun, Champoux, and Alder Ridge.

BEST BETS

Syrah $$ A big, dense, opulent wine showing jammy black fruit, chocolate, and coffee tendencies and a long, lush finish. Drink young with lamb or venison.

Klipsun Merlot $$ Showing rich cherry and vanilla aromas, this medium-bodied wine offers ripe cherry and blueberry flavors with overtones of cedar and mocha. A wine to enjoy with grilled meats or vegetables.

BSH $$$ A blend of mostly Cabernet Sauvignon that is deep, dark, and dense with penetrating black fruit and chocolate and big, balanced tannins. A wine for tucking away in the cellar or pairing with a big, rare ribeye. The name is an acronym (think "Big as a brick . . .").

WHERE TO BUY: WINERY, WINE SHOPS

4497 S. 134th Place, Tukwila, WA 98168; 206-243-3427; www.owen sullivan.com. Open by appointment.

PARADISOS DEL SOL

YAKIMA VALLEY   ESTABLISHED 1999

After two decades of making wines for a variety of Washington wineries, Paul Vandenberg launched his own boutique operation using grapes primarily from his estate vineyard.

BEST BETS

Rosé Paradisos $ A delicious picnic wine that shows off bright aromas and flavors of strawberries and rhubarb, this will pair well with chicken or ham.

Angelica $ This soft, sweet wine shows off a nutty aroma with orchard and citrus fruit flavors. A fine sipper.

WHERE TO BUY: WINERY, WINE SHOPS

881 Holmason Road, Sunnyside, WA 98944; 509-839-9632; www.paradisosdelsol.com. Open Friday–Monday or by appointment.

PASEK CELLARS

SKAGIT VALLEY   ESTABLISHED 1995

Gene and Kathy Pasek are well situated in the idyllic Skagit Valley north of Seattle, crafting delicious red and white wines from Eastern Washington grapes, as well as a few well-made fruit wines. In 2001 they moved their tasting room from downtown Mount Vernon to the hamlet of Conway, where it is conveniently located in a country store just off Interstate 5. Their style is fruit-driven, fresh wines that celebrate the beauty of their locale.

BEST BETS

Merlot–Cab $ A bright red blend with plenty of up-front fruit, this is built and priced for everyday enjoyment. Match this with most meat or pasta dishes.

Red Quartette $ A blend of Cabernet Sauvignon, Syrah, Merlot, and Cabernet Franc, this is rich with bright fruit aromas and spicy, medium-bodied flavors.

Syrah Port $ One of the better Ports you'll find in the Northwest, this uses grapes from the Yakima Valley and is loaded with sweet jam, plum, and raisin aromas and flavors. Perfect with Stilton or Gorgonzola.

Blackberry $ Remember picking blackberries on warm late-summer days? You will when you smell and sip this beauty. It bursts with aromas and is delicate on the palate, with good acidity to match barbecued chicken or ribs.

WHERE TO BUY: WINERY

18729 Fir Island Road, Conway, WA 98238; 888-350-9463. Open daily.

PATRICK M. PAUL VINEYARDS

WALLA WALLA VALLEY   ESTABLISHED 1988

Mike Paul makes wine just down the road from Leonetti Cellar's Gary Figgins. Paul and Figgins have been near each other much of their lives, as they grew up on the same street and worked for the same company before getting into the wine industry. Paul planted a small Cabernet Franc vineyard in 1984 and is one of the valley's smallest producers, with just 500 cases per year. His wines are approachable in price as well as in flavor.

BEST BETS

Cabernet Franc $$ Patrick M. Paul's signature wine is a bright and fruity red that is delightfully rich and approachable in its youth.

Merlot $$ This handcrafted red has well-balanced oak and fruit components. A classy, well-done Merlot.

Cabernet Sauvignon $$ Nicely integrated fruit and oak are Patrick M. Paul's trademark, and this Cab is a textbook example. Tame tannins make this approachable in its youth.

WHERE TO BUY: WINERY, WINE SHOPS

1554 School Ave., Walla Walla, WA 99362; 509-525-6502. Seasonal hours.

PAUL THOMAS WINERY

SEATTLE AREA   ESTABLISHED 1979

Paul Thomas was a pioneer of Washington's modern wine history, producing primarily non-grape wines and also top Chardonnay and Cabernet Sauvignon. Brian Carter of Washington Hills Cellars fame got his start at Paul Thomas, helping the winery gain early momentum. Eventually the winery was sold to Associated Vintners and now is owned by the giant Canandaigua Wine Company. The wines tend to offer good quality at value prices.

BEST BETS

Merlot $ Delicious fruit with well-integrated oak nuances, this always delicious—and occasionally great—red is built to enjoy early and often.

Cabernet Sauvignon $ Ridiculously priced for under $10, this Cab shows rich fruit, complex spiciness, and well-structured tannins.

Razz $ A consumer favorite, this raspberry wine is a delicious sipper with intense fruit and terrific structure. A consistent gold medal winner.

WHERE TO BUY: GROCERY STORES

14030 N.E. 145th St., Woodinville, WA 98072; 425-488-2776; www.paulthomaswinery.com. No tasting facility.

PEPPER BRIDGE WINERY

WALLA WALLA VALLEY   ESTABLISHED 1998

Named after vaunted Pepper Bridge Vineyard, one of the Walla Walla Valley's youngest and hottest wineries is turning heads and gaining fans with its deep, intense Bordeaux-style reds. The effort is led by Norm McKibben, who manages the winery as well as the vineyard and nearby Seven Hills Vineyard, and winemaker Jean-François Pellet. Collectors might consider getting on the winery's mailing list while they still can.

BEST BETS

Cabernet Sauvignon $$$$ A rich, concentrated wine with classic vanilla, black currant, and blackberry aromas and ripe, penetrating flavors. It's difficult to imagine drinking this without a rare ribeye on the table.

Merlot $$$$ This long, smooth red is nearly as big as the Cab, with bright berry fruit and vanilla aromas and deep, brooding flavors. It's plenty approachable in its youth but also will age gracefully for a half-decade or more. Pair with beef, lamb, chocolate, or hard cheeses.

WHERE TO BUY: WINERY, WINE SHOPS

1704 J. B. George Road, Walla Walla, WA 99362; 509-525-7505; www.pepperbridge.com. Open by appointment.

PONTIN DEL ROSA

YAKIMA VALLEY   ESTABLISHED 1984

The Pontin family owns and operates this longtime Yakima Valley producer in the Roza district near the town of Prosser. The wine styles range from gorgeous Pinot Gris to succulent Sangiovese. The family has been farming in the valley for four decades, and the winemaking efforts are led by Scott Pontin.

BEST BETS

Cabernet Sauvignon $$ A warm, creamy, approachable red offering dark fruit flavors and ripe tannins. Pair with beef in a mushroom sauce.

Pinot Grigio $ One of the best Pinot Gris in Washington, this provides delicate tropical fruit and vanilla bean aromas with superlative balance and crisp, cleansing acidity. Try this with veal, mussels or pork.

Angelo Pontin Sangiovese $$ This tribute to the family patriarch who emigrated from Italy to the United States in the early twentieth century is a classic Sangiovese with dusty cherry and spice aromas and a fruit driven, cleansing mouth feel. Enjoy with lasagna.

Chenin Blanc $ Often forgotten amid more popular white wines, this is a star in its own right with luscious pear, apple, and orange flavors backed up with great acidity. Enjoy with chicken, pasta, or shellfish.

WHERE TO BUY: WINERY, WINE SHOPS, GROCERY STORES

35502 N. Hinzerling Road, Prosser, WA 99350; 509-786-4449. Open daily.

PORTTEUS WINERY

YAKIMA VALLEY   ESTABLISHED 1984

Paul Portteus grows highly sought-after grapes in the Yakima Valley and crafts a wide variety of wines, primarily focusing on reds. All of his wines are made from grapes grown on his sixty acres of vineyards. Portteus, a gentle soul who has gained a strong following, perhaps is best known for pioneering Zinfandel in Washington, where little of this grape is grown.

BEST BETS

Zinfandel $$ A zesty wine showing ripe strawberry and black pepper notes with a lush, jammy, spicy midpalate. A wonderful wine for barbecued ribs or rare steaks.

Cabernet Sauvignon $$ A fresh, approachable red exhibiting rich blueberry and blackberry notes with plenty of tannins.

Rattlesnake Ridge Red $ This red table wine is a fine Bordeaux-style blend that is fresh and approachable in style and priced for everyday enjoyment.

Estate Reserve $$$ Portteus's finest wine, this is a blend of Cab, Merlot, Cab Franc, and Syrah. It's a huge wine with penetrating yet elegant aromas and flavors of black fruit, chocolate, and aromatic spices. A wine to pull out for a special occasion.

WHERE TO BUY: WINERY, WINE SHOPS

5201 Highland Drive, Zillah, WA 98953; www.portteus.com. Open daily.

PRESTON PREMIUM WINES

COLUMBIA VALLEY   ESTABLISHED 1976

When Bill Preston planted grapes in his alfalfa field in 1972, his fellow farmers and businessmen thought he was crazy. There were only a handful of wineries in Washington at the time, and the industry was struggling. But Preston was a shrewd entrepreneur who proved his naysayers wrong. Thanks primarily to the talented Rob Griffin, who came up from California in 1977, Preston gained early fame with a string of delicious wines. After Griffin left, Preston proved that more isn't always better, and the winery struggled with quality as it grew to about fifty thousand cases annually. In the '90s, however, the second generation began to take over, with son Brent as winemaker and daughter Cathy running the business. They scaled back production and concentrated on quality, and Preston now produces about fifteen thousand cases of exceptional wine. Bill Preston, who died in 2001, left a legacy of quality and hard work, and a heritage as a pioneer of the Washington wine industry.

BEST BETS

Reserve Cabernet Sauvignon $$ This wine defines the "new" Preston Premium Wines. Supple and loaded with complexity, this is one of the Northwest's finest Cabs.

Reserve Merlot $$ A rich, layered, and delicious Merlot that will change a lot of minds about Preston's quality.

Beaujolais Rosé $ A delicious off-dry wine that is a great introduction for newer wine drinkers and a perfect party or deck wine.

WHERE TO BUY: WINERY, WINE SHOPS, GROCERY STORES

502 E. Vineyard Drive, Pasco, WA 99301; 509-545-1990; www.preston wines.com. Open daily.

QUILCEDA CREEK VINTNERS

SEATTLE AREA   ESTABLISHED 1979

Considered for more than two decades to be one of America's finest producers of Bordeaux-style wines, Quilceda Creek Vintners continues to craft stunning Cabernet Sauvignons and Merlots. Alex Golitzin, a chemical engineer by training, began his winery north of Seattle just as the modern Washington wine industry was beginning, and his commitment to quality has been second to none. Alex's son Paul has assumed the winemaker's role, and the father-and-son team ensures the wines live up to their fame.

The Golitzens begin with top-quality grapes from the Columbia Valley's finest regions, from their part ownership in venerable Champoux Vineyards in the Horse Heaven Hills, and their own vineyard on highly acclaimed Red Mountain, a ridge in the eastern Yakima Valley. Each vintage, all Quilceda wine is aged in 100 percent new French oak. The results are smooth, rich Cabs and Merlots that can be con-sumed on the spot or cellared for two decades or more. From vintage to vintage, Quilceda Creek is guaranteed to be one of the most consis-tently great wines you'll purchase.

BEST BETS

Cabernet Sauvignon $$$$ Even with 100 percent new French oak, the ripe fruit shines through. The balance of fruit, oak, acidity, and tannin is impeccable and virtually guarantees exceptional aging potential. Save this wine for the most special occasions and serve with the finest cuts of beef.

Merlot $$$$ Like its Cab counterpart, the Quilceda Merlot is rich in bright, accessible fruit with great balance, qualities that will make it difficult to cellar. This is one of America's best Merlots.

Red table wine $$$ About a third of Quilceda's wine is declassified each vintage, meaning Paul and Alex sort out barrels that don't quite make the cut for the top-end wines. In the tradition of the grand Bordeaux chateaux, these wines, while still wonderful by any measurement, go into a second, more affordable blend. This is the result and, while not priced for everyday enjoyment, it is perfect for regular consumption at casual get-togethers.

WHERE TO BUY: WINERY, WINE SHOPS

11306 52nd St. S.E., Snohomish, WA 98290; 360-568-2389; www.quilcedacreek.com. Open by appointment.

REININGER WINERY

WALLA WALLA VALLEY   ESTABLISHED 1997

Chuck and Tracy Reininger moved to Walla Walla in the early '90s and started making their own wine in 1993 while working at nearby Waterbrook Winery. They started Reininger in 1997 and quickly struck gold, literally, with medals for their Merlots, Cabs, and Syrahs in regional and international competition. In an appellation loaded with stars, Reininger Winery is one of the brightest.

BEST BETS

Merlot $$$ This fruit-driven beauty is loaded with cherries and berries, with supple tannins and just enough oak treatment to give it a little extra depth. The finish is as smooth and tasty as they come.

Cabernet Sauvignon $$$ This delicious Cab offers great complexity with black cherries, blackberries, fresh cedar, tobacco, cocoa, and spice. A superior wine with exceptional character that is easy to get excited about.

Syrah $$$ A hedonistic red that explodes with big, brooding aromas and flavors of blackberry jam, vanilla, spices, and more. A wine to savor with lamb, pasta, or sweetbreads.

WHERE TO BUY: WINERY, WINE SHOPS

720 C Street, Walla Walla, WA 99362; 509-522-1994; www.reininger winery.com. Open by appointment.

ROBERT KARL CELLARS

SPOKANE   ESTABLISHED 1999

One of Spokane's newest wineries is dedicated to producing high-quality and approachable Cabernet Sauvignon. Buying fruit from the Yakima Valley and Columbia Basin, the Gunselman family began with the celebrated 1999 vintage. In future vintages, look for releases including a Bordeaux-style blend and a Sauvignon Blanc.

BEST BETS

Cabernet Sauvignon $$$ From first whiff, you'll be hard pressed not to be seduced by this deeply aromatic Cab. It opens with black currants, cedar, and blackberries and provides complex layers of black fruit, spice, oak, tobacco, and more. Cellar for up to a decade or enjoy now with a T-bone, prime rib, or lamb.

WHERE TO BUY: WINERY, WINE SHOPS

115 W. Pacific Ave., Spokane, WA 99201; 509-363-1353; www.robertkarl.com. Open Saturdays and by appointment.

RULO WINERY

WALLA WALLA VALLEY   ESTABLISHED 2000

This boutique winery, the creation of Kurt Schlicker and Vicki Ritzinger, is south of downtown Walla Walla near the Oregon border amid a cluster of several other new wineries. Rulo's first efforts are focused on high-quality whites and a delicious rosé, with plans for reds in the works.

BEST BETS

Viognier $$ This white wine is brimming with incredible flavors and complexity. It's a huge wine with rich, clean tropical and orchard fruit with hints of lilac, petrol, mineral, guava, and ripe apricot. Enjoy this with most seafoods or fowl.

Rosé $ Made primarily from Cabernet Franc, this offers bright cherry and strawberry flavors and would pair well with cold fried chicken or medium cheeses.

Sundance Vineyard Chardonnay $$ Rulo makes two Chardonnays, and this is a rich, fruit-driven wine that shows fresh flavors and good density. A certain match with shellfish or grilled chicken.

3525 Pranger Road, Walla Walla, WA 99362; 509-525-7856; www.rulowinery.com. Open by appointment.

RUSSELL CREEK WINERY

WALLA WALLA VALLEY   ESTABLISHED 1998

Owner/winemaker Larry Krivosheln focuses on high-quality red wines and holds his own among Walla Walla's superpremium producers. In addition to his Bordeaux-style wines, keep an eye out for his delicious Sangiovese.

BEST BETS

Merlot $$$ A classy red with great balance of black cherry fruit, supple tannins, and perfect acidity, this is a pleasing sipper from first whiff through the lengthy finish. Pair with beef, veal, lasagna, or lamb.

Cabernet Sauvignon $$$ A rich, harmonious wine with concentrated aromas and flavors and layers of complexity. Enjoy with a thick steak, dark chocolates, or firm cheeses.

WHERE TO BUY: WINERY, WINE SHOPS

301 Aeronca Ave., Walla Walla, WA 99362; 509-386-4401; www. russellcreek-winery.com. Open by appointment.

RYAN PATRICK VINEYARDS

COLUMBIA VALLEY   ESTABLISHED 1999

With three estate vineyards in Washington's Columbia Basin, this exciting young winery is poised to build on its early success. The winery is the brainchild of Terry Flanagan, who grew up near the farming community of Quincy, then worked overseas and gained a love of wine. In the mid-'90s, he planted his first vineyard on the banks of the Columbia River and started to make wine beginning with the 1999 vintage.

BEST BETS

Ryan Patrick Red $$$ A classic Bordeaux-style blend of Cabernet Sauvignon, Merlot, and Cabernet Franc, this is a massive wine loaded with black fruit, mocha, and complex spice components, backed up with approachable tannins and a satisfying finish. Pair with prime rib.

Chardonnay $ An appealing white that shows off its good balance of fruit and oak aging. The palate is filled with citrus and tropical flavors and offers a crisp backbone that makes this a good match for grilled fish, scallops, or pasta.

WHERE TO BUY: WINERY, WINE SHOPS

80 4th St., Rock Island, WA 98850; 509-667-0921; www.ryanpatrick vineyards.com. Open weekends and by appointment.

SAGELANDS VINEYARD

YAKIMA VALLEY   ESTABLISHED 1984

Sagelands began life as Staton Hills Winery, a property that showed uneven quality in its first fifteen years. The Chalone Wine Group purchased the operation in 1999, giving the Napa, California, company two Washington wineries, one in the western Yakima Valley (Sagelands) and one to the east in Walla Walla (Canoe Ridge). With this new lease on life, Sagelands is expected to offer wines of increasing quality.

BEST BETS

Merlot $ A tasty, straightforward red with soft berry aromas and flavors. A good wine for everyday consumption.

Cabernet Sauvignon $ Delicious with classic currant and vanilla aromas, this big, tannic wine offers good black fruit and spicy flavors. Cellar for a half-decade or enjoy with a rare steak.

Ellipse $$ This Cab-based Port opens with rich, raisiny aromas and deep, concentrated flavors. Enjoy with dark chocolate or a cigar.

Orange Nectar $$ A rare white Port made from Muscat grapes, this offers intriguing raisin, pear, and orange oil aromas. A good after-dinner sipper.

WHERE TO BUY: WINERY, WINE SHOPS, GROCERY STORES

71 Gangl Road, Wapato, WA 98951, 800-967-0921; www.sagelands vineyard.com. Open daily.

SAINTPAULIA VINTNERS

SEATTLE AREA   ESTABLISHED 1994

Paul Shinoda Jr. is a horticulturist by trade and a winemaker by passion. His winery, named after a variety of African violet, focuses on Bordeaux-style wines from Red Mountain vineyards. Shinoda believes in long barrel aging (often more than thirty months for his Cabernet Sauvignon) and in releasing his wines later than those of other wineries, often four years after vintage.

BEST BETS

Cabernet Sauvignon $$ Extensive oak aging gives this a rich European feel with aromas of cedar and black fruit with blackberry flavors, big tannins, and a lingering finish.

Sauvignon Blanc $ A veritable basket of aromas and flavors, primarily stone, citrus, and tropical fruits, are backed up with a touch of residual sugar and good, clean acidity.

WHERE TO BUY: WINERY, WINE SHOPS

18302 83rd Ave. S.E., Snohomish, WA 98296; 360-668-8585. Open by appointment.

SALISHAN VINEYARDS

SOUTHWEST WASHINGTON   ESTABLISHED 1975

Seattle Times *reporter-turned-winegrower Joan Wolverton is a maverick in every sense of the word. She and her husband, Lincoln, cheerfully note they make wine in a vacuum. Their vineyards are nowhere near Seattle or the vast Columbia Valley in Eastern Washington. Instead they're just across the Columbia River from Portland, growing Pinot Noir. So they are ignored by the Oregon wine industry and virtually forgotten by Washington. Joan has been through a lot in the past quarter-century—including the eruption of nearby Mount St. Helens—all along happily making highly regarded Pinot Noir and Chardonnay that has a stronger following in the United Kingdom than in the Seattle area, thanks to British merchants who appreciate her style.*

BEST BETS

Pinot Noir $ Washington's answer to Oregon Pinot Noir and a vastly underpriced red that is consistently high quality. Earthy with lovely violet aromas and brooding flavors of cherries, licorice, and spices. A classic Burgundian-style wine with a velvety finish.

Chardonnay $ A clean, crisp, fruit-laden white that would match well with shellfish, lightly grilled chicken, or various cheeses.

WHERE TO BUY: WINERY, WINE SHOPS

35011 N. Fork Ave., La Center, WA 98629; 360-263-2713. Open seasonally or by appointment.

SAMISH ISLAND WINERY

NORTHWEST WASHINGTON   ESTABLISHED 1997

This small winery in Skagit County produces wines from blueberries, strawberries, and blackberries, including a blend of all three. The wines are available only at retailers and liquor stores in the Burlington and Mount Vernon areas.

BEST BETS

Blackberry $ With rich berry aromas and tasty flavors, this soft, off-dry red would pair well with barbecued ribs.

Blueberry $ Inviting aromas and soft, sweet, succulent flavors make this an approachable and enjoyable sipper. Try this with Stilton or chocolate.

Samish Island Blend $ Strawberries dominate the aromas and flavors of this sweet, delicious red wine. Enjoy this with barbecued chicken or vanilla ice cream.

WHERE TO BUY: GROCERY STORES

10990 Samish Island Road, Bow, WA 98232; 360-766-6086. Not open to the public.

SAN JUAN VINEYARDS

PUGET SOUND   ESTABLISHED 1996

The folks at San Juan Vineyards may have figured out how to have the best of all worlds. The winery is in an 1896 schoolhouse in picturesque Friday Harbor on San Juan Island. The grapes come from the estate vineyards and the Columbia Valley. They're far enough away from it all not to be hampered by traffic, yet a Washington State Ferry conveniently drops off customers every few hours. And the wines? Consistently delicious and value-priced.

BEST BETS

Merlot $ A soft, supple, elegant wine that shows off a complex blend of black tea, sweet spice, oak, and bright berries. The palate is balanced with rich flavors of blackberry jam, good acidity, and approachable tannins. A great everyday wine.

Semillon–Chardonnay $ This white blend is so good because it shows off the best of both varieties, including tropical citrus, bananas, figs, and hints of herbs. A terrific wine for seafood, including Dungeness crab or halibut.

Madeleine Angevine $ This cool-climate grape from island vineyards makes a fresh, juicy wine with good crispness to back up a bit of sweetness. A fun sipper or something to go with grilled chicken or fish.

Syrah $$ A palatial red with yummy aromas and flavors of black olives, chocolate, ripe plums, and jammy blackberries. This approachable wine would pair well with lamb or, perhaps, lasagna.

WHERE TO BUY: WINERY, WINE SHOPS, GROCERY STORES

3136 Roche Harbor Road, Friday Harbor, WA 98250; 360-378-9463; www.sanjuanvineyards.com. Seasonal hours.

SANDHILL WINERY

RED MOUNTAIN   ESTABLISHED 1998

John Dingethal knows the value of location. He owns Red Mountain Vineyard and Sandhill Winery just down the hill from Hedges Cellars and has come out with one of Washington's most delicious Cabernet Sauvignons.

BEST BETS

Cabernet Sauvignon $$ A stunning wine loaded with black currants, chocolate, and oak aromas followed by layers of dark fruit flavors and oak. Supple tannins back this wine's full-bodied flavors.

Merlot $$ Equally delicious is Sandhill's delightful Merlot, a mouth-filling red loaded with the likes of bright fruit, vanilla, and spice. Enjoy this with rare cuts of beef.

48313 N. Sunset Road, Benton City, WA 99320; 509-588-2699. Open by appointment.

SAVIAH CELLARS

WALLA WALLA VALLEY   ESTABLISHED 2000

One of a growing group of tiny wineries popping up south of Walla Walla, Saviah Cellars is off to a strong start, thanks to a careful selection of grapes from throughout the vast Columbia Valley, including Red Mountain, the Wahluke Slope and, of course, the Walla Walla Valley. The early wines by winemaker/owner Richard Funk are worthy efforts, and consumers can expect this trend to continue.

BEST BETS

Syrah $$ This dense, spicy red is rich with jammy plum, cedar, and dark chocolate aromas and flavors and will pair well with lamb or pasta with a full-bodied red sauce.

Une Vallée $$ A classic Bordeaux-style blend with fruit from three top vineyards, this is a big, cellar-worthy red showing cedar and vanilla from French oak aging, plum and blackberry flavors, and rich, chewy tannins. Team this up with prime rib.

WHERE TO BUY: WINERY, WINE SHOPS

1979 J. B. George Road, Walla Walla, WA 99362; 509-520-5166; www.saviahcellars.com. Seasonal hours.

SETH RYAN WINERY

RED MOUNTAIN   ESTABLISHED 1983

Jo and Ron Brodzinski and their son Kirk run this boutique winery that is a Red Mountain pioneer. They specialize in classic Washington varieties, including Cabernet Sauvignon, Cabernet Franc, Merlot, Gewürztraminer, Riesling, and Chardonnay. The Seth Ryan Gewürztraminer is one of the best you'll run across in the Pacific Northwest.

BEST BETS

Gewürztraminer $ With luscious aromas of peaches, grapefruit, and nutmeg, this is a classic white with fresh, delicious flavors and plentiful acidity. Buy early and often.

Cabernet Sauvignon $$ A classy red showing off long, elegant aromas and flavors of plums, chocolates, black pepper, oak spice, and vanilla. Enjoy with a thick steak.

Jessica's Meritage $$$ Blending the five classic red grapes of Bordeaux, this opens with warm milk chocolate and black currant aromas that lead to lush flavors of blackberries, blueberries, dark chocolate, and pepper, all balanced with solid tannins and plenty of acidity.

Late Harvest Riesling $ A smooth, ripe, sweet white with aromas and flavors of apricots and nectarines with good acidity. A good brunch or cheese plate wine.

WHERE TO BUY: WINERY, WINE SHOPS, GROCERY STORES

35306 Sunset Road, Benton City, WA 99320; 509-588-6780; www.sethryan.com. Open weekends and by appointment.

SEVEN HILLS WINERY

WALLA WALLA VALLEY   ESTABLISHED 1988

Seven Hills began its life as an Oregon winery, but in 2000 it moved from Milton-Freewater to downtown Walla Walla—about fifteen miles. The winery is in the historic Whitehouse-Crawford building, where owners Casey and Vicky McClellan produce highly regarded reds and bright, delicious whites. They're no longer owners of the regionally famous vineyard of the same name, though they purchase grapes from it.

BEST BETS

Reserve Cabernet Sauvignon $$$ A massive wine loaded with spicy black fruit, chocolate, oak, and layers of complexity. This is one for the cellar.

Klipsun Vineyard Cabernet Sauvignon $$ A classy wine from a great Red Mountain vineyard, this is loaded with black currants, leather, tobacco, chocolate, vanilla, and sweet spices.

Seven Hills Vineyard Merlot $$$ In some years, Seven Hills will make a regular and a reserve from this vineyard-designated fruit. Well-integrated oak and fruit make this a food-friendly wine with plenty of bright fruit and approachable tannins.

Syrah $$ A tasty and complex red wine with aromas and flavors of berries, sweet oak, spice, tar, and chocolate.

Pinot Gris $ A bright, rich, delicious wine from Oregon grapes. Citrus, crushed hazelnuts, and touches of sweet spice are hallmarks of this satisfying summer wine.

WHERE TO BUY: WINERY, WINE SHOPS

212 N. 3rd Ave., Walla Walla, WA 99362; 509-529-7198; www.seven hillswinery.com. Open Tuesday-Saturday.

SHERIDAN VINEYARD

SEATTLE AREA   ESTABLISHED 2000

Sheridan Vineyard is fast becoming one of the Yakima Valley's premier vineyards. Planted in 1997, the seventy-six-acre site produces Cabernet Sauvignon, Merlot, Syrah, and Cabernet Franc. The first releases are a delicious Syrah and a red blend of Cabernet Sauvignon, Merlot, and Cabernet Franc. The business operations are west of the Cascades in Bellevue.

BEST BETS

Red Wine $$ A tasty blend that shows off earthy and ripe cherry aromas and black fruit flavors with chocolate overtones and plenty of tannins. A good wine to pair with a rare steak.

Syrah $$ A dark, intense red with penetrating flavors of plums, blackberries, and chocolate. Perfect for lamb.

WHERE TO BUY; WINERY, WINE SHOPS

4957 Lakemont Blvd. S.E., Bellevue, WA 98006; 425-401-0167; www.sheridanvineyard.com. Open by appointment.

SILVER LAKE WINERY

SEATTLE AREA AND YAKIMA VALLEY   ESTABLISHED 1989

What began as a hobby for three University of Washington professors now is one of Washington's ten largest wineries and is consumer owned: Customers can purchase shares in the winery. Led by winemaker Cheryl Barber-Jones for most of the winery's existence, Silver Lake produces good-quality wines at affordable prices. You'll find just about anything you want at Silver Lake, from big reds and crisp whites to sparkling wines. Hard ciders are sold under the Spire Mountain label. In 2001, Silver Lake moved to a new facility around the corner from Chateau Ste. Michelle in Woodinville and also opened a Yakima Valley tasting room in the former Covey Run facility near Zillah.

BEST BETS

Reserve Chardonnay $ A great wine at a good price, this fruit-filled white is loaded with tropical, citrus, and orchard fruits and hints of vanilla from oak aging, leading to huge fruit flavors and tremendous viscosity. Enjoy with salmon, grilled chicken, and prawns.

Roza Riesling $ A crisp, fresh wine that might remind you of a bite from a Red Delicious. This shows off classic mineral aromas and offers a light kiss of sweetness. A good wine for sipping or with turkey or Chinese dishes.

Cabernet Sauvignon $ Black currants mingle with light oak on the aromas, and solid tannins back up a spicy, layered red that pairs well with lamb chops, a T-bone, or hearty stews.

Claret $$ An Old World name for a Bordeaux blend is appropriate for this classy red. Thanks to long barrel and bottle aging, this begins to show off subtle bottle bouquet and penetrating black fruit, tar, and white pepper. A wine to enjoy with prime rib.

Woodinville: 15029 Woodinville-Redmond Road, Woodinville, WA 98072; 425-486-1900. Yakima Valley: 1500 Vintage Road, Zillah, WA 98953; 509-829-6235; www.silverlakewinery.com. Open daily.

SKY RIVER MEADERY

NORTH-CENTRAL WASHINGTON   ESTABLISHED 1999

One of two full-time mead producers in Washington, Sky River makes three styles of honey wine: dry, semi-sweet, and sweet. All are delicious and can be enjoyed chilled or heated. The meadery is run by Denise and Derek Ingalls and sprouted from Pure Foods, a honey processor and wholesaler run by Derek's father.

BEST BETS

Dry Mead $ Telltale alfalfa aromas and flavors of honey as well as baked apple flavors. Would match well with poultry.

Semi-Sweet Mead $ A light, delightful aroma with essence of clover and light grassiness. Soft, delicate flavors would make this a tasty aperitif.

Sweet Mead $ Sweet and elegant, this wine would match well with cheeses or stand by itself as an after-dinner treat.

WHERE TO BUY: WINERY, WINE SHOPS, GROCERY STORES

32533 Cascade View Drive, Sultan, WA 98294; 360-793-6761; www.skyriverbrewing.com. Open weekdays.

SNOQUALMIE VINEYARDS

YAKIMA VALLEY   ESTABLISHED 1984

In every respect, Snoqualmie Vineyards is a joy. Winemaker Joy Andersen crafts wines with great expression and offers them at a tremendous value. The wines are made nowhere near Snoqualmie (the city, falls, or mountain pass). Instead, this Stimson Lane property's products are made in Prosser, the heart of the Yakima Valley. Snoqualmie's wines are consistently good, often great, and occasionally spectacular.

BEST BETS

Reserve Cabernet Sauvignon $$ Approachable in its youth yet with aging potential, this Cab is rich with supple black fruit, chocolate, cedar, and more. Smooth, delicious, and capable of greatness.

Cab–Merlot $ The 1995 version of this blend shocked the Northwest wine world in '97 by winning Best of Show at the Tri-Cities Wine Festival, then showed great character as it aged. It's unfair for a wine this inexpensive to be this good.

Riesling $ Beautifully balanced between classic orchard fruit and crisp acidity, this white is a great match with seafood, Asian-inspired dishes, and pasta in cream sauces.

Chenin Blanc $ A much-maligned variety, especially in California where it is grown for bulk production. But treated with care, it can produce a nicely aromatic and crisp wine with excellent food-matching potential.

WHERE TO BUY: WINE SHOPS, GROCERY STORES

660 Frontier Road, Prosser, WA 99350; 509-786-2104; www snoqualmie.com. Open daily.

SOOS CREEK WINE CELLARS

SEATTLE AREA   ESTABLISHED 1989

Dave Larsen got into the Washington wine scene just as it was taking off, and as a result he has established great relationships with top vineyards, including Champoux, Ciel du Cheval, Pepper Bridge, and Charbonneau. Soos Creek makes only Bordeaux-style reds, all of which are dark, rich, and powerful. You can expect consistently outstanding wines from Soos Creek.

BEST BETS

Reserve Cabernet Sauvignon $$$ Opening with aromas of black fruit, pencil shavings, spice, and chocolate, this rich wine offers compelling flavors. A wine with massive tannins that are so in balance with the fruit, they aren't overwhelming. Cellar or pair with a rare cut of beef.

Stampede Pass $$ A red blend that shows aromas of cedar and berries and black, inky flavors of ripe berries and freshly roasted coffee. Enjoy with lamb or venison.

Sundance $$ A blend dominated by Merlot, this opens with elegant blackberry, vanilla, and sweet spice aromas that lead to dense fruit flavors. Try this with lasagna.

WHERE TO BUY: WINERY, WINE SHOPS

20404 140th Ave. S.E., Kent, WA 98402; 253-631-8775; www.soos creekwine.com. Open by appointment.

SORENSEN CELLARS

OLYMPIC PENINSULA   ESTABLISHED 1998

Richard Sorensen's foray into winemaking is a familiar tale. He was part of a group of serious wine collectors and consumers in the Port Townsend area and decided to try his hand at the noble profession. Purchasing grapes from Red Mountain as well as the Walla Walla Valley, Sorensen quickly gained a reputation for producing some of the top red wines in Washington, especially with his outstanding Cabernet Sauvignon.

BEST BETS

Cabernet Sauvignon $$ Alluring aromas of black currants, cedar, and vanilla lead to massive amounts of fruit and chewy tannins. This is a huge wine that is supremely balanced for consumption now or to age for a decade or more.

Cabernet Franc $$ A bright, approachable wine with varietal herbal characteristics and tasty cranberry and cherry flavors. An elegant red wine that can be enjoyed in its youth.

WHERE TO BUY: WINERY, WINE SHOPS

274 Otto St., Suite S, Port Townsend, WA 98368; 360-379-6416; www.sorensencellars.com. Seasonal hours.

SPRING VALLEY VINEYARD

WALLA WALLA VALLEY   ESTABLISHED 1999

With vines planted in 1993, Spring Valley Vineyard fruit has quickly become a favorite among winemakers from Walla Walla to Seattle. In 1999 the Corkrum-Derby family at Spring Valley began to make wine. The first was a well-received Bordeaux-style blend called Uriah. Also look for bottlings of Syrah and Merlot.

BEST BETS

Uriah $$ A blend of Cabernet Franc, Merlot, and Petit Verdot, this opens with aromas of black cherries and peppercorns and jammy flavors of cherries and plums. With well-integrated oak and a good balance of tannin, fruit, and acidity, this will go well with prime rib or a thick steak.

WHERE TO BUY: WINERY, WINE SHOPS

1682 Corkrum Road, Walla Walla, WA 99362; 509-337-6915; www.springvalleyvineyard.com. Open by appointment.

SYNCLINE WINE CELLARS

COLUMBIA GORGE   ESTABLISHED 1999

Two young wine lovers, James and Poppie Mantone, followed their dreams from Michigan and New England to Oregon's Willamette Valley and then the Washington side of the Columbia River Gorge to begin Syncline Wine Cellars. The focus is on Syrah from the warm Wahluke Slope and Pinot Noir from nearby Celilo Vineyard. Also look for releases of Viognier, Grenache, Cabernet Sauvignon, and Merlot.

BEST BETS

Sundance Vineyard Syrah $$ A classy red with rich, deep fruit and layers of complex flavors, this Syrah from the Wahluke Slope is a hedonistic wine with superlative food-matching ability. Try with lamb, veal, or chicken.

Celilo Vineyard Pinot Noir $$ Violet, bright cherry, and vanilla aromas with delicious pie cherry flavors and hints of black pepper. A tasty wine from a wonderful vineyard.

WHERE TO BUY: WINERY, WINE SHOPS

307 W. Humboldt St., Bingen, WA 98605; 541-912-7960; www.syncline wine.com. Open seasonally.

TAGARIS WINERY

TRI-CITIES   ESTABLISHED 1988

Third-generation grape grower Mike Taggares launched his family winery in 1988, changing the spelling to honor the original name from his Greek origins. The wines are crafted from estate organic vineyards by Greg Powers of Powers Winery/Badger Mountain Vineyards.

BEST BETS

Cabernet Sauvignon $$ A bright, fruit-driven Cab that offers clean, tasty berry and oak flavors. A wine to enjoy with everyday cuisine.

Merlot $$ This smooth, ripe red shows off plum and cherry notes amid underlying spicy oak. A good wine to pair with spaghetti and meatballs.

Chardonnay $ A rich, fruit-laden white with a balanced mouth feel and flavors of bananas, melon, citrus, and vanilla.

Riesling $ Peach and ripe apple aromas and flavors are backed up with a good hit of sweetness and crisp acidity. Try this with chicken or pasta in a cream sauce.

WHERE TO BUY: WINERY, WINE SHOPS, GROCERY STORES

1625 W. A St., Unit E, Pasco, WA 99301; 509-547-3590; www.tagariswines.com. Open weekdays.

TAMARACK CELLARS

WALLA WALLA VALLEY   ESTABLISHED 1998

Ron Coleman has been a lot of things in life, most of them related to the wine business. He's been a wholesaler and a sommelier and now he's making some of the Northwest's best Merlot. Coleman produces three thousand cases a year in a converted firehouse at the Walla Walla Airport. Like many of the neighboring wineries, Coleman's operation focuses on red wines.

BEST BETS

Merlot $$ A rich yet smooth red wine with black cherries, smoky vanilla, bittersweet chocolate, leather, coffee, and cedar.

Firehouse Red $ This is a prime blend of Cabernet Sauvignon, Syrah, Merlot, and Cabernet Franc. This fruit-driven wine has plenty of character for a nice price.

Cabernet Sauvignon $$$ A big, complex red showing off black currants, pipe tobacco, bittersweet chocolate, and dark, ripe fruit. Savor this with prime rib.

WHERE TO BUY: WINERY, WINE SHOPS

700 C St., Walla Walla, WA 99362; 509-526-3533; www.tamarack cellars.com. Open by appointment.

TANJULI

YAKIMA VALLEY   ESTABLISHED 1997

Tom Campbell has a long history in the Yakima Valley, starting Horizon's Edge Winery in the town of Zillah as well as Mission Mountain Winery near Flathead Lake in Western Montana. After he sold Horizon's Edge, he launched Tanjuli, which focuses on red blends.

BEST BETS

Konnowack Red $$ A rich blend of Cabernet Sauvignon, Malbec, and a splash of Merlot, this Bordeaux-style wine is ripe with black fruit and earthy notes. The winemaker suggests bottle aging for a half-decade or more.

Red Rocket $$ Blending the five classic grapes of red Bordeaux (Cabernet Sauvignon, Merlot, Cabernet Franc, Malbec, and Petit Verdot), this is a ripe, ready-to-enjoy red with bright currant and blackberry fruit and some oak.

Northern Lights Chardonnay Ice Wine $ A tasty after-dinner sipper with plenty of sugar and clean, tasty fruit. Match with cheesecake.

WHERE TO BUY: WINERY

4530 E. Zillah Drive, Zillah, WA 98953; 406-883-0803. Open by appointment.

TAPTEIL VINEYARD WINERY

RED MOUNTAIN   ESTABLISHED 1998

With vineyards first planted in 1985 high on venerable Red Mountain, Tapteil has gained a reputation for producing first-class grapes for wineries statewide. In the late '90s, vineyard owner Larry Pierson decided to launch his own winery, with his first wines released in 2002.

BEST BETS

Merlot $$ Classic Red Mountain aromas of ripe blackberries and black cherries with toasty oak, hints of bittersweet chocolate, and solid tannins. Pair this with a rare steak.

Chenin Blanc $ Showing off sweet pineapple aromas and light citrus notes, this sipper will pair well with lemon chicken or pasta salad.

WHERE TO BUY: WINERY, WINE SHOPS

20206 E. 583 PR N.E., Benton City, WA 99320; 509-588-4460. Open by appointment.

TERRA BLANCA

RED MOUNTAIN   ESTABLISHED 1993

Keith Pilgrim is a geologist by trade, so when he decided to open a winery on Red Mountain, he also decided to dig. The results are twin 200-foot-deep caves into the mountain where Terra Blanca ages its red wines in naturally cool temperatures. As the estate vineyards come into full fruition, Terra Blanca's wines are becoming more focused, with Syrah the most popular. Those who appreciate dessert wines should seek out the ice and botrytis-affected offerings.

BEST BETS

Syrah $$ A complex red wine showing off such notes as black fruit, toasty oak, spices, and anise. A good match with beef or lamb.

Onyx $$$ A blend of Cabernet Sauvignon, Merlot, Cabernet Franc, Malbec, and Petit Verdot, this provides ripe, complex layers of bright fruit, smoky vanilla, and plenty of structure. Try this with venison or pasta.

Semillon Ice Wine $$ A rich, thick, lip-smacking white that is filled with aromas and flavors of honey, nutmeg, pineapples, pears, and peaches. Try this with poached pears stuffed with gorgonzola and chopped walnuts.

WHERE TO BUY: WINERY, WINE SHOPS, GROCERY STORES

34715 N. Demoss Road, Benton City, WA 99320; 509-588-6082; www.terrablanca.com. Open daily.

TEFFT CELLARS

YAKIMA VALLEY   ESTABLISHED 1991

If Joel Tefft can't live in Italy, then he'll bring a taste of the world's leading wine-producing nation to the Yakima Valley. The owner/ winemaker of this small producer west of Sunnyside loves Tuscany and has entertained thoughts of relocating. Northwest wine lovers who enjoy his repertoire of Italian-style vino will hope he doesn't. Tefft also produces several styles of Port as well as Syrah, Merlot, and Cabernet Sauvignon, among others.

BEST BETS

Sangiovese $$ Year in and year out, Tefft creates a Chianti-style red that is bright and luscious with good depth from blending with

Cabernet Sauvignon. Delicious with most red meat dishes and perfect with thick slabs of lasagna.

Nebbiolo $$ This red wine is relatively unknown in the Northwest and is the main grape in the Piedmont region of Italy. Darker and more serious than Sangiovese, this should become a quick favorite and a great match with lamb dishes and finer cuts of beef.

Pinot Grigio $ Looking for an alternative to Chardonnay? This little beauty is it. Crammed with fruit aromas and wonderfully balanced on the palate, this Italian-style Pinot Gris is a summer sipper that matches nicely with shellfish, grilled chicken, or salmon.

Huckleberry Starboard $$$ Made from 100 percent Cascade huckleberries, this fortified red dessert wine can't legally be called a Port, so Tefft calls it Starboard. It's a definite sipper that tastes best on rainy or snowy winter evenings.

WHERE TO BUY: WINERY, WINE SHOPS, GROCERY STORES

1320 Independence Road, Outlook, WA 98938; 509-837-7651; www.tefftcellars.com. Open daily.

THREE RIVERS WINERY

WALLA WALLA VALLEY   ESTABLISHED 1999

This showcase winery just west of Walla Walla features hugely expressive wines, a classy tasting room, and even a three-hole golf course. Three Rivers got out of the gate quickly with longtime Washington winemaker Charlie Hoppes at the helm. He left in 2002 to start his own winery, leaving Three Rivers in capable hands. Three Rivers produces big, juicy wines showing plenty of varietal character and oak from barrel aging.

BEST BETS

Chardonnay $$ Well-integrated oak gives this white wine good buttery characteristics that meld nicely with its tropical fruit aromas and flavors.

Merlot $$ A delicious red wine with sweet oak aromas and tons of fruit. Round, flavorful, and smooth, this will not disappoint.

Sangiovese $$$ This red, Italian-style wine is mesmerizing on the nose with sweet oak, vanilla, black fruit, and characteristic dusty peppercorns. An exceptional wine.

Syrah $$ A fruit- and oak-driven red Rhône-style wine that offers light plums, bing cherries, peppercorns, chocolate, and a tangy finish.

WHERE TO BUY: WINERY, WINE SHOPS

5641 W. Hwy. 12, Walla Walla, WA 99362; 509-526-9463; www.threeriverswinery.com. Open daily.

THURSTON WOLFE WINERY

YAKIMA VALLEY   ESTABLISHED 1987

Before Wade Wolfe joined nearby Hogue Cellars as general manager, he and his wife, Becky Yeaman, launched their small family winery, Thurston Wolfe. Together they produce an impressive array of delicious wines, including a Pinot Gris–Viognier blend, a number of rich reds, and an always tasty Port. The winery specializes in Lemberger, called Blue Franc after an anglicized form of the grape's Austrian name.

BEST BETS

Sangiovese $$ You won't find this in some cheesy straw-covered Chianti jug. Rather, this is more like a Super-Tuscan with its sweet, ripe plum and blackberry aromas and flavors, smoky oak, and supple tannins. Pair with lamb or spicy meat dishes.

Blue Franc $ In an area known for its world-class Lemberger, Thurston Wolfe makes one of the best. It's a juicy, fruit-driven wine with aromas of vanilla, berry, and sweet spices. A delicious everyday wine, so enjoy it with lasagna, burgers, or casseroles.

Pinot Gris–Viognier $ This blend brings out the tropical fruitiness of the Viognier and the bold mouth feel and acidity of the Pinot Gris. Chill it and pair with pasta tossed with chicken.

JTW Port $$ A delightful winter sipper, this is a rich, spicy dessert red thick with blackberry and plum flavors. A fine match with Stilton.

WHERE TO BUY WINERY, WINE SHOPS

2880 Lee Road, Suite C, Prosser, WA 99350; 509 786-3313. Open seasonally.

TOWNSHEND CELLAR

SPOKANE AREA   ESTABLISHED 1998

The Townshend family began its winery with the heralded 1998 vintage using fruit primarily from the Columbia Valley. The first wines, released in 2001, showed tremendous depth of flavor and approachability. In addition to the Cabernet Sauvignon and Merlot, also look for a Chardonnay and a huckleberry Port using North Idaho fruit.

BEST BETS

Merlot $$ Huge up-front aromas of plums, blackberries, cedar, and vanilla lead to luscious flavors and a velvety finish. A superb effort that would pair well with flank steak, sirloin, firm cheeses, and hearty stews.

Cabernet Sauvignon $$ A silky, seductive red with brooding black fruit aromas and flavors that include plums, black raspberries, freshly ground espresso, and intense dark chocolate. Pair with rare beef, spare ribs, or pheasant.

16112 N. Greenbluff Road, Colbert, WA 99005; 509-238-4346; www.townshendcellar.com. Open by appointment.

TUCKER CELLARS

YAKIMA VALLEY   ESTABLISHED 1981

The Tuckers are one of the oldest grape-growing families in the Yakima Valley, with a history stretching back to the repeal of Prohibition in 1933, when the Tuckers grew grapes for the legendary William Bridgman and his Upland Winery in Sunnyside. Today, the Tuckers make a number of wines and are always happy to share their joy about wines and fresh produce with visitors.

BEST BETS

Muscat Canelli $ A wonderfully perfumy white with soft, delicious aromas and flavors of peaches, rose petals, and grapefruit. A perfect wine for brunches and picnics.

Cabernet Sauvignon $ This red offers black currant and blackberry aromas and smooth, tasty black-fruit flavors. Priced for everyday enjoyment; pair this with beef cuts, pasta, or stews.

Lemberger $ A bright, peppery red with strawberry jam and pomegranate flavors. This is just right for pizza, pasta, or steak sandwiches.

Late Harvest Riesling $$ A honey of a wine with 8 percent residual sugar, this is rich in apple and orange flavors with great acidity and a long, lovely finish. A dessert unto itself.

WHERE TO BUY: WINERY, WINE SHOPS, GROCERY STORES

70 Ray Road, Sunnyside, WA 98944; 509-837-8701; www.tucker cellars.com. Open daily.

VASHON WINERY

PUGET SOUND   ESTABLISHED 1990

Ron Irvine has had his hands in the Washington wine industry for decades. He was a founder of Pike & Western Wine Shop in Seattle's Pike Place Market, he has judged wine competitions, and in 1997 he wrote the definitive history of Washington wine with his self-published book The Wine Project. *After several years of running Vashon Winery, he purchased the property in 2001. Irvine is known for his passion for Semillon, an underappreciated white Bordeaux grape, and he also crafts classic red wines. In his spare time, Irvine pursues his passion for high-end varietal ciders.*

BEST BETS

Semillon $ This white wine shows off lovely aromatics of perfumy rose water and light grassy notes that follow into the flavors. This is a full-flavored wine with plenty of acidity and could be paired with chicken, shellfish, or salmon.

Merlot $$ A classic red that offers aromas of black currants, cedar, and blueberries and big, chalky flavors of lush plums and blackberries. A big wine to pair with lamb or beef.

Cabernet Sauvignon $$ This outstanding, food-friendly red opens with dusty cherry and oak aromas that lead to huge fruit flavors backed up with racy acidity and a rich finish. A candidate for prime rib or duck.

WHERE TO BUY: WINERY, WINE SHOPS

10317 S.W. 156th St., Vashon, WA 98070; 206-567-0055; www.vashonwinery.com. Seasonal hours.

WALLA WALLA VINTNERS

WALLA WALLA VALLEY   ESTABLISHED 1995

From their winery east of town, Myles Anderson and Gordy Venneri have been producing wines of complexity and quality since their first vintage and have gained a strong following among discerning lovers of red wine. Walla Walla Vintners is about as close as you can come to a can't-miss winery, and it would be wise to get on its mailing list while you can.

BEST BETS

Merlot $$ Jammy and fruit-driven with hints of oak treatment, this is a complex and layered wine.

Cabernet Franc $$ Classic Cab flavors and aromas with approachable tannins. Vanilla and cherries highlight this terrific wine.

Sangiovese $$ This Italian variety is expertly blended with Cabernet Sauvignon, creating a jammy and mouth-watering red wine that should be highly sought-after.

WHERE TO BUY: WINERY, WINE SHOPS

226 Vineyard Lane, Walla Walla, WA 99362; 509-525-4724; www.wallawallavintners.com. Open Saturdays and by appointment.

WASHINGTON HILLS CELLARS

YAKIMA VALLEY   ESTABLISHED 1988

Led by winemaker Brian Carter, Washington Hills Cellars produces some of Washington's best wines and best values, vintage in and vintage out. Using three labels—Washington Hills, W. B. Bridgman, and Apex—Carter is able to give consumers of every taste and bank account what they want. The Washington Hills brand is dedicated to high-quality, cost-conscious wines. W. B. Bridgman pays homage to Washington wine pioneer William Bridgman and fills in the mid-level value, and Apex is the premium brand.

BEST BETS

Apex Cabernet Sauvignon $$$ A dense wine showing off black fruit, chocolate, and spice, as well as vanilla and cedar from French oak aging. A big wine for a special event.

W. B. Bridgman Merlot $$ An up-front and fruit-driven red with dark chocolate–covered cherries, vanilla extract, and excellent balance of fruit, acidity, and tannin. A perfect match for ribeye.

Washington Hills Dry Riesling $ Balance is everything for this seriously delicious white. The ripe fruit, racy acidity, and long flavors exemplify everything that is good about Washington Riesling.

Washington Hills Semillon $ Simply one of the best the state has to offer (and usually found at bargain prices). It's a delicate wine laced with fig and citrus aromas and flavors. Pair with pasta, salmon, or chicken.

WHERE TO BUY: WINERY, WINE SHOPS, GROCERY STORES

111 E. Lincoln Ave., Sunnyside, WA 98944; 509-839-9463; www.washingtonhills.com. Open Thursday–Monday.

WATERBROOK WINERY

WALLA WALLA VALLEY   ESTABLISHED 1984

After working crush in 1983 for the new L'Ecole No. 41 in Lowden, Eric Rindal was hooked on winery life. He founded Waterbrook Winery a year later. Waterbrook makes one of the widest varieties of wine in the Walla Walla Valley and was one of the state's first producers of Viognier, a white-wine darling in Washington. In the late '90s, Waterbrook opened a tasting room in downtown Walla Walla, though the winery still is south of the town of Lowden. Since the tasting room opened, several other Walla Walla wineries have followed suit and gravitated toward the historic downtown area.

BEST BETS

Cabernet Sauvignon $$ Blending from multiple vineyards across the vast Columbia Valley gives this wine abundant complexity. This is a big, chewy wine loaded with black, jammy fruit and shows off oak aging. Serve with venison, lamb, or ribs.

Melange $ A nicely priced blend of Sangiovese, Syrah, Cab, Merlot, and Cab Franc. This shows off ripe currants, cherries, and herbal notes. It's a bright, supple, ready-to-drink wine that will pair well with pizza, lasagna, or beef stew.

Sauvignon Blanc $ Using grapes from famed Klipsun Vineyard on Red Mountain, this white is crisp and refreshing, with pear, orange, and lemon flavors. Try this with a shrimp salad, pork, chicken, or shellfish.

Chardonnay $ This richly structured wine shows off oak aging and creamy flavors of apples, pineapples, and lemons. Plenty of acidity for pairing with seafood.

WHERE TO BUY: WINERY, WINE SHOPS, GROCERY STORES

31 E. Main St., Walla Walla, WA 99362; 509-522-1262; www.water brook.com. Open daily.

WEDGE MOUNTAIN WINERY

NORTH-CENTRAL WASHINGTON   ESTABLISHED 2001

Charlie McKee, a retired engineer and longtime orchardist in the Wenatchee area, turned to winemaking and grape growing in the late '90s. He focuses on small lots of a variety of wines using grapes from Red Mountain and the Columbia Valley.

BEST BETS

Cabernet Sauvignon $$ An austere red showing off aromas and flavors of moist earth, cherry, and mocha. Enjoy this with pork or pasta.

Merlot $$ A bright red showing off hints of oak amid cherry and berry aromas and flavors. A tasty wine to enjoy with grilled chicken.

WHERE TO BUY: WINERY, WINE SHOPS

9534 Saunders Road, Peshastin, WA 98847; 509-548-7068; www.wedgemountainwinery.com. Open daily.

WHIDBEY ISLAND VINEYARDS & WINERY

PUGET SOUND   ESTABLISHED 1990

Greg and Elizabeth Osenbach enjoy the best of many worlds with their Western Washington winery. They operate the winery on the southern end of beautiful Whidbey Island, where they grow grapes on seven acres of vineyards, and they purchase classic wine grapes from east of the Cascades, where Merlot, Chardonnay, and Syrah thrive. They enjoy a rural, rustic lifestyle, yet can jump on a ferry and be in downtown Seattle in an hour or so. And because they run a small winery, producing just under three thousand cases a year, they get to do everything from caring for the vineyards to making wine to running the tasting room.

The Osenbachs's most interesting wines come from the Puget Sound grapes. Though most consumers won't be as familiar with such wines as Madeleine Angevine or Siegerrebe, they shouldn't shy away from these white beauties that match perfectly with the Northwest's fresh seafood.

BEST BETS

Island White $ One of the winery's best-sellers is a blend of Madeleine Angevine, Madeleine Sylvaner, and Siegerrebe. It's a steely wine with rich apple aromas and flavors that has enough residual sugar to back up the acidity.

Madeleine Angevine $ Crisp citrus and lemon aromas meld with pear and white fruit flavors. Enjoy with scallops, prawns, or crab legs.

Siegerrebe $ Outrageously aromatic with spice, orange zest, and apples, this deliciously steely wine cries out for Asian-inspired dishes.

Lemberger $$ From Eastern Washington grapes comes this fruit-driven, food-friendly red wine that oozes with cherry and raspberry aromas and flavors. A delicious, quaffable wine.

Merlot $$ Spicy cherry aromas lead to a smooth and flavorful wine loaded with bright fruit, peppercorns, and berry jam. Everything you'd hope for in an approachable Washington Merlot.

WHERE TO BUY: WINERY, WINE SHOPS

5237 S. Langley Road, Langley, WA 98260; 360-221-2040; www.whidbeyislandwinery.com. Seasonal hours.

WHITE HERON CELLARS

COLUMBIA BASIN   ESTABLISHED 1986

Cameron and Phyllis Fries learned to love wine while living in Switzerland. The Washington natives returned home in the mid-'80s, and Cameron became winemaker for Worden in Spokane, then Champs de Brionne in George. They now own and operate White Heron Cellars in the ghost town of Trinidad in the Columbia Basin and are known for producing robust red wines, including a Bordeaux-style blend called Chantepierre.

BEST BETS

Mariposa Vineyard Red Wine $ A fabulous red blend at a great price, this provides delicious herbal, oak, and cherry aromas and flavors with bright acidity and approachable tannins. Enjoy this with pasta, chicken, or beef.

Mariposa Vineyard Syrah $ Richly structured with jammy cherry and berry aromas and flavors, this will pair well with lamb or beef.

WHERE TO BUY: WINERY, WINE SHOPS

10035 Stuhlmiller Road, Quincy, WA 98848; 509-797-9463; www.whiteheronwine.com.

WHITMAN CELLARS

WALLA WALLA VALLEY   ESTABLISHED 1999

Whitman Cellars came out of the block quickly in 2001 with its initial release from the 1999 vintage. A Cabernet Sauvignon and Merlot, both from fruit grown at venerable Seven Hills Vineyard, were highly regarded by critics and consumers alike. In 2002 the winery lured Steve Lessard from Hedges Cellars on Red Mountain, giving the budding operation a winemaker who is well versed in top-quality Bordeaux-style blends in Washington.

BEST BETS

Merlot $$$ An incredibly concentrated and complex red that explodes with black fruit, spice, coffee, and chocolate aromas and flavors, all backed up by rich tannins. A huge wine worthy of the Walla Walla Valley appellation.

Cabernet Sauvignon $$$ Equally impressive is this Cab, though the subtleties of the variety make this somewhat more subdued and, ultimately, perhaps more interesting. This wine starts slowly, with layers of fruit, spice, and more brewing in the background. It then builds momentum on the palate, developing complexity like a symphony until the final note rings out on the lingering finish.

WHERE TO BUY: WINERY, WINE SHOPS

228 E. Main St., Suite A, Walla Walla, WA 99362; 509-529-1142; www.whitmancellars.com. Open by appointment.

WIDGEON HILL WINERY

SOUTHWESTERN WASHINGTON   ESTABLISHED 1991

The Mills family has been producing good-quality wines primarily from Yakima Valley grapes for more than a decade. The winery in Chehalis is near a watershed that is home to the Widgeon duck, giving winemaker Joel Mills a natural choice for his operation's name. Mills focuses on small lots of Cabernet Sauvignon, Merlot, Chardonnay, Syrah, and others, and the quality of the wine and its distinctive label (using watercolors from local artist Dixie Rogerson-Bill) have made Widgeon a favorite with consumers.

BEST BETS

Cabernet Sauvignon $ This nicely priced Cab offers a complex blend of herbal and spice aromas with jammy fruit and concentrated depth of flavor.

Merlot $ A spicy red with lingering fruit that shows off its oak aging. Bold acidity gives this plenty of backbone. A versatile food wine.

Syrah $ Everything you'd expect in a Syrah, with black cherry and plum flavors, sweet tannins, and a bold, sassy finish. Match with lamb.

Chenin Blanc $ A crisp, slightly sweet, refreshing white wine that might remind you of a summer rainstorm. A great match with Asian cuisine, pasta, chicken, or shellfish.

121 Widgeon Hill Road, Chehalis, WA 98532; 360-748-0432; www.widgeonhill.com. Open daily.

WILLOW CREST WINERY

YAKIMA VALLEY   ESTABLISHED 1995

Dave Minick is a Yakima Valley farmer who launched his winery in the mid-'90s. He makes a variety of wines and has become most noted for two Rhône-style varieties: Syrah and Mourvedre. His wines are distinctive in style and should be sought after by the discerning wine lover.

BEST BETS

Syrah $$ A regular gold medal winner, this might not remind you of the rich, almost sweet Syrahs you'll find elsewhere in Washington. Instead, it's more elegant than brash in style with smooth flavors of plums, nutmeg, and vanilla.

Mourvedre $$ A grape found in the Côtes du Rhône, this is a rare discovery in the New World. Willow Crest's version is fresh and approachable with bright and delicious fruit. This might pair well with Thai-inspired dishes.

Black Muscat $ An off-dry rosé, this is a perfumy wine with deep aromas of strawberry and rhubarb and smooth, elegant flavors of cherries and peaches. An appealing wine to enjoy on picnics.

Winsome $$ This late-harvest Cabernet Franc is loaded with aromas and flavors of strawberries and ripe cherries. A smooth, rich mouth feel makes this a delicious sipper.

WHERE TO BUY: WINERY, WINE SHOPS

55002 Gap Road, Prosser, WA 99350; 509-786-7999. Open weekends.

WILRIDGE WINERY

SEATTLE AREA   ESTABLISHED 1988

The Wilridge Winery name combines the names of its owners, Lysle Wilhelmi and Paul Beveridge. Located in Seattle's Madrona neighborhood, Wilridge focuses on small lots of single-vineyard wines from Washington and Oregon. The wines have a strong following and are worth seeking out in Puget Sound wine shops, and the whimsical labels add to the enjoyment.

BEST BETS

Melange $$ A Bordeaux-style blend of Merlot, Cabernet Sauvignon, and Cabernet Franc, this cellar-worthy red is rich in deep, black fruit with tremendous structure and balance. A big, serious wine to enjoy with the finest cuts of meat.

Spring Valley Vineyard Merlot $$ This hearty Merlot often is part of the Melange blend. Long on flavor with big, sweet tannins, this can be enjoyed now or over the next few years.

Nebbiolo di Klipsun $$ This northern Italian grape thrives in one of Washington's most celebrated vineyards, Klipsun on Red Mountain. This is rich in black fruit and bittersweet chocolate and smooth throughout, making it an approachable wine in its youth.

Klipsun Vineyard Cabernet Sauvignon $$ This highly prized Cab will be difficult to find, but if you do, hold onto it dearly, as it will reward a decade or more of patience in the cellar.

WHERE TO BUY: WINERY, WINE SHOPS

1416 34th Ave., Seattle, WA 98122; 206-325-3051; www.wilridge winery.com. Open by appointment.

WIND RIVER CELLARS

COLUMBIA GORGE   ESTABLISHED 1995

High in the hills above the Columbia River Gorge is Wind River Cellars, a winery with one of the most spectacular vistas in the Northwest. Looking out upon Mount Hood and up toward Mount Adams, the winery is situated in the old Hooper Family Winery facility. Its bold and delicious wines range from bright Pinot Noirs and Gewürztraminers to big Cabernet Sauvignons and a luscious Port.

BEST BETS

Port of Celilo $$ One of the Northwest's finest Ports, this Lemberger-based red dessert wine is loaded with plum, raisin, and chocolate nuances. A perennial award-winner, this and Stilton are a match made in the Gorge.

Riesling $ Slightly sweet and long on orchard fruit and honey aromas and flavors, this is a terrific summer sipper. Pair with seafood, Asian-inspired cuisine, chicken, or pasta.

Pinot Noir $$ Bright cherry and strawberry aromas and flavors with clean acidity and an inspired finish.

WHERE TO BUY: WINERY, WINE SHOPS, GROCERY STORES

196 Spring Creek Road, Husum, WA 98623; 509-493-2324; www.windrivercellars.com. Open daily.

WINEGLASS CELLARS

YAKIMA VALLEY   ESTABLISHED 1994

Thanks to producing consistently high-quality reds, David and Linda Lowe have created a near-cult following among Washington wine lovers. The bicycling enthusiasts are particularly well known for their Merlot, and they also make wines with California Zinfandel.

BEST BETS

Reserve Merlot $$$ A luscious red exhibiting deep, penetrating aromas and flavors of blueberries, huckleberries, and cherries, backed up with exotic spices and big tannins.

Merlot $$ An elegant wine showing rich flavors of blackberries and huckleberries with vanilla and oak spice aromas. An excellent wine to pair with a rare ribeye.

Rich Harvest $$$$ A Bordeaux-style blend of Cabernet Sauvignon, Merlot, and Cabernet Franc, this shows off huge berry and vanilla aromatics with deep flavors of dark fruit, chocolate, and spices. Save for your finest cuts of beef.

Elerding Vineyard Cabernet Sauvignon $$$ A deep, dark, serious wine showing aromas of pipe tobacco, espresso, and ripe plums and thick, elegant flavors. Enjoy with prime rib.

WHERE TO BUY: WINERY, WINE SHOPS

260 N. Bonair Road, Zillah, WA 98953; 509-829-3011; www.wine glasscellars.com. Seasonal hours.

WOODHOUSE FAMILY VINEYARDS

SEATTLE AREA   ESTABLISHED 1998

Bijal and Sinead Shah head up this young venture with veteran wine-maker Tom Campbell, who owns Tanjuli winery in the Yakima Valley and Mission Mountain Winery in western Montana. The wines show up under various names, including Dussek Family Cellars, Maghie Cellars, and Darighe. The early efforts have resulted in big, delicious, spendy wines.

BEST BETS

Darighe $$$$ A Gaelic word for "Red," this blend of Cabernet Sauvignon, Merlot, Petit Verdot, and Malbec shows off deep, rich, concentrated flavors with black licorice notes on the finish. A sure bet for a marbled ribeye steak.

Maghie Cellars Reserve Merlot $$$$ Spice and black fruit aromas give way to deep flavors of blueberries and huckleberries. A tasty wine to pair with lamb or beef.

WHERE TO BUY: WINERY, WINE SHOPS

604 Boren Avenue N., Seattle, WA 98109; 509-382-1805. Call for hours.

WOODINVILLE WINE CO.

SEATTLE AREA   ESTABLISHED 1999

*Located in the old Silver Lake Winery building in Woodinville, Wood-
inville Wine Co. is focused on making small lots of high-quality wines
from vineyards of the Yakima and Columbia Valleys.*

BEST BETS

Syrah $$ This jammy, fruit-driven red offers black cherry and toasty
oak aromas with flavors of bright berries and cloves. Enjoy with
lamb.

WHERE TO BUY: WINERY, WINE SHOPS

*17721 132nd Ave. N.E., Woodinville, WA 98072; 425-481-7500. Open
by appointment.*

WOODWARD CANYON WINERY

WALLA WALLA VALLEY   ESTABLISHED 1981

*Driving by on Highway 12, you might not get the impression that
Woodward Canyon is one of the top wineries in the country. In fact,
you might not think it's a winery at all. But Rick Small is more inter-
ested in crafting world-class wines than in making sure the sign out
front is nicely painted. The energetic, unassuming Small is meticulous
about quality, and it shows at every level, from his deep, concentrated,
age-worthy Cabs to his big, buttery Chardonnays.*

BEST BETS

Old Vine (Dedication Series) Cabernet Sauvignon $$$$ The distinctively
labeled wine simply is one of the country's best Cabs every year.
A vertical tasting of nineteen years of the Old Vines shows the old-
est still are fruity, youthful, and supple, with two of the best being
from 1983 and 1981. Small's Old Vine Cab comes from a few dis-
tinct vineyards and has proven to be good for the cellar for two
to three decades.

Artist Series Cabernet Sauvignon $$$ The grapes for this wine come from
Canoe Ridge, an area along the Columbia River facing south
toward Oregon. The wine is rich and complex, yet approachable
within five years of vintage. Another home run by Small.

Chardonnay $$$ Small makes a few different Chardonnays depending
on grape availability. Perhaps his best is from Celilo Vineyard,
which is on the Washington side of the Columbia Gorge. A buttery,
oaky wine, this is a crowd pleaser that serves nicely as an aperitif
or will match with scallops or salmon. His outstanding Estate
Chardonnay also should be considered one of the Northwest's best.

WHERE TO BUY: WINERY, WINE SHOPS, GROCERY STORES

*11920 W. Hwy. 12, Lowden, WA 99360; 509-525-4129; www.woodward
canyon.com. Open daily.*

WYVERN CELLARS

SPOKANE   ESTABLISHED 1980

For two decades, Wyvern Cellars was Worden's Washington Winery, until the winery changed ownership in the late '90s. A Wyvern is a mythical dragon that protects vineyards, and it's doing a good job, as the wines coming from Wyvern Cellars offer both good quality and good value.

BEST BETS

Cabernet Sauvignon $$ A complex, approachable red with tangy fruit and an array of spices with smooth, food-friendly tannins. Enjoy this with London broil, lasagna, lamb, or a hearty stew.

Cab–Merlot $$ Pioneered in Washington by Worden's, this smooth, tasty blend of two classic grapes is loaded with good stuff, including bright cherries, black pepper, and sweet tobacco. A tasty pizza wine.

Merlot $$ A fruit-driven red with up-front plums and cherries, smooth tannins, and a silky finish. Enjoy with roast, lamb, or mild cheeses.

Gewürztraminer $ Made in a dry style, this refreshing and aromatic wine is a great match with Thai dishes, curried chicken, or turkey.

WHERE TO BUY: WINERY, WINE SHOPS, GROCERY STORES

7217 W. Westbow Road, Spokane, WA 99224; 509-455-7835; www.wyverncellars.com. Open daily.

YAKIMA CELLARS

YAKIMA VALLEY   ESTABLISHED 2000

Yakima Cellars is off to a strong start, crafting a handful of wines that are all top-notch. The winery was started and is run by an energetic group of friends who wanted a winery in this central Washington city's fading downtown area.

BEST BETS

Millennium Red $$ A succulent, Bordeaux-style red that is loaded with complex layers of blackberries, plums, sweet spices, toasted oak, and more. Cook mine rare.

Cabernet Franc $$$ This smooth, approachable red is another out-standing effort with lovely oak spice and black currant aromas and luscious bright fruit flavors. A good wine for lamb or pasta.

Sangiovese $$$ A ripe, youthful wine that beckons the wine lover to explore its intricacies. Classic smoky cherry fruit with a luscious midpalate and chocolate notes through the finish. Try this with lasagna.

Semillon $$ This rich, creamy white shows off barrel aging with its toasty, butterscotch aromas and flavors with hints of lemons. Enjoy with appetizers or salmon.

WHERE TO BUY: WINERY, WINE SHOPS

32 N. 2nd St., Yakima, WA 98901; 509-577-0461; www.yakima cellars.com. Open Friday-Sunday.

YAKIMA RIVER WINERY

YAKIMA VALLEY   ESTABLISHED 1977

Under the direction of John Rauner, Yakima River Winery is best known for crafting barrel-aged red wines. Yakima River Winery is one of the valley's oldest producers, and Rauner has gained a following for his Lemberger, Merlot, and Port.

BEST BETS

Lemberger $ A spicy red with smooth aromas and flavors of bright berries and vanilla notes. A tasty everyday wine to enjoy with pasta or stew.

Sof Lem $ This Lemberger is a refreshing red with a bit of residual sugar that highlights the aromas and flavors of fresh strawberries and raspberries. A nouveau-style wine to enjoy just slightly chilled. Perfect for barbecued chicken or ribs.

Merlot $$ Just what Yakima River Winery is famous for, this mouth-filling red shows off plenty of rich, ripe fruit and vanilla backed up with big, long tannins. A wine to enjoy with a thick steak.

Port $$ Made from Merlot, this provides full, ripe aromas of spicy plums and a long, creamy mouth feel. A good wine for blue cheeses or by itself.

WHERE TO BUY: WINERY, WINE SHOPS

143302 W. North River Road, Prosser, WA 99350; 509-786-2805; www.yakimariverwinery.com. Seasonal hours.

YELLOW HAWK CELLAR

WALLA WALLA VALLEY   ESTABLISHED 1998

Dedicated to "interesting wines that are reasonably priced," Yellow Hawk is one of the Walla Walla Valley's bright young stars, producing delicious, food-friendly wines. The winery, in a century-old barn along Yellow Hawk Creek, is the creation of winemaker Tim Sampson and manager Barbara Hetrick.

BEST BETS

Sangiovese $$ A delightful and bright red with well-integrated oak amid the raspberry, cherry, and chocolate aromas and flavors. Enjoy this with a thick slab of lasagna or grilled lamb.

Muscat Canelli $ Aromatic and fruit-driven, this white picnic sipper is generous with its flavors of apples, grapefruit, and tropical fruits. Good sweetness is backed up with crisp acidity.

WHERE TO BUY: WINERY, WINE SHOPS

395 Yellowhawk St., Walla Walla, WA 99362; 509-529-1714. Open by appointment.

OREGON WINES AND WINERIES

When contemplating Oregon wine country, one's thoughts automatically drift toward Pinot Noir. And rightly so, because the United States' fourth-largest wine-producing region excels at the red grape that makes France's Burgundy region great.

The bulk of Oregon's wine production takes place in the Willamette Valley, which stretches from the Columbia River in the north to Eugene, roughly halfway down the state. Within this large American Viticultural Area, or appellation, are a number of important microclimates for growing Pinot Noir. Of greatest importance is Yamhill County, southwest of Portland, which is home to more than sixty wineries and many of the state's most prominent wineries and vineyards. South of Yamhill County is another important region, known as the Eola Hills, near Salem.

Unlike Washington's Columbia Valley, the Willamette Valley can't rely on low rainfall. Willamette Valley producers often live in suspense during harvest as they hope the inevitable autumn rainstorms will hold off long enough for the prized Pinot Noir to ripen and be harvested.

Like growers in some of Europe's great wine regions, Oregon's top producers usually are able to produce quality crops even in marginal years. In fact, many Oregon grape growers and vintners are pioneering ways to promote balanced ripening earlier in an effort to stay a step ahead of Mother Nature. Crop thinning is vital, and crop loads are half (or less) that of Washington reds, to ensure that the grapes left on the vine have the best chance of making a great bottle of wine.

But Oregon isn't just about Pinot Noir. As in Burgundy, the key white grape in Oregon has been Chardonnay, and Oregon vintners have worked hard to find the right clones of Chardonnay for the Willamette Valley. Consumers will see the clone names on the bottle (with Dijon being the most popular).

In recent years, Chardonnay has been supplanted by Pinot Gris, a white grape that is related to Pinot Noir. This crisp wine commonly associated with the Alsace region of France goes exceedingly well with the fresh seafood that graces Northwest restaurant menus, and as a result it has become the most-planted white grape in the state.

Often overlooked is Southern Oregon, which is beginning to emerge from the Willamette Valley's shadow as an important grape-growing region. In the south, Pinot Noir is largely ignored and Bordeaux varieties gain in prominence. In fact, Southern Oregon wine producers usually have more in common with the Napa and Sonoma Valleys than with their neighbors to the north.

Oregon Appellations

Willamette Valley. This valley is a giant stretch of land that begins at the Columbia River in the north and finishes around the city of Eugene. The primary grapes are Pinot Noir, Pinot Gris, and Chardonnay, but many other varieties are planted as well, including Gewürztraminer, Pinot Blanc, Pinot Meunier, Riesling, and Müller-Thurgau.

Umpqua Valley. This region around Roseburg is warmer and drier than the Willamette Valley and is growing in popularity. Here, consumers will find Pinot Noir, Chardonnay, Merlot, Syrah, and Tempranillo, as well as many other varieties.

Rogue Valley. In the southwestern part of the state, this appellation is arid and rugged, perfect for growing bold red-wine grapes. The Rogue has the greatest potential for Bordeaux and Rhône varieties in Oregon, and many Willamette Valley producers are looking in this direction for alternatives to Pinot Noir.

Applegate Valley. Oregon's newest appellation is within the Rogue Valley around the historic town of Jacksonville. It's a warm and picturesque area that is ideal for grape growing and wine touring.

Columbia and Walla Walla Valleys. An extension of these two major Washington appellations dips into Oregon from around The Dalles in the Columbia Gorge to Milton-Freewater on the eastern side of the state. Many Washington wineries take advantage of these vineyards, as do a handful of Oregon vintners.

Oregon Subappellations and Regions of Interest

Though these areas aren't yet recognized by the government, they are seen by winemakers and consumers alike as key grape-growing regions.

Yamhill County. The center of winemaking activity for Oregon, this county southwest of Portland is loaded with significant wineries, vineyards, and microclimates. Future potential appellations within Yamhill County include Chehalem Mountains, Ribbon Ridge, Red Hills, Yamhill/Carlton District, and McMinnville Foothills.

Eola Hills. This area near the capital city of Salem is home to several important vineyards. The area is a potential future appellation.

Columbia Gorge. The Oregon side of the Columbia River along this gorgeous stretch of the Northwest plays an important role in Oregon's winemaking past, present, and future. Because the area is usually warm and dry (more so farther east), winemakers are finding success with Merlot, Cabernet Sauvignon, Riesling, and even Zinfandel.

Key Oregon Vineyards

The Pines (Columbia Gorge). This century-old Zinfandel vineyard near The Dalles has been revitalized in recent years and now is supplying grapes to a handful of Oregon vintners.

Del Rio Vineyard (Rogue Valley). Del Rio is a relatively young vineyard that has quickly gained a following, primarily for its Syrah. Many Willamette Valley winemakers are using Del Rio grapes, and this vineyard could become the state's most famous in a hurry.

Seven Hills Vineyard (Walla Walla Valley). Grapes from Seven Hills are primarily used by Washington winemakers, but a few Western Oregon winemakers also buy from the vineyard.

Shea Vineyard (Willamette Valley). Dick Shea grows consistently great Pinot Noir for a number of top producers, and consumers will come across many Shea Vineyard–designated wines. In the mid-'90s, Shea launched his own winery.

ABACELA VINEYARDS

UMPQUA VALLEY   ESTABLISHED 1997

Earl and Hilda Jones have a passion for the extraordinary. That, perhaps, is why they decided to plant and promote grapes that are out of the mainstream in North America. Abacela, an old Castilian word that means "to plant grapevines," specializes in such classic (but little-grown in the United States) wines as Tempranillo, Dolcetto, and Malbec. It also grows and blends Graciano, Bastardo, and Tinta Roriz (from Spain and Portugal), Refosco and Fresia (from Italy), and Petit Verdot (from France). Additionally, Abacela makes such "normal" wines as Grenache, Sangiovese, Syrah, Merlot, Cabernet Franc, and Viognier. The wines of Abacela regularly win medals and praise from judges and critics.

BEST BETS

Cabernet Franc $$ Consistently one of the top Cab Francs in the Northwest, this offers rich, round flavors of black fruit, classic black currant aromas, and a charming mouth feel.

Tempranillo $$ This Spanish variety is a robust wine with sweet spice and black fruit aromas and flavors. This is an intriguing and rare wine with big tannins. Age for a half-decade or enjoy now with a thick steak.

Dolcetto $$ This early ripening grape normally associated with Italy's Piedmont region is full-flavored and full-bodied with bright cherry flavors and soft, approachable tannins. Match with pasta in a red meat sauce.

Syrah $$ A smooth and delicious red displaying dusty cherry and vanilla aromas and ripe, jammy berries and cherries. The moderate tannins make this a good match for lamb.

WHERE TO BUY: WINERY, WINE SHOPS, GROCERY STORES

12500 Lookingglass Road, Roseburg, OR 97470; 541-679-6642; www.abacela.com. Open daily.

THE ACADEMY

APPLEGATE VALLEY   ESTABLISHED 1996

Owner/winemaker Barney Smith was the driving force in the establishment of the Applegate American Viticulture Area, Southern Oregon's newest appellation. Smith specializes in Cabernet Sauvignon, Merlot, Chardonnay, and Pinot Noir.

BEST BETS

Pinot Noir $ A delicious and inexpensive red, this is fruit-driven, with aromas and flavors of cherries, raspberries, cranberries, and hints of bright spice. Pair with lamb or beef.

WHERE TO BUY: WINERY, WINE SHOPS

18200 Hwy. 238, Grants Pass, OR 97527; 541-846-6817. Open by appointment.

ADEA WINE COMPANY

YAMHILL COUNTY   ESTABLISHED 1995

What started as Fisher Family Cellars became ADEA Wine Company in 1998 because of a name conflict with another vineyard. ADEA, an acronym for the first names of the family members, produces small lots of Burgundian-style wines.

BEST BETS

Pinot Noir $$$ Supple and understated, this opens with inviting berries, vanilla, and oak spice that lead to a broad mouth feel highlighted with creamy notes of black cherries and bittersweet chocolate. Try this with a thick steak.

Chardonnay $$ A luscious white rich in bright fruit aromas and flavors with plenty of acidity to back it up. Savor this with a plate of scallops sautéed in butter or grilled halibut with an herb sauce.

WHERE TO BUY: WINERY, WINE SHOPS

26423 N.W. Hwy. 47, Gaston, OR 97119; 503-662-4509; www.adeawine.com. Open by appointment.

ADELSHEIM VINEYARD

YAMHILL COUNTY ESTABLISHED 1973

David Adelsheim proves that three decades of experience growing grapes and making wine in Yamhill County mean something. Revered as one of Oregon's modern pioneers, Adelsheim Vineyard continues to produce some of the best wines in the state, as it proves annually with its wide array of Pinot Noirs and its wonderful Pinot Gris, as well as elegant Chardonnays and Pinot Blanc. Though the reserve-level wines often are the highlights at Adelsheim, don't overlook the Oregon Series wines, which are delicious wines at good prices. In 1994, Jack and Lynn Loacker joined Adelsheim as co-owners. In addition to the wines, Adelsheim is known for its distinctive labels, drawn by co-founder Ginny Adelsheim.

BEST BETS

Reserve Pinot Noirs $$$–$$$$ With no fewer than four reserve and vineyard-designated Pinot Noirs, Adelsheim is able to express the different styles of different sites. Each is elegant and sophisticated, with the Bryan Creek Vineyard showing off powerful fruit and layers of berries, spice, leather, and bittersweet chocolate. Enjoy with sirloin, salmon, or pork.

Pinot Gris $ A stunning white that shows off everything good about Oregon Pinot Gris. It's ripe with fruit and long on flavor, bright acidity, and balance. A superb match with grilled halibut, steamed oysters, or sautéed scallops.

Stoller Vineyard Chardonnay $$$ This richly structured white shows off great integration of fruit and oak, with orchard fruits and sweet spices backed up with crisp acidity. Enjoy this with chicken, turkey, or shellfish.

Pinot Blanc $ Floral, pear, and honeydew aromas and flavors are backed up with solid acidity. A steely, flinty finish gives this good food-matching potential. Try this with a Cobb salad or grilled prawns.

WHERE TO BUY: WINERY, WINE SHOPS, GROCERY STORES

16800 N.E. Calkins Lane, Newberg, OR 97132; 503-538-3652; www.adelsheimvineyard.com. Open by appointment.

AIRLIE WINERY

WILLAMETTE VALLEY ESTABLISHED 1986

Under the guidance of owner Mary Olson and winemaker Suzy Gagne, Airlie is producing consistently good wines from the estate vineyard northwest of Corvallis. Like the balloon on the label, Airlie's wines are bright, uplifting, and could go far. In addition to the wines reviewed here, Airlie produces Chardonnay, Müller-Thurgau, and Riesling.

BEST BETS

Dunn Forest Vineyard Pinot Noir $$ The winery's first vineyard-designated wine was this delicious red that shows elegant cherry and spice aromas and penetrating blackberry and plum flavors, all backed up with good acidity and firm tannins. Try this with venison or duck.

Gewürztraminer $ Alsatian in style, this is loaded with aromas and flavors of grapefruit, pear, and apple, as well as a good dose of clove and cardamom.

Pinot Gris $ A delicate wine with appealing stone fruit aromas and flavors. Clean and crisp through the palate, this will pair well with cheese or cold chicken.

Maréchal Foch $ A deep, black wine with toasty, charred, spicy aromas that meld with ripe plum and blackberry flavors. Try this with Tex-Mex.

WHERE TO BUY: WINERY, WINE SHOPS, GROCERY STORES

15305 Dunn Forest Road, Monmouth, OR 97361; 503-838-6013; www.airliewinery.com. Seasonal hours.

AMITY VINEYARDS

YAMHILL COUNTY   ESTABLISHED 1976

Myron Redford has proven for more than a quarter-century that you can stubbornly do things your way—and prove you're right. The founder of Amity Vineyards remains as rebellious today as he was in his youth, shunning varieties he doesn't think will do well and embracing those he has faith in. He eschews new oak, with the result being some of the state's consistently best wines. In addition to multiple bottlings of Pinot Noir, Amity also excels in Pinot Blanc, Gamay Noir, Riesling, Gewürztraminer, and others.

BEST BETS

Schouten Vineyard Pinot Noir $$ With its complex array of fruit, spice, and other classic components, this will push your pleasure button.

Winemaker's Reserve Pinot Noir $$$ Subtle yet complex, this layered red reveals its berry, spice, and cedar components with a bit of coaxing in the glass. This is one to age a half-decade or more.

Dry Gewürztraminer $ Classic grapefruit and sweet spice aromas lead to an intensely flavored wine that would match well with Thai dishes or Asian-inspired duck.

Ravenous Rosé $ Crafted from Gamay Noir grapes, this is no California Kool-Aid, but rather a crisp wine with fresh berry flavors. Match with grilled chicken, turkey, or ham.

Gamay Noir $ This is a somewhat rare grape for the Northwest, and Amity takes great pride in its embrace of the variety. The resulting wine offers bright, fresh cherry aromas and strawberry flavors. Serve this food-friendly wine slightly cooler than room temperature for greatest enjoyment.

WHERE TO BUY: WINERY, WINE SHOPS, GROCERY STORES

18150 Amity Vineyards Road S.E., Amity, OR 97101; 503-835-2362; www.amityvineyards.com. Open daily, closed January.

ANDREW RICH WINES

PORTLAND   ESTABLISHED 1995

Andrew Rich is not one to go with the flow, perhaps a trait he learned (or at least solidified) while working at famed Bonny Doon Winery in California. The former magazine editor came north from California to make Rhône-style wines in the Northwest, and he doesn't much care if the grapes are from Washington or Oregon. In addition to a fabulous Syrah, Rich makes remarkable Pinot Noir, late-harvest Gewürztraminer, and Sauvignon Blanc.

BEST BETS

Pinot Noir $$ A superior red with elegant aromas and flavors of sweet herbs, coffee, pipe tobacco, moist earth, strawberry jam, and hints of cranberries. Try this with a rare steak.

Syrah $$ A complex and jammy Syrah loaded with blackberry preserve flavors with a fine balance of acidity and smooth, supple tannins. Try this with lamb or venison.

Late Harvest Gewürztraminer $$ A luscious white wine that is as complex as it is sweet. It opens with aromas and flavors of cardamom, honey, poached pears, and vanilla ice cream. A real treat with remarkably good acidity.

Sauvignon Blanc $$ A richly structured white that shows off orchard fruit aromas with hints of toasty oak. Pears, apples, and kiwis dominate the palate. A classic Sauvignon Blanc to pair with scallops, chicken, or pasta in a cream sauce.

WHERE TO BUY: WINERY, WINE SHOPS

3287 N.E. Alameda St., Portland, OR 97212; 503-284-6622. Not open to the public.

ANKENY VINEYARD

WILLAMETTE VALLEY   ESTABLISHED 1999

In the early '80s, Joe Olexa planted a vineyard and opened a little winery, an operation that didn't last long because, well, life got in the way. He continued to grow Pinot Gris and Pinot Noir, some of which went into some of the state's best wines, including King Estate's venerable

Reserve Pinot Gris. Now retired, Olexa is giving winemaking another chance. And thankfully so. His Pinot Gris ranks among the Northwest's best, and his Pinot Noir also is highly regarded.

BEST BETS

Reserve Pinot Gris $ This crisp white bursts with juicy orchard fruit with subtle vanilla undertones and a rich mouth feel. A versatile food match.

Pinot Noir $$ Berry and earth aromas lead to a richly structured wine with up-front fruit and silky tannins. Try with turkey or other sweet meats.

WHERE TO BUY: WINERY, WINE SHOPS

2565 Riverside Road S., Salem, OR 97306; 503-378-1498. Open weekends and by appointment.

ANTICA TERRA VINEYARDS

PORTLAND   ESTABLISHED 1996

This tiny winery gets much of its fruit from its estate vineyard in Yamhill County, and its focus is on small lots of highly sought-after Pinot Noir. The winery is owned and operated by Marc Peters and Marty Weber.

BEST BETS

Croft Vineyard Pinot Noir $$$ A deep, delicious wine with earthy, oaky, black cherry aromas and rich pepper and black fruit flavors. Match with a thick, rare steak.

WHERE TO BUY: WINERY, WINE SHOPS

6120 N.E. 22nd Ave., Portland, OR 97211; 503-281-7696. Open by appointment.

ARCHERY SUMMIT WINERY

YAMHILL COUNTY   ESTABLISHED 1993

Archery Summit has established itself as a gem in star-studded Yamhill County. It produces some of Oregon's best—and most expensive— Pinot Noirs. Founder Gary Andrus started Archery Summit on the right course with energy in the vineyards, and constant trials and experiments in the cellar. In 2001, Andrus sold Archery Summit and the new owners changed winemakers, with the early releases showing the winery continuing on a course of high quality.

BEST BETS

Archery Summit Estate Pinot Noir $$$$$$$ A huge, intense wine and one of Oregon's most expensive, this is a gangbuster wine with perfect balance and finesse that should be a must-have for any serious collector.

Red Hills Estate Pinot Noir $$$$$ A dark, brooding wine with complex layers of elegant black fruit, this is rich yet gentle, with a finish that goes on forever.

Arcus Estate Pinot Noir $$$$$ A more delicate wine with aromas of raspberries in cream, with rich yet refined tannins and a superior balance of fruit and acidity.

Premiere Cuvée Pinot Noir $$$ Layers of soft, gentle, silky fruit with wonderful texture, this is a wine of elegance and finesse.

WHERE TO BUY: WINERY, WINE SHOPS

18599 N.E. Archery Summit Road, Dayton, OR 97114; 503-864-4300; www.archerysummit.com. Open by appointment.

ARGYLE WINERY

YAMHILL COUNTY   ESTABLISHED 1987

Pick up any good wine list in Oregon and you're likely to find an Argyle sparkling wine. And it isn't just good marketing: Argyle excels at great bubbly, especially its Brut. But don't overlook Argyle's still wines, including Pinot Noir, Chardonnay, and Riesling. Argyle, in an old hazelnut processing plant on the highway going through the wine village of Dundee, produces thirty-five thousand cases annually from 500 acres of premium vineyards above Dundee and in the Eola Hills to the south.

BEST BETS

Brut $$ A refreshing sparkler with rich bubbles, apple aromas, and cake, citrus, and spice flavors. A creamy midpalate balances this wine perfectly. Imagine this with oysters.

Dry Riesling $ Classic German-style aromas with petrol notes and refreshing apple, pear, and mineral flavors. Match with spicy dishes or cold chicken.

Reserve Pinot Noir $$ Richly textured with deep velvety and earthy flavors along with chocolate and cherry notes.

Chardonnay $ Rich vanilla, pear, and tropical fruit aromas. A wine that shows off oak aging and abundant food-matching potential. Serve with pasta in a cream sauce or with salmon.

WHERE TO BUY: WINERY, WINE SHOPS, GROCERY STORES

691 Hwy. 99W, Dundee, OR 97115; 503-538-8520; www.argyle winery.com. Open daily.

ASHLAND VINEYARDS

ROGUE VALLEY   ESTABLISHED 1987

Since taking over in 1994, Phil and Kathy Kodak have been transforming Ashland Vineyards into a winery of distinction, focusing on

Bordeaux-style reds that are suited to the arid climate of southwestern Oregon. In addition to a Chardonnay and Pinot Gris, the winery makes a wildly popular blend called Shakespeare's Love, in recognition of the world-famous Shakespeare Festival in Ashland.

BEST BETS

Merlot $ A rich red loaded with cherries, vanilla, and black pepper aromas. The well-balanced palate offers smooth, ripe flavors with mellow tannins. Priced for everyday enjoyment. Pair this with pasta or beef dishes.

Pinot Gris $ This luscious white offers honeydew and tropical aromas with smooth, fruity, nutty flavors. Enjoy with halibut or salmon.

Cabernet Sauvignon $ Perfumy aromas of currants and black fruit. A smooth, approachable wine to be enjoyed with lasagna or steak.

Shakespeare's Love $ A blend of six grapes, this is a fresh, fruity, sweet delight with bright fruit aromas and flavors. A lovely sipper perfect for brunches and hot tubs.

WHERE TO BUY: WINERY, WINE SHOPS, GROCERY STORES

2775 E. Main St., Ashland, OR 97520; 541-488-0088; www.winenet.com. Open Tuesday–Sunday.

BEAR CREEK WINERY

ROGUE VALLEY   ESTABLISHED 1998

The former Siskiyou Vineyards is owned and operated by Bridgeview winemaker Rene Eichmann, who produces wines under the Bear Creek and Siskiyou labels. The wines tend to be big, full-bodied, and nicely priced.

BEST BETS

Bear Creek Merlot $ A deep, penetrating wine with complex aromas and flavors of coffee, plum, and blackberry. An elegant wine that pairs well with marinated meats.

Siskiyou La Cave Rouge $ This Cab–Merlot blend is huge and richly aromatic with blackberries, plums, chocolate, coffee, and sweet spice. One of the best wines you'll find in Southern Oregon.

Siskiyou Gewürztraminer $ A soft, spicy white with light floral aromas and slightly sweet flavors. A pleasant sipper.

Siskiyou Pinot Blanc $ A crisp, delicious white with a plethora of fruit flavors, especially oranges and pears. Enjoy with shellfish.

WHERE TO BUY: WINERY, WINE SHOPS

6220 Caves Hwy., Cave Junction, OR 97523; 541-592-3977. Open daily from Memorial Day through Labor Day or by appointment.

BEAUX FRÈRES

YAMHILL COUNTY   ESTABLISHED 1987

Like many of the great estates of Burgundy, Beaux Frères focuses on just one wine: Pinot Noir. Begun in 1987 as a partnership between Michael and Jacqueline Etzel and Robert M. Parker Jr., the famed East Coast wine writer and Michael's brother-in-law, Beaux Frères has excellence as its goal, and it rarely misses. Michael is the winemaker and also keeps a watchful eye over the estate vineyards, from which all the fruit for the flagship Pinot Noir emanates. He consistently demonstrates that attention to detail is the key to success with this most fickle of wine grapes.

BEST BETS

Beaux Frères Pinot Noir $$$ This is one of Oregon's top Pinots and stands up well against the best from California and Burgundy. This silky, seductive Pinot is rich with characteristic cherry and raspberry aromas and is layered with pepper, spice, and delicious fruit. Beaux Frères wines are age-worthy, and top vintages are likely to improve for a decade or more.

Belles Soeurs Pinot Noir $$ A delicious and fun contrast to the Beaux Frères, this Pinot comes from non-estate grapes, usually Shea or another top Yamhill vineyard. Its style, typically much different than the Beaux Frères, is more approachable as a younger wine.

WHERE TO BUY: WINERY, WINE SHOPS

15155 N.E. North Valley Road, Newberg, OR 97132; 503-537-1137; www.beauxfreres.com. Open Memorial Day and Thanksgiving weekends.

BELLE PENTE VINEYARD AND WINERY

YAMHILL COUNTY   ESTABLISHED 1996

After the 1989 Loma Prieta earthquake, Brian and Jill O'Donnell decided to migrate north from California. Oregon wine lovers can be thankful for that move because the couple created Belle Pente (pronounced "bell pont," meaning "beautiful slope"). The first vineyards were planted in 1994, with the first vintage in '96. Today, Belle Pente produces 4,400 cases annually of expressive wines, including Riesling, Pinot Gris, Chardonnay, a rosé, and several Pinot Noirs. For their quality, Belle Pente wines are remarkably good values.

BEST BETS

Pinot Noir $$–$$$ No fewer than four different Pinot Noirs are crafted at Belle Pente. Each is expressive of its style and vineyard, and all show off classic aromas and flavors, from earth, cherry, and berry aromas to rich spices and dark flavors that are deep with structure and complexity.

Riesling $ A classic wine that shows off apple, petrol, honey, and spice aromas with crisp, refreshing flavors of apples and orange oil.

Pinot Gris $ Two styles are made: a regular and reserve. Both show off tropical and clove aromas with crisp yet creamy mouth weight and opulent flavors. Pair with turkey, ham, Asian dishes, or pork.

Chardonnay $$ Forget about a California oak bomb here, as this offers the essence of the grape with delicate lemon, butter, vanilla, and tropical aromas and clean, crisp flavors with a creamy midpalate. Try this with smoked meats.

WHERE TO BUY: WINERY, WINE SHOPS

12470 N.E. Rowland Road, Carlton, OR 97111; 503-852-9500; www.bellepente.com. Open Memorial Day and Thanksgiving weekends and by appointment.

BENTON-LANE WINERY

WILLAMETTE VALLEY   ESTABLISHED 1991

Benton-Lane makes some of Oregon's silkiest and most elegant Pinot Noir. Started by former California vintners Steve Girard (Girard Winery) and Carl Duomani (Stag's Leap Winery), Benton-Lane focuses narrowly on Pinot Noir, making no fewer than three styles depending on the vintage. Winemaker Gary Horner creates the wines with grapes from the estate vineyard in the southern Willamette Valley.

BEST BETS

Reserve Pinot Noir $$ A luscious wine with sweet vanilla aromas and ripe, penetrating black fruit. An underlying spiciness with hints of chocolate and leather makes this a memorable red.

Pinot Noir $$ Bright, spicy aromas with hints of violets and flavors of strawberry jam and moderate tannins. Enjoy this with fine cuts of beef.

WHERE TO BUY: WINERY, WINE SHOPS

23924 Territorial Road, Monroe, OR 97456; 541-847-5792; www.benton-lane.com. Open by appointment.

BERAN VINEYARDS

WILLAMETTE VALLEY   ESTABLISHED 1997

After more than two decades as grape growers, Bill and Sharon Beran launched Beran Vineyards, a small winery in a former dairy dating from World War II. The Berans focus on high-end Pinot Noir, and they may have found their niche, as the wines show off great elegance and complexity.

BEST BETS

Pinot Noir $$ Graceful throughout, this wonderful red opens with layers of aromas, including violet, cherry, vanilla bean, forest floor, and sweet spice. The complex flavors include hints of Rainier cherries and bittersweet chocolate. A serious effort that should be highly sought after.

WHERE TO BUY: WINERY, WINE SHOPS

30088 S.W. Egger Road, Hillsboro, OR 97123; 503-628-1298; www.beranvineyards.com. Open Memorial Day and Thanksgiving weekends or by appointment.

BERGSTRÖM WINERY

YAMHILL COUNTY   ESTABLISHED 1999

The focus is on small lots of handcrafted wines from two estate vineyards and two contracted vineyards in Yamhill County. Winemaker Josh Bergström, trained in Burgundy, leads the effort, which includes Pinot Noir, Chardonnay, and Pinot Gris. A new winery, completed in 2001, promises great things as this small producer develops.

BEST BETS

Pinot Noir $$ An elegant and refined red showing austere aromas and flavors of violets, cherries, sweet spices, and vanilla. Enjoy with veal or salmon.

WHERE TO BUY: WINERY, WINE SHOPS

18405 N.E. Calkins Lane, Newberg, OR 97132; 503-554-0468; www.bergstromwines.com. Open Memorial Day and Thanksgiving weekends or by appointment.

BETHEL HEIGHTS VINEYARD

WILLAMETTE VALLEY   ESTABLISHED 1984

Twin brothers Ted and Terry Casteel form the backbone of this family-operated winery in the Eola Hills near Salem. With some fifty acres of vineyards first planted in 1977, the winery relies primarily on estate-grown grapes but also purchases grapes from vineyards elsewhere in the vast Willamette Valley to give its wines more complexity.

BEST BETS

Estate Grown Pinot Noir $$ Huge, warm berry aromas lead to a luscious mouth feel and flavors of soft berries and vanilla. An elegant wine to savor with lamb.

Pinot Blanc $ A bright wine rich in orchard and tropical fruit aromas and flavors. Backed with plenty of acidity, this pairs well with pasta in a cream sauce, chicken, or shellfish.

Chardonnay $ This richly structured wine is a classic example of Oregon Chardonnay with its smoky, flinty aromas that give way to fruit-driven flavors with hints of oak and a fine balance of fruit and acidity. Try this with salmon, ahi, or scallops.

Pinot Gris $ A deliciously balanced wine with tropical and citrus fruit flavors, crisp acidity, and a zesty finish. Perfect with shellfish, chicken, or pasta.

WHERE TO BUY: WINERY, WINE SHOPS, GROCERY STORES

6060 Bethel Heights Road N.W., Salem, OR 97304; 503-581-2262; www.bethelheights.com. Seasonal hours.

BISHOP CREEK CELLARS / URBAN WINEWORKS

PORTLAND   ESTABLISHED 1998

Longtime Yamhill County grower Reuel Fish launched Bishop Creek Cellars and Urban Wineworks in the late '90s, complete with a Portland winery and tasting room that offers blending classes, art tours, and a lot of fun. The Bishop Creek label denotes the operation's high-end wines, and the Urban Wineworks label is more value-driven and gets its grapes from Oregon and Washington.

BEST BETS

Bishop Creek Special Cuvée Pinot Gris $ This delicate wine opens with perfumy aromas of mint and orange oil and offers plenty of fruit aromas backed up with a crisp, clean mouth feel. Enjoy with pork or shellfish.

Bishop Creek Barrel Selection Pinot Noir $$ A classy red that opens with dusty cherry and vanilla aromas with bright, tangy cherries and spices. A good wine for fish or chicken.

WHERE TO BUY: WINERY, WINE SHOPS

407 N.W. 16th Ave., Portland, OR 97209; 503-226-9797; www.urbanwineworks.com. Open daily.

BRICK HOUSE VINEYARDS

YAMHILL COUNTY   ESTABLISHED 1994

Soil is a subject of discussion no matter what wine region you're in. When you're at Brick House Vineyards, the soil takes center stage. The vineyard has been certified organic since 1990, and the vines are carefully tended to ensure low tonnage and high quality. In addition to Pinot Noir and Chardonnay, Brick House also produces Gamay Noir, an often-overlooked but delicious red variety.

BEST BETS

Cuvée du Tonnelier Pinot Noir $$$ A reserve wine made when quality allows, this is an expressive red that reveals great finesse in the glass, with rich aromas and flavors of raspberries, blackberries, sweet spice, violets, and light oak. A wine to savor with lamb, beef, or fowl.

Pinot Noir $$ This deep, intense wine shows off great balance of flavors, acidity, and tannin with sweet spice aromas and an elegant mouth feel. Silky through the palate, this is a wine to enjoy with delicate meat dishes.

Gamay Noir $$ A wonderfully rich and fruit-driven red that shows off ripe plum, blackberry, and floral notes with a creamy midpalate. This versatile food wine will match well with turkey or whatever's in the picnic basket.

Chardonnay $$ This richly structured wine exemplifies Oregon Chardonnay with its aromas and flavors that include spiced apples, pears, and pineapple. A creamy midpalate gives this good mouth weight, and the balance of fruit and acidity is superb.

WHERE TO BUY: WINERY, WINE SHOPS

18200 Lewis Rogers Lane, Newberg, OR 97132; 503-538-5136; www.brickhousewines.com. Open Thanksgiving weekend or by appointment.

BRIDGEVIEW VINEYARDS

ROGUE VALLEY   ESTABLISHED 1986

You can't get much closer to California and still be in Oregon than Cave Junction. Bridgeview Vineyards, one of Oregon's largest wineries, takes advantage of Southern Oregon's warmer climate to grow top-rated Pinot Noir, Riesling, Chardonnay, Pinot Gris, and Merlot. The winery's approach pays off for consumers who are looking for delicious wines at bargain prices. If you're looking for a fun gift, check out the Blue Moon Riesling in a blue bottle shaped like a crescent moon.

BEST BETS

Reserve Pinot Noir $$ Smooth, velvety red with violet aromas, black cherry and light cedar flavors, and supple tannins. A top Oregon Pinot Noir.

Reserve Pinot Gris $ A delicate and refined white with crisp lemon, orange, and tropical flavors.

Blue Moon Riesling $ A nice bit of sweetness is backed up with crisp acidity and bright apple and pear fruit flavors.

Blue Moon Pinot Noir $$ One of Oregon's best inexpensive Pinot Noirs, this silky and complex wine keeps winning top awards. It provides berry, vanilla, and violet aromas with richly structured strawberry jam flavors. Enjoy with veal, lamb, or pork loin.

WHERE TO BUY: WINERY, WINE SHOPS, GROCERY STORES

4210 Holland Loop Road, Cave Junction, OR 97523; 541-592-4688; www. bridgeviewwine.com. Open daily.

BRIGGS HILL VINEYARD

WILLAMETTE VALLEY   ESTABLISHED 1998

Ron Kuhn makes tiny amounts of Pinot Noir and a white blend from his four-acre vineyard near Eugene. His wines are highly sought after by wine aficionados who appreciate high quality at reasonable prices.

BEST BETS

Pinot Noir $$ Rich spice and fruit aromas give way to distinct berry, rhubarb, and tart berry flavors. A wine with a lot of character.

Briggs Hill White $ This consumer favorite offers floral and orange aromas with clean, refreshing flavors and a good dose of sweetness. A lovely summer sipper.

WHERE TO BUY: WINERY, WINE SHOPS

27127 Briggs Hill Road, Eugene, OR 97405; 541-341-3974.

BROOKS / MORNE WINE COMPANY

YAMHILL COUNTY   ESTABLISHED 1999

Jimi Brooks makes small amounts of high-quality wines, including three Pinot Noirs, a Riesling, and a white blend. Brooks is starting off doing everything right, from judicious use of new oak and filtering to working closely with vineyard sources.

BEST BETS

Amycas $ This whimsical blend of Riesling, Pinot Gris, and Gewürz-traminer is a fresh, flavorful sipper with aromas and flavors of apples and citrus fruit, a mellow mouth feel, and a lingering finish. Enjoy with brunches or picnics.

Riesling $ Classic apple and petrol aromas lead to rich, pleasing flavors backed up with a bit of residual sugar. Enjoy this with ham, duck, or firm cheeses.

Pinot Noir $$ Earthy, European aromas give way to round, rich flavors of cherries, berries, and hints of vanilla. Solid acidity gives this plenty of length, and it should pair well with turkey, Cornish game hen, or sirloin.

WHERE TO BUY: WINERY, WINE SHOPS

1043 N.E. 4th St., McMinnville, OR 97128; 503-435-1278. Call for hours.

CAMERON WINERY

YAMHILL COUNTY   ESTABLISHED 1984

Brilliant and irreverent, winemaker John Paul does things his own way at his winery in the hills above Dundee. His sardonic wit, revealed in his annual newsletter, is legendary, and his Pinot Noirs are intense. Paul crafts Pinot Noir in small lots with grapes from select

vineyards, as well as producing other wines such as Chardonnay and
Pinot Blanc.

BEST BETS

Clos Electrique Pinot Noir $$$ Forget about over-oaked wines at
Cameron. Winemaker John Paul believes in allowing the wine to
express itself. This, perhaps his finest Pinot Noir, is deep and earthy
with gobs of complex black fruit aromas and flavors. This is a
can't-miss for Pinot lovers.

Abbey Ridge Pinot Noir $$$ Rich and intense, this offers complex berry
flavors and a silky mouth feel.

Arley's Leap Pinot Noir $$$ Perhaps Cameron's most approachable
Pinot in its youth, this exhibits great cherry and raspberry charac-
ter with telltale earthiness and a velvety mouth feel.

WHERE TO BUY: WINERY, WINE SHOPS

*8200 Worden Hill Road, Dundee, OR 97115; 503-538-0336. Open
by appointment.*

CARABELLA VINEYARD

WILLAMETTE VALLEY   ESTABLISHED 1998

*Like so many before him, winemaker Mike Hallock was drawn to the
Willamette Valley for its lush surroundings, steelhead fishing, and
great Pinot Noir. With fruit from its forty-nine-acre vineyard on Par-
rett Mountain near Wilsonville, Carabella produces Pinot Noir,
Chardonnay, and Pinot Gris.*

BEST BETS

Chardonnay $$ A fruit-driven beauty loaded with aromas and flavors
of oranges, lemons, and apples. A bright, approachable wine with
medium mouth weight, this pairs well with salmon, chicken, or
pasta in a cream sauce.

Pinot Gris $ Pleasing from start to lengthy finish, this is laden with
orchard and citrus fruit notes as well as mouth-pleasing acidity.
A sure match for Thai-inspired shrimp.

Pinot Noir $$$ A complex red with aromas of bright cherries and
sweet oak spice. The penetrating flavors reveal black fruit, licorice,
chocolate, tobacco, and more. Try this with a pepper steak.

WHERE TO BUY: WINE SHOPS

*Edminston Road, Wilsonville, OR; 303-423-3272; www.carabella
wine.com. Not open to the public.*

CARLO & JULIAN WINERY

YAMHILL COUNTY   ESTABLISHED 1996

This tiny producer in the wine hamlet of Carlton is named after the twin sons of owners Felix and Annette Madrid. The winery is a family labor of love, with a loyal consumer following for its small lots of high-quality Pinot Noir.

BEST BETS

Croft Vineyard Pinot Noir $$ A complex wine with violet and earthy aromas and rich black fruit and leather flavors. A classy wine from a great vineyard.

Pinot Noir $$ This blend of grapes from Croft and estate vineyard grapes offers delicious cherry and raspberry fruit with hints of smoke, spice, and herbs.

Sauvignon Blanc $$ Honey and orchard fruit aromas are backed up with deliciously steely flavors and a rich mouth feel with hints of orange oil.

WHERE TO BUY: WINERY, WINE SHOPS

1000 E. Main St., Carlton, OR 97111; 503-852-7432. Open Memorial Day and Thanksgiving weekends or by appointment.

CHAMPAGNE CREEK CELLARS

UMPQUA VALLEY   ESTABLISHED 1987

The former Callahan Ridge Winery doesn't produce any sparkling wines. Rather, it's named after a creek that meanders through the region. The new owners are off to a good start with several savory wines, all of which are nicely priced.

BEST BETS

Gamay Noir $ A somewhat rare variety in the Northwest, this Gamay Noir is a bright, pretty wine with up-front fruit flavors that will make you a fan. Try this with barbecued chicken or ribs.

Pinot Noir $ Nothing pretentious here, just an exotic, fruit-driven red with strawberry and mint flavors. It's priced for everyday enjoyment, so serve this with salmon, steak, or spicy chicken.

Pinot Gris $ A bright white with luscious fruit and floral nuances, this is a gentle wine that pairs well with clams, mussels, or a seafood bisque.

WHERE TO BUY: WINERY, WINE SHOPS, GROCERY STORES

340 Busenbark Lane, Roseburg, OR 97470; 541-673-7901; www.champagnecreek.com. Open daily.

CHAMPOEG WINE CELLARS

WILLAMETTE VALLEY   ESTABLISHED 1990

With vineyards planted in the mid-1970s, Champoeg changed owner-ship in 2000. Louanna and Chuck Eggert are focused on high quality that starts in the vineyard. When visiting the winery, bring a picnic lunch and enjoy the view of Mount Hood.

BEST BETS

Reserve Pinot Noir $$ This tasty, affordable wine is a ripe, drink-now crowd pleaser with complex aromas and flavors including those of black cherries, plums, anise, and vanilla. Enjoy with beef or chicken.

White Riesling $ A classic Oregon Riesling with aromas and flavors of apples, tangerines, white flowers, and hints of pears. Enjoy with chicken, cheese, and fruit plates or Asian-inspired cuisine.

French Prairie Blanc $ This tasty blush is named for the nearby French Prairie region and is loaded with luscious flavors of peaches, pears, and strawberries. Enjoy on a picnic or with turkey.

Reserve Chardonnay $ A pleasant white that offers vanilla, spice, and oak aromas with orchard fruit flavors. Pair with mussels, salmon, or cod.

WHERE TO BUY: WINERY, WINE SHOPS, GROCERY STORES

10375 Champoeg Road N.E., Aurora, OR 97002; 503-678-2144; www.champoegwine.com. Open daily.

CHATEAU BENOIT WINERY

YAMHILL COUNTY   ESTABLISHED 1979

One of Oregon's oldest wineries has a new attitude. Through the years Chateau Benoit built its reputation on white wines, particularly Müller-Thurgau. An ownership change in 1999 brought a new dispo-sition, giving winemaker Scott Huffman the tools and opportunity to craft top wines. The winery has replaced a lot of equipment and is reducing vineyard yields to increase quality. The result is high-quality Pinot Noirs that are beginning to turn heads.

BEST BETS

Pinot Gris $ Showing some oak aging, this has touches of vanilla and butter with long flavors of pears and tangerines and crisp acidity. Serve with shellfish, pasta, or chicken.

Pinot Noir $$ Classy violet and bright fruit aromas with cherry and berry flavors and supple tannins. A delicious, food-friendly wine.

Vineyard-designated Pinot Noirs $$$ Chateau Benoit crafts no fewer than three vineyard-designated Pinots, each showing off the sites' quali-ties. Perhaps the best is from Doe Ridge Vineyard, a complex red loaded with layers of fruit, spice, earth, and mocha backed with a deliciously creamy palate and a long, juicy finish.

Anne Amie Pinot Noir $$$$ A high-end brand for Benoit, this is a refined, elegant wine with gentle black fruit, spice, and a rich mouth feel. A collector's wine.

WHERE TO BUY: WINERY, WINE SHOPS, GROCERY STORES

6580 N.E. Mineral Springs Road, Carlton, OR 97127; 503-864-2991; www.chateaubenoit.com. Open daily.

CHATEAU BIANCA WINERY

WILLAMETTE VALLEY   ESTABLISHED 1987

The winemaking history of the Wetzel family goes back no fewer than six generations to Germany. The family's Chateau Bianca produces a wide variety of delicious wines at affordable prices. Visitors might want to consider staying at the estate B&B.

BEST BETS

Estate Reserve Pinot Noir $$ An intense red showing classic earth and cherry aromas with complex fruit, spice, and oak flavors. Great balance between fruit, acidity, and tannins makes this a perfect match for pheasant, lamb, or beef dishes.

Pinot Blanc $ A rich and tasty white with tropical aromas and fresh, fruit-driven flavors. A touch of sweetness makes this a nice sipper, or enjoy it with a seafood bisque.

Pinot Gris $ A delicate white that shows off complex aromas and flavors of flint, citrus, orchard fruit, and tropical notes. A delicious example of Oregon Pinot Gris that will pair well with chicken.

Gewürztraminer $ This classic example offers grapefruit and nutmeg aromas with fresh citrus flavors and refreshing acidity. Perfect for turkey, duck, or lightly spiced dishes.

WHERE TO BUY: WINERY, WINE SHOPS, GROCERY STORES

17485 Hwy. 22, Dallas, OR 97338; 503-623-6181; www.chateaubianca.com. Open daily (by appointment in January).

CHATEAU LORANE

WILLAMETTE VALLEY   ESTABLISHED 1991

In the southern end of the long Willamette Valley is a winery producing a dizzying and unusual array of varieties. Owner/winemaker Linde Kester produces more than a dozen different varieties, from the mainstream (Pinot Noir, Chardonnay, Cabernet Sauvignon, and Merlot) to the rarely seen (Huxelrebe, Petite Sirah, Melón, Chancellor, and Pinot Meunier) and sweet and fruit wines.

BEST BETS

Durif $$ A rare variety for the Northwest, this Petite Sirah provides blackberry and plum aromas with good richness on the midpalate with smooth blackberry and black cherry flavors.

Pinot Meunier $$ A red wine that most often is used in classic Champagne, this relative of Pinot Noir shows off similar characteristics. This example provides strawberry jam and raspberry aromas and flavors with a clean, racy mouth feel. A good wine to pair with salmon.

Huxelrebe $$ An unusual grape for the Northwest, this is made in a late-harvest style with about 2.5 percent residual sugar. It provides tart apple, orange oil, rose petal, and dried grapefruit nuances with plenty of backbone and a lengthy finish. A fine end-of-the-meal sipper.

WHERE TO BUY: WINERY, WINE SHOPS, GROCERY STORES

27415 Siuslaw River Road, Lorane, OR 97451; 541-942-8028; www.chateaulorane.com. Seasonal hours.

CHEHALEM

YAMHILL COUNTY   ESTABLISHED 1990

Under the direction of Harry Peterson-Nedry and co-winemaker Cheryl Francis, Chehalem is well known for its high-quality and distinctive wines. The grapes come primarily from three estate vineyards, two run by Peterson-Nedry and one run by Chehalem co-owners Bill and Cathy Stoller. The wines are elegant in style and reflect care from vineyard to bottle.

BEST BETS

Ridgecrest Vineyard Pinot Noir $$$ A bold wine showing dark berry, spice, and oak aromas and flavors and richly structured tannins. Pair this with steak.

Rion Reserve Pinot Noir $$$$ Chehalem calls this its best Pinot Noir to date, and it's difficult to disagree. It is a complex wine with aromas of berries, pencil shavings, and earthiness and flavors of black olives, freshly ground pepper, and deep, dark fruit. The finish is long and richly structured.

Ian's Reserve Chardonnay $$$ A luscious example of Oregon Chardonnay with its butterscotch aromas and orchard and citrus fruit flavors with a creamy midpalate and a long finish. A great wine to pair with shellfish or ahi.

Reserve Pinot Gris $$ This hugely aromatic and flavorful wine opens with aromas of oranges, flowers, and hazelnuts and flavors of citrus and tropical fruit. The rich acidity makes this a perfect match for shellfish or chicken.

31190 N.E. Veritas Lane, Newberg, OR 97132; 503-538-4700; www.chehalemwines.com. Open Memorial Day and Thanksgiving weekends.

COLEMAN VINEYARD

YAMHILL COUNTY   ESTABLISHED 1999

Randy and Kim Coleman produce small amounts of high-quality Pinot Noir and Pinot Gris. The couple do all the work, from tending the vineyards to making the wines and putting in the corks.

BEST BETS

Reserve Pinot Noir $$$ Heady aromas of cherries, vanilla, cedar, earth, and herbs give way to deep, dark flavors of blackberries, sweet oak spices, and bittersweet chocolate. A lengthy wine with ripe tannins; pair this with beef.

Pinot Noir $$ A bright, elegant red showing off cherry, violet, and red currant aromas and flavors with a nicely balanced mouth feel and approachable tannins. A good wine to try with salmon.

WHERE TO BUY: WINERY, WINE SHOPS

22734 Latham Road, McMinnville, OR 97128; 503-843-2707; www.colemanvineyard.com. Open Memorial Day and Thanksgiving weekends and by appointment.

COOPER MOUNTAIN VINEYARDS

WILLAMETTE VALLEY   ESTABLISHED 1987

Named for an old volcano that overlooks the Tualatin Valley west of Portland, Cooper Mountain Vineyards focuses on small amounts of wines made from estate organic vineyards. The winery produces a wide variety of Pinot Noir, Chardonnay, and Pinot Gris.

BEST BETS

Dijon Reserve Chardonnay $ This richly structured white is loaded with aromas and flavors of spiced apples, butter, and citrus. A smooth Oregon Chardonnay with a lingering mouth feel. Try this with breaded chicken in a lemon cream sauce.

Reserve Pinot Gris $ Loaded with orchard and tropical fruit, this luscious white is backed up with food-friendly acidity and a hint of sweetness. Try this with shellfish or ahi.

Pinot Noir $ A big, delicious red with dark fruit flavors laced with black pepper, approachable tannins, and fresh strawberries on the finish. Enjoy with pork loin.

WHERE TO BUY: WINERY, WINE SHOPS, GROCERY STORES

9480 S.W. Grabhorn Road, Beaverton, OR 97007; 503-649-0027; www.coopermountainwine.com. Open daily (January by appointment).

CRISTOM

WILLAMETTE VALLEY   ESTABLISHED 1992

Cristom is focused on high-quality wines primarily from estate vine-yards near Salem. It also secures grapes from throughout the Willamette Valley as well as from vaunted Celilo Vineyard in the Columbia Gorge. Depending on vintage quality, Cristom will make a half-dozen Pinot Noirs, two Chardonnays, Pinot Gris, and Viognier. Cristom's wines are highly regarded, and the Pinot Noirs should be highly sought after.

BEST BETS

Mt. Jefferson Cuvée Pinot Noir $$ A blend of Pinot Noir from more than a dozen Willamette Valley vineyards, this is a delicious wine at a fair price. It provides complex aromas of bright cherries and raspberries with underlying violets and forest floor. The flavors are deep and intense with a fine balance of fruit, tannins, and acidity.

Reserve Pinot Noir $$$ Blended from several vineyards, this top-end Pinot Noir is a penetrating red with earthy, spicy, and berry aromas with undertones of vanilla and deep, dark fruit flavors with rich tan-nins. A great wine to age a few years or enjoy now with a thick steak.

Louise Vineyard Pinot Noir $$$ This smooth and balanced wine provides notes of ripe dark fruit, vanilla, and violets, with plenty of com-plexity throughout. An elegant wine to enjoy with pheasant, lamb, or beef.

Celilo Vineyard Chardonnay $$ A big white wine with aromas and flavors of toasty oak, apples, lemons, and butter. A dense, rich wine to enjoy with fresh crab or pasta tossed with smoked salmon.

WHERE TO BUY: WINERY, WINE SHOPS

6905 Spring Valley Road N.W., Salem, OR 97304; 503-375-3068; www.cristomwines.com. Seasonal hours.

CROFT BAILEY VINEYARDS

YAMHILL COUNTY   ESTABLISHED 1998

This southern Willamette Valley vineyard began to make minute amounts of Pinot Noir and Pinot Gris beginning with the heralded 1998 vintage. With only a few hundred cases scattered here and there, buy this wine when you find it.

BEST BETS

Reserve Pinot Noir $$$$ A huge, complex wine with layers of intriguing leather, toast, cherry, raspberry, and anise aromas and a fruit-laden palate with mouth-filling acidity. A giant of a wine to serve with prime rib.

Pinot Noir $$$ A refined and low-key red with aromas and flavors of earthy cherry, leather, and white pepper. Enjoy with lamb.

Pinot Gris $ A delicious white showing off toasty pear and lemon aromas with tasty citrus flavors. A well-balanced wine to pair with scallops or steamed oysters.

WHERE TO BUY: WINERY, WINE SHOPS

1301 N. Hwy. 99 #144, McMinnville, OR 97128; 505-881-8300; www.croftbailey.com. Not open to the public.

CUNEO CELLARS

YAMHILL COUNTY   ESTABLISHED 1993

Gino Cuneo knows what he likes and has no fear about going after it. Though situated deep in Yamhill County, Cuneo Cellars is about more than Pinot Noir. Gino also loves Italian varieties and hot-climate grapes, so he looks north, where he procures grapes from some of Washington's finest vineyards, and he also is planting some of his own vines. Cuneo's Cana's Feast wines are his finest and are eminently age-worthy.

BEST BETS

Cana's Feast Red Mountain Bordeaux $$$ A deep, dense, and intense wine, loaded with rich fruit, including black currants and blackberries. It's a bold wine with smooth tannins. Savor this wine with lamb or beef.

Ciel du Cheval Sangiovese $$ From Washington's Red Mountain comes this elegant wine with aromas and flavors of cherries, plums, and spices. A lush wine to enjoy with lasagna or beef.

Cana's Feast Pinot Noir, Cuveé G $$$ This opens with aromas of coffee, chocolate, blackberries, and sweet spices and intense flavors of cherries and plums. Richly structured with ripe tannins, this will stand up to lamb or prime rib.

Cana's Feast Del Rio Vineyard Bordeaux $$$ From Southern Oregon grapes, this opens with stylish aromas of cola and black fruit. A thick, tannic wine that will go well with a thick steak.

WHERE TO BUY: WINERY, WINE SHOPS

750 Lincoln St., Carlton, OR 97111; 503-852-0002; www.cuneo cellars.com. Seasonal hours.

DAEDALUS CELLARS

YAMHILL COUNTY   ESTABLISHED 2000

This tiny producer in Dundee is the creation of Rex Hill Vineyards winemaker Aron Hess and his wife, Pam Walden. They focus on Yamhill County Pinot Noir as well as a bit of Syrah from The Dalles, Oregon. They intend to plant an estate vineyard on a seventeen-acre site and to slowly build their production.

BEST BETS

Pinot Noir $$ Inviting aromas of dark berries, vanilla, and bacon fat lead to silky, luscious flavors of ripe cherries and cream. This is an elegant wine to savor with duck, veal, or even salmon.

WHERE TO BUY: WINE SHOPS

10505 N.E. Red Hills Road, Dundee, OR 97115; 503-537-0727; www.daedaluscellars. Not open to the public.

DAVID HILL VINEYARD AND WINERY

WILLAMETTE VALLEY   ESTABLISHED 1991

David Hill led the territorial government of Oregon before it became a state and is the namesake of Hillsboro, a nearby city. The estate that honors him has a long history of grape growing that dates back to before Prohibition, and vineyards were re-established in the mid-1960s. Today the winery makes a wide array of wines, primarily with grapes from nearby vineyards and also from California.

BEST BETS

Reserve Pinot Noir $$ A toasty, spicy red with rich aromatics and delicious concentration of ripe fruit. A good match for salmon, pork, or chicken.

Gewürztraminer $ A fresh, tasty white with good citrus and spice in the aromas and flavors. A steely wine that will match well with Thai-inspired dishes.

Muscat Port $$ A rare white Port from Muscat grapes, this is an intensely rich wine with nectarine and pear aromas and honeyed, spicy flavors. A tasty winter sipper.

WHERE TO BUY: WINERY, WINE SHOPS, GROCERY STORES

46350 David Hill Road, Forest Grove, OR 97116; 503-992-8545; www.davidhillwinery.com. Open Tuesday–Sunday.

DENINO UMPQUA RIVER ESTATE

UMPQUA VALLEY   ESTABLISHED 1988

The DeNino family knows all about good food and wine. The winery focuses on off-dry white wines, and the family's restaurant, Dino's Ristorante Italiano in downtown Roseburg, has a reputation as one of the best and most authentic Italian eateries in Oregon.

BEST BETS

Le Tre Sorelle $ A blend of Semillon, Sauvignon Blanc, and Chenin Blanc, this bright, food-friendly white offers delicious aromas and flavors of pears, Fuji apples, and figs with a touch of sweetness, cleansing acidity, and long flavors.

Semillon $ An off-dry white showing aromas and flavors of baked apples, light spice, and a pleasant finish. Enjoy with cheese.

Select Cluster Semillon $$ A sweeter wine at about 2 percent residual sugar, this has plenty of acidity to back up the refreshing flavors of apples and figs. A delicious brunch wine.

WHERE TO BUY: WINERY, WINE SHOPS, GROCERY STORES

451 Hess Road, Roseburg, OR 97470; 541-673-1975. Seasonal hours.

DOMAINE DROUHIN OREGON

YAMHILL COUNTY   ESTABLISHED 1989

With a few hundred years of making Pinot Noir under its belt, the decision by the Drouhin family of France to build a world-class winery in the hills above Dundee was a defining moment for the Oregon wine industry. Robert Drouhin fell in love with the Willamette Valley during a visit in the early 1960s and got to know some of the area's wine pioneers in the '70s. When The Eyrie Vineyard's 1975 South Block Pinot Noir whipped Burgundy's best in a now-famous French competition, Drouhin knew it was time to look seriously at Oregon Pinot Noir.

The vineyards were started in 1988, and the winery was built a year later. It's Oregon's first gravity-flow operation (a system that uses gravity rather than pumps to move wine around a winery), and the Drouhins also pioneered high-density vineyards and clonal selection. They leave little to chance, as they grow their own rootstock, graft their own vines, make their own barrels, and craft their wine with a gentle touch. All of this adds up to some of the finest Pinot Noir outside of Beaune.

BEST BETS

Laurène Pinot Noir $$$$ Named for winemaker Veronique Drouhin's oldest daughter, this reserve-style Pinot Noir is a richly textured wine loaded with cherries, raspberries, jammy black fruit, and velvety tannins. Its gently oaked origins are hinted at with a whisper of vanilla, and its elegant, complex layers reveal earthy, peppery nuances.

Pinot Noir $$$$ Brighter and more approachable in its youth than the Laurène, the classic Pinot Noir is loaded with rich, delicious raspberries and cherries. Violets dance with light touches of vanilla on the aromas, and its clean, pure flavors make this a delicate and complex wine.

Chardonnay $$ Worth seeking out is this Chardonnay, an elegant white that shows off huge amounts of ripe apples, grapefruit, and minerals. A delicious wine from front to back.

P.O. Box 700, Dundee, OR 97115; 503-864-2700; www.domaine drouhin.com. Open Memorial Day and Thanksgiving weekends and by appointment.

DOMAINE MERIWETHER

WILLAMETTE VALLEY   ESTABLISHED 1998

Domaine Meriwether is a young winery full of tradition. The winery is named after Meriwether Lewis of Lewis and Clark fame, the first wine is the Capt. Wm Clark Cuvée, and the sparkling wines are made in the traditional Methode Champenoise. The wines are made by sixth-generation Champagne winemaker Jean-Louis Denois, and the winery is run by John Bagdade, a founder of the famed Pike & Western Wine Shop in Seattle's Pike Place Market.

BEST BETS

Capt. Wm Clark Cuvee Brut $$ A classy sparkler with aromas of berries, hazelnuts, and cake and a rich mouth feel from fine bubbles. A good match for oysters, scallops, or a toast to the explorer in you.

Pinot Noir $$ This medium-bodied red offers delicate berry and vanilla aromas with tangy cherry and spice flavors. An elegant wine for salmon.

WHERE TO BUY: WINERY, WINE SHOPS, GROCERY STORES

801 N. Scott St., Carlton, OR 97111; 503-852-6100. Open Saturdays.

DOMAINE SERENE

YAMHILL COUNTY   ESTABLISHED 1990

With a beautiful new gravity-flow facility high above the wine village of Dundee, Domaine Serene is set to increase the success it's had since its inception. Domaine Serene was fortunate to have Ken Wright as its winemaker until 1998, when Tony Rynders arrived from Hogue Cellars in Washington. Good fruit sources and Wright's talent gave Domaine Serene early praise from critics and consumers alike, and its focus is on Pinot Noir and Chardonnay. In 2001, Serene introduced a new label, Rockblock, which focuses on Syrah from the Walla Walla Valley and Southern Oregon.

BEST BETS

Evenstad Reserve Pinot Noir $$$$ Carefully controlled crop levels of about two tons per acre from estate vineyard fruit produce a silky and rich Pinot with violet aromas and smooth, layered flavors. Eighty percent new French oak shows as a component with a hint of spice and vanilla.

Côte Sud Vineyard Chardonnay $$$ Fragrant tropical and butterscotch aromas abound in this richly flavored and complex white from one of Serene's estate vineyards. Light toastiness shows from nearly 50 percent new French oak aging, and a long, delicious farewell can be attributed to "sur lie" aging, in which yeast sediment left from fermentation is allowed to remain in the wine.

Clos du Soleil Vineyard Chardonnay $$$ Richer and creamier than its Côte Sud sibling, this delicious Chardonnay shows off butterscotch, buttery, toasty oak, and hints of ripe white fruit.

Seven Hills Vineyard Rockblock Syrah $$$ With fruit from one of Walla Walla Valley's top vineyards, this supple, textured red shows off ripe plums, sweet oak aromas, vanilla, and balanced tannins. A huge mouth feel and tremendous depth make this a winner.

WHERE TO BUY: WINERY, WINE SHOPS

6555 N.E. Hilltop Lane, Dayton, OR 97114; 503-864-4600; www.domaineserene.com. Open Memorial Day and Thanksgiving weekends and by appointment.

DUCK POND CELLARS

YAMHILL COUNTY   ESTABLISHED 1993

One of Oregon's largest wineries, Duck Pond Cellars also produces a large amount of Washington wine from its highly regarded vineyard on Eastern Washington's Wahluke Slope. Duck Pond is known for good-quality, value-priced wines. In 2001 it introduced a new label, Desert Wind Vineyard, a line of high-end, Bordeaux-style wines from its best Washington grapes. Plans are in the works for a tasting room in the Yakima Valley.

BEST BETS

Desert Wind Vineyard Merlot $$ A chewy red with gobs of flavor, including bright fruit, chocolate, cedar, vanilla, and spice. A versatile, food-friendly wine.

Pinot Noir $ One of Oregon's best-priced Pinots that is consistently tasty and occasionally great. Good cherry and raspberry aromas with fruity, earthy, spicy flavors. A good wine for pork or salmon.

Chardonnay $ Duck Pond makes two Chardonnays, one from Oregon and one from Washington. They show the contrasting styles of the two regions, with the Washington version often providing the best qualities.

Desert Wind Vineyard Semillon $$ A fruit-driven white offering layers of flavors, including citrus and fig. A delicious alternative to Chardonnay that matches well with seafood and chicken.

23145 Hwy. 99W, Dundee, OR 97115; 503-538-3199; www.duck pondcellars.com. Open daily.

DUNDEE SPRINGS WINERY

YAMHILL COUNTY   ESTABLISHED 1992

With its focus on Pinot Noir, Pinot Gris, and Pinot Blanc, Dundee Springs is the House of the Three Pinots. The three related grapes make up the sixty-acre vineyard that stretches from Highway 99W in the wine village of Dundee up the hill behind town. Concentrating on these three varieties is paying off as Dundee Springs wines gain consistency and quality.

BEST BETS

Pinot Blanc $$ A fresh, fruity white wine with orchard fruit aromas and flavors and sufficient acidity to back it up.

Pinot Gris $$ Neutral oak aging gives this crisp, food-friendly wine a hint of light vanilla aromas and a creamy mouth feel. Spicy nuances make this a good match with boldly flavored cuisine.

Reserve Pinot Noir $$$ This complex red is loaded with cerebral aromas, including earth, anise, herbs, and mint. Bright berry flavors highlight this smooth and inviting wine.

WHERE TO BUY: WINERY, WINE SHOPS

9605 Fox Farm Road, Dundee, OR 97115; 503 551 8000. Winery open daily.

EDGFFIELD WINERY

PORTLAND   ESTABLISHED 1990

Owned by the regionally famous McMenamin brothers, who also own a string of brewpubs throughout the greater Portland area, this winery near the mouth of the Columbia Gorge makes a variety of wines from Oregon and Washington grapes. Across the board, the wines are approachable and free of inhibition.

BEST BETS

Layne Vineyard Merlot $$ From a Rogue Valley vineyard come grapes for this tangy, youthful wine that is delicious and unpretentious.

Syrah $$ A smooth, richly structured red with plenty of black fruit, spices, and chocolate. A good match for lamb.

Old Vine Zinfandel $$ From ninety-year-old vines in The Dalles, Oregon, this rare Northwest Zin is long on lush berry flavors with hints of vanilla. Smooth through the finish.

Pinot Gris Ice Block $$ This white dessert wine is loaded with honey and orchard fruit aromas and soft, lovely flavors. Plenty of sugar with a good acidic backbone. Pair with cheesecake.

WHERE TO BUY: WINERY

2126 S.W. Halsey St., Troutdale, OR 97060; 503-665-2992; www.mcmenamins.com. Open daily.

ELK COVE VINEYARDS

YAMHILL COUNTY   ESTABLISHED 1978

One of Oregon's oldest wineries has been going through a renaissance of sorts as the second generation has taken over. Pat and Joe Campbell planted their first vineyards in 1973 high in the hills above the town of Gaston and began producing vineyard-designated Pinot Noirs in 1979. Now, their son Alex has taken Elk Cove's helm as winemaker and general manager. He has replaced equipment, moved the wine-making procedures to a gravity-flow system, and has reduced vineyard yields to increase fruit quality. The results are intense wines that show the character of Elk Cove's estate vineyards.

BEST BETS

Roosevelt Pinot Noir $$$$ From the estate Roosevelt Vineyard (named after a herd of Roosevelt elk that still migrates to the area), this is a richly textured red that shows off big, ripe berries, smoky, spicy tannins, and earthy undertones. With yields of just about a ton per acre and delicate cellar treatment, this wine was coddled from vineyard to bottle.

Pinot Noir $$ Elk Cove's mainline Pinot Noir is an affordable red with ripe fruit, rich, smoky cherries, and a smooth, delicious finish.

Pinot Gris $ One of the Northwest's top Pinot Gris comes from Elk Cove. This is one of the winery's main whites since phasing out Chardonnay in the late '90s. It's a graceful yet richly textured, food-friendly wine loaded with fresh tropical and citrus fruit.

Viognier $$ This is a rare but fashionable variety in the Northwest, and Chardonnay lovers will enjoy its butter and vanilla aromas backed up with mineral and ripe fruit flavors. A tasty wine made in small lots.

WHERE TO BUY: WINERY, WINE SHOPS, GROCERY STORES

27751 N.W. Olson Road, Gaston, OR 97119; 503-985-7760; www.elkcove.com. Open daily.

ELVENGLADE VINEYARDS

YAMHILL COUNTY   ESTABLISHED 1998

This vineyard in the Gaston area decided to launch a winery in the late '90s and also makes a blend for 24 Brix, a nearby wine shop. Its first efforts are with Pinot Gris, but also look for Pinot Noir and Chardonnay in future vintages.

BEST BETS

Pinot Gris $ This offers everything you'd expect from a quality Oregon Pinot Gris, from the lemon and tropical aromas to the crisp citrus and pineapple flavors, all backed up with food-friendly acidity. Imagine this with prawns or scallops.

Late Harvest Pinot Gris $ With aromas of honey, nuts, apples, and oranges and flavors of pears and tangerines, this wine offers bright, clean acidity that expertly backs up the well-balanced sweetness. Try this with baked apples with French vanilla ice cream.

WHERE TO BUY: WINE SHOPS

3500 Bridgefarmer Road, Gaston, OR 97119. No tasting facility.

EOLA HILLS WINE CELLARS

WILLAMETTE VALLEY   ESTABLISHED 1986

One of Oregon's largest wineries, Eola Hills also is one of the state's most diverse. It produces powerful Chardonnays, elegant Pinot Noirs, sassy Pinot Gris, sensual dessert wines, and even some Bordeaux-style reds. The wines are good to great depending on vintage, and consistently delicious.

BEST BETS

Mystery Block Chardonnay $$ One of the Northwest's finest Chardonnays, this is an intense wine loaded with butter and vanilla, yet it is well-balanced with tropical and orchard fruit. A luscious wine throughout, this pairs well with scallops in a butter and herb sauce.

Pinot Noir $$ Light, bright berry aromas and flavors with a supple mouth feel. A wine to enjoy with salmon or pasta.

Vin d'Epice Late Harvest Gewürztraminer $ A spicy honey wine with long, clean, delicious flavors and an extravagant mouth feel. A sweet dessert unto itself or serve with a fruit plate.

La Creole Cabernet Sauvignon $$ A thick, dark wine showing herbal and coffee aromas with a good balance of ripe plum flavors, good acidity, and a silky finish. Try this with beef in a mushroom sauce.

WHERE TO BUY: WINERY, WINE SHOPS, GROCERY STORES

501 S. Pacific Hwy. 99W, Rickreall, OR 97371; 503-623-2405; www.eolahillswinery.com. Open daily.

ERATH VINEYARDS WINERY

YAMHILL COUNTY   ESTABLISHED 1972

One of Oregon's Pinot pioneers, Dick Erath is going as strong today as he was three decades ago. A gentle bear of a man, Erath is a California native who came north to craft Pinot Noir. A multiyear tasting of Erath Pinot, held on 2000, showed that even his 1974 Pinot Noir (put in a Riesling-style "hock" bottle because it cost less than a Burgundy bottle) still shows plenty of youthful fruit and impressive acidity. The quality of Erath's wines makes him one of the state's most highly regarded producers. Don't overlook his late-harvest wines as well as his dry Pinot Blanc and Pinot Gris.

BEST BETS

Leland Vineyard Pinot Noir $$$ Erath has a special relationship with Leland Vineyard, going back to the 1980s, and this nurturing shows in this wine rich in complex layers of bright fruit, violets, earthiness, and spices.

Pinot Noir $ The "basic" Pinot also is one of the best around (and one of the best bargains among high-end Pinots). Resplendent with lush fruit, this is a wine built to drink sooner rather than later and matches well with everything from salmon to lamb.

Pinot Gris $ A crisp, fresh, unpretentious wine that shouts, "Bring me shellfish!" Loaded with bright fruit and good complexity, it shows why Oregon is Pinot Gris country.

WHERE TO BUY: WINERY, WINE SHOPS, GROCERY STORES

9409 N.E. Worden Hill Road, Dundee, OR 97115; 503-538-3318; www.erath.com. Open daily.

EVESHAM WOOD WINERY

WILLAMETTE VALLEY   ESTABLISHED 1986

Russ Raney quietly goes about making graceful wines of distinction, and Evesham Wood wines are highly sought after by consumers in the know. Raney learned winemaking in Germany before he and his wife, Mary, moved to Oregon in the early '80s. Much of his fruit comes from his Eola Hills vineyard, but he also buys grapes from throughout the Willamette Valley, including those for the Cuvée J from the famed Shea Vineyard in Yamhill County.

BEST BETS

Cuvée J Pinot Noir $$ A deep and elegant wine with complex aromas and flavors of moist earth, nutmeg, violets, and blackberries with herbal and vanilla undertones. A wine to enjoy with veal or lamb.

Le Puits Sec Pinot Noir $$ A classy red showing dark, earthy aromas and deep fruit and blackberry flavors with lavender notes on the finish. A superb wine to enjoy with duck or turkey.

Pinot Gris $$ A crisp Oregon Pinot Gris that shows off flinty, herbal, and tropical notes with flavors of apples, citrus, and star fruit. Plenty of acidity gives this backbone and lets it match up with scallops or chicken.

Chardonnay \$\$ A fruit-driven white that provides grassy, citrus, and tropical notes with a creamy midpalate and a crisp finish. Enjoy with salmon or chicken.

WHERE TO BUY: WINERY, WINE SHOPS

3795 Wallace Road N.W., Salem, OR 97304; 503-371-8478. Open by appointment.

EYRIE VINEYARDS

YAMHILL COUNTY   ESTABLISHED 1970

David Lett came to Oregon and planted his vineyard in the mid-1960s. The winery opened in 1970, and his 1975 South Block Pinot Noir put Oregon on the world Pinot Noir map when it whipped several famous Burgundies in Paris. That judging eventually led Robert Drouhin to launch his Oregon winery. Lett also pioneered Pinot Gris, now Oregon's favorite white wine. He planted it in the '60s and has been making it since the first vintage.

BEST BETS

Pinot Gris \$\$ A bright, flavorful white showing off orchard fruit aromas and flavors and backed up with plenty of food-friendly acidity.

Pinot Noir \$\$ This solid standard-bearer for Oregon Pinot Noir provides classic varietal tendencies with bright cherry aromas and flavors, approachable tannins, and a smooth finish. Pair with sirloin or turkey.

Chardonnay \$\$ Little oak is apparent in this smooth, tasty white, which offers butterscotch, apple, and pear aromas and flavors. Good creaminess through the midpalate leads to a tasty finish. Serve with chicken or seafood.

WHERE TO BUY: WINERY, WINE SHOPS, GROCERY STORES

935 N.E. 10th Ave., McMinnville, OR 97128; 503-472-6315. Open Memorial Day and Thanksgiving weekends.

FLERCHINGER VINEYARDS

COLUMBIA GORGE   ESTABLISHED 1994

Like many wineries, Flerchinger started innocently enough: The family bought a little land, planted a few grapes, and one day ended up making it a commercial venture. In Flerchinger's case, it has become a mecca for Alsatian-style white wines, creating some of the Northwest's best Riesling and Pinot Gris. Additionally, the father-and-son team of Joe and Don Flerchinger produces some delicious reds, most notably the award-winning Syrah, as well as Cabernet Sauvignon, Merlot, and a blend of both.

BEST BETS

Riesling $ An absolutely stunning wine and consistently one of the best in the Northwest. It's loaded with bright apple and citrus flavors and has plenty of acidity to back up the bright residual sugar.

Pinot Gris $ A huge, juicy white with full-bodied flavors of orchard and tropical fruit with racy acidity and a long, satisfying finish. A perfect match for oysters, salmon, pork, or pasta in a clam sauce.

Reserve Syrah $ A big wine that is heavy on spice, jammy plum, and good structure. Pair this with lamb, venison, or spicy stews.

Cabernet Sauvignon $ A bright, tasty red showing spice, cedar, and berry aromas and flavors. Its racy acidity and lighter body should pair well with pasta, beef stew, or pork chops.

WHERE TO BUY: WINERY, WINE SHOPS

4200 Post Canyon Road, Hood River, OR 97031; 541-386-2882; www.flerchinger.com. Open daily.

FLYING DUTCHMAN WINERY

OREGON COAST   ESTABLISHED 1997

The Cutler family launched its winery in the late 1990s and earned quick success with an award-winning Pinot Noir. The winery, at the Inn at Otter Crest between Lincoln City and Newport, is a popular stop for coastal travelers. The wines are approachable, delectable, and should serve well for any palate.

BEST BETS

Pinot Noir $$ An elegant wine made from Willamette Valley grapes, this shows off aromas of bright cherries, violets, and rose petals and rich, jammy flavors. Enjoy this with surf or turf.

Chardonnay $$ A crisp, clean wine that highlights the fruit instead of oak barrels. This would pair well with salmon, halibut, shellfish, or chicken.

Merlot $$ A bigger red from Rogue Valley grapes, this provides bold varietal aromas and flavors of vanilla, plum, cherry, and more. Match with lasagna or lamb.

WHERE TO BUY: WINERY, WINE SHOPS

915 First St., Otter Rock, OR 97369; 541-765-2553. Open daily.

FORIS VINEYARDS WINERY

ROGUE VALLEY   ESTABLISHED 1989

Oregon's southernmost winery is deep in the heart of the Illinois Valley, a subregion of the Rogue Valley appellation, and is just a few miles from the California border. Foris has earned a reputation for high-quality reds and whites not only from estate fruit and grapes from nearby vineyards, but also for its Klipsun Vineyard red from Washington's famed Red Mountain. From vintage to vintage, Foris shows exceptional consistency in high-quality wines.

BEST BETS

Pinot Blanc $ A wonderfully complex white wine with aromas of orange oil, white flowers, and hints of freshly mowed hay. Lovely pear and orange flavors give this great matching potential with pasta, chicken, and shellfish.

Maple Ranch Pinot Noir $$ Classic aromas of violets and berries with smooth, silky flavors of berries, cherries, hints of vanilla, and sweet spices. Enjoy with salmon or steak.

Gewürztraminer $ A clean and delicious wine showing off grapefruit and clove aromas and rich, lovely honey, citrus, tropical, and sweet spice flavors.

Chardonnay $ A food-friendly and approachable wine showing orchard and citrus aromas with hints of butter and a smooth, creamy mouth feel. Enjoy with seafood.

WHERE TO BUY: WINERY, WINE SHOPS, GROCERY STORES

654 Kendall Road, Cave Junction, OR 97523; 541-592-3752; www.foriswine.com. Open daily.

FREJA VINEYARDS

WILLAMETTE VALLEY   ESTABLISHED 1998

Owner/winemaker Willy Gianopulos focuses on a small production of high-quality Pinot Noir from estate vineyards on Chehalem Mountain in the North Willamette Valley. Gianopulos moved to Oregon in the late 1980s after trying unsuccessfully to grow grapes on the East Coast. The wines are expressive of the vineyard and should be highly sought after by Pinot Noir lovers.

BEST BETS

Winemaker's Reserve Pinot Noir $$$ A rich, deep wine with sensual berry and cherry aromas and flavors with hints of oak spice and vanilla. Smooth and velvety throughout.

Pinot Noir $$ An elegant and approachable wine showing classic hay, earth, cherry, strawberry, and violet aromas and flavors. A food-friendly wine to match with lamb, chicken, or pasta.

WHERE TO BUY: WINERY, WINE SHOPS

16691 S.W. McFee Place, Hillsboro, OR 97123; 503-628-7843; www.frejacellars.com. Open by appointment.

GIRARDET WINE CELLARS

UMPQUA VALLEY   ESTABLISHED 1983

One of the Umpqua Valley's pioneers, Girardet makes a wide variety of wines and a number of styles of Pinot Noir (no fewer than four at last count). The winery was started by Phillippe Girardet, a Swiss immigrant, and his wife, Bonnie. Today, their son Marc is head winemaker and has a following for his Baco Noir, a French hybrid that has adapted quite well to warm Southern Oregon.

BEST BETS

Reserve Pinot Noir $$$ A rich wine that shows the care that went into it. This opens with ripe cherry and earth aromas and deep, dark flavors. A classy wine.

Baco Noir $$ A customer favorite that doesn't exhibit the grapy aromas that often hinder hybrids. This opens with black pepper and dark berry scents as well as rich, smooth berry flavors with supple tannins.

Cabernet Sauvignon $ A spicy red with rich berries, black currants, and smooth cherry flavors. A nicely priced Cab.

Late Harvest Pinot Gris $ This is like strolling through a tropical paradise with banana, orange, and pineapple aromas and pear and orange oil flavors. Sugar and acidity are nicely balanced.

WHERE TO BUY: WINERY, WINE SHOPS, GROCERY STORES

895 Reston Road, Roseburg, OR 97470; 541-679-7252; www.girardet wine.com. Open daily.

GRANITE PEAK WINERY

UMPQUA VALLEY   ESTABLISHED 1998

This small winery in the Umpqua Valley focuses on Bordeaux varieties from the Rogue Valley. Winemaker Andy Swan has worked with Cabernet Sauvignon and Merlot from the Rogue since 1991 and plans to include Sauvignon Blanc, Syrah, and Zinfandel in future releases.

BEST BETS

Cab–Merlot $ This easy-drinking blend from Southern Oregon opens with hints of raspberries, black currants, and chocolate and offers flavors of spicy black fruit with modest tannins. Enjoy with roast, pasta, chicken, and other everyday meals.

WHERE TO BUY: WINERY, WINE SHOPS

P.O. Box 115, Umpqua, OR 97486; 541-840-0299. Not currently open to the public.

GRANVILLE

YAMHILL COUNTY   ESTABLISHED 1998

After running one of Yamhill County's oldest vineyards for two decades, Allen and Sally Holstein launched their own small winery with the highly regarded 1998 vintage. Their focus is on high-end Pinot Noir and Pinot Gris.

BEST BETS

Pinot Noir $$ A smooth, supple wine showing cherry and cola aromas with flavors of black fruit backed up with cedar and oak spice. A silky wine to pair with lamb.

Pinot Gris $ A bright, crisp wine showing off citrus, pear, and tropical notes. A good white to go with shellfish or grilled chicken.

WHERE TO BUY: WINERY, WINE SHOPS

P.O. Box 566, Dundee, OR 97115; 503-554-1831; www.granville.com. Not open to the public.

HAMACHER WINES

YAMHILL COUNTY   ESTABLISHED 1995

Launched by Eric Hamacher and his wife, Luisa Ponzi, this boutique operation produces small amounts of well-regarded Pinot Noir and Chardonnay. Hamacher also was the driving force behind the Carlton Winemakers Studio, a co-op winery in Yamhill County used by a number of small producers.

BEST BETS

Pinot Noir $$$ Spicy berry aromas lead to a richly structured mouth feel with flavors such as ripe cherries, anise, and an herbal undertone in this deep, complex red. Try this with lamb or Cornish game hen.

WHERE TO BUY: WINERY, WINE SHOPS

801 N. Scott St., Carlton, OR 97119; 503-852-6100; www.hamacher wines.com. Open Memorial Day and Thanksgiving weekends.

HAUER OF THE DAUEN

YAMHILL COUNTY   ESTABLISHED 1998

Carl Dauenhauer is a longtime Yamhill County grape grower who decided in the late 1990s to hold back some of his fruit to make his own wines. Hauer of the Dauen wines are consistently good to great, at reasonable prices.

BEST BETS

Pinot Noir $ A lovely and approachable red offering aromas of cherries and vanilla with bold flavors of strawberry jam and a long, lingering finish. Try this with pork, beef, or salmon.

Late Harvest Pinot Gris $ This might remind you of the holidays with its baked apple and cinnamon aromas and flavors with a creamy midpalate. Enjoy on its own or with poached pears.

Pinot Gris $ A slightly off-dry white showing orchard and tropical fruit and a crisp, clean finish. Enjoy with pasta, oysters, or pork.

Late Harvest Chardonnay $ A rich, viscous dessert wine showing pear and tropical aromas with bold fruit and honey flavors. It's all backed up with plenty of acidity. Enjoy with a plate of cheeses and table grapes.

WHERE TO BUY: WINERY, WINE SHOPS, GROCERY STORES

16425 S.W. Webfoot Road, Dayton, OR 97114; 503-868-7359. Open weekends.

HELVETIA VINEYARDS

WILLAMETTE VALLEY   ESTABLISHED 1996

John Platt and Elizabeth Furse planted their vineyard in 1982 and were content to sell grapes to others for about a decade. Their wine was made by Laurel Ridge from 1992 to 1996, when John and Elizabeth (a retired congresswoman) began to make their own wine. They focus on Oregon's favorite grapes: Pinot Noir, Pinot Gris, and Chardonnay.

BEST BETS

Pinot Gris $ A lovely white with peach and other orchard fruit aromas and flavors. This is a fresh, fruit-forward wine that is a tasty summer sipper or will pair well with pork or scallops.

Chardonnay $ This tropical fruit–driven wine might remind you of piña colada with its pineapple and coconut aromas, crisp acidity, and flavorful finish.

Pinot Noir $$ A classic wine with bright cherry and earthy aromas and tasty berry and pepper notes on the palate.

WHERE TO BUY: WINERY, WINE SHOPS, GROCERY STORES

22485 N.W. Yungen Road, Helvetia, OR 97124; 503-647-5169; www.helvetiawinery.com. Open seasonally.

HENRY ESTATE WINERY

UMPQUA VALLEY   ESTABLISHED 1978

The Henry family is widely recognized for producing delicious, often outstanding wines, yet the winery is perhaps best known for the Scott Henry Trellis, a grape-growing system invented by founder Scott Henry III and now in use around the world. Henry makes a wide variety of wines, from Pinot Noir, Cabernet Sauvignon, Merlot, and Syrah to Chardonnay, Gewürztraminer, Pinot Gris, and Müller-Thurgau. Scott Henry IV is heavily involved in the marketing and winemaking, and his son, Scott Henry V, likely will be a third-generation winemaker.

BEST BETS

Syrah-Cab $$ A big, lush yet approachable red blend with ripe plums and blackberries. A wine that would pair well with lamb or a thick ribeye.

Pinot Gris $ Tropical and mineral notes open this crisp white, which offers apricot and coconut flavors on a creamy midpalate. Enjoy this with grilled chicken or pork.

Dry Gewürztraminer $ Ripe grapefruit and nutmeg aromas give way to a rich mouth feel loaded with fruit and mineral flavors. Put this on the Thanksgiving table or with Tex-Mex.

Müller-Thurgau $ A fresh and fruity wine that is a perfect Oregon summer sipper. This is a mouthful of apples, oranges, and peaches with a good bit of sugar yet plenty of acidity to back it up. Shellfish, cheeses, or a fresh fruit salad would be great matches.

WHERE TO BUY: WINERY, WINE SHOPS, GROCERY STORES

687 Hubbard Road, Umpqua, OR 97486; 541-459-5120; www.henry estate.com. Open daily.

HIGH PASS WINERY

WILLAMETTE VALLEY   ESTABLISHED 1994

Dieter Boehm grew up in East Germany and fled to Western Europe in the mid-1970s. He later discovered the beauty of Oregon and dreamed of growing grapes and making wine there. In the mid-1980s he planted a vineyard and a decade later opened his winery. In addition to growing and producing Pinot Noir and Chardonnay, Boehm makes Cabernet Sauvignon, Merlot, Sauvignon Blanc, and Pinot Gris, as well as a couple of rare wines, Scheurebe and Huxelrebe. His Walnut Ridge Pinot Noir is one of the best you'll find.

BEST BETS

Walnut Ridge Pinot Noir $$ A seductive wine with ripe fruit, violet, and sweet oak aromas, as well as long, intense, complex flavors and supple tannins. A great wine at a great price.

Late Harvest Scheurebe $$ A white dessert wine that sings with honey, apricot, and tangerine aromas and rich, sweet fruit flavors. Plenty of acidity backs up all the sugar. Try this with poached pears with a scoop of vanilla ice cream.

Pinot Gris $ With its rich tropical fruit aromas and flavors, this is a bright, clean, crisp wine to pair with steelhead or shellfish.

Sauvignon Blanc $ A bright, grassy wine with lovely fruit-driven flavors. Enjoy this with chicken or pork.

24757 Lavell Road, Junction City, OR 97448; 541-998-1447; www.highpasswinery.com. Open Memorial Day and Thanksgiving weekends or by appointment.

HILLCREST VINEYARD

UMPQUA VALLEY   ESTABLISHED 1961

In the late 1950s, Richard Sommer came north from California and established HillCrest, now Oregon's oldest winery producing purely European grape wines. Other pioneers followed his lead, including Dick Erath, David Adelsheim, and David Lett. Sommer continues to craft his own styles of wine, from Pinot Noir, Cabernet Sauvignon, and Zinfandel to Riesling, Semillon, and Gewürztraminer.

BEST BETS

Cabernet Sauvignon $$$ This shows off bottle bouquet from extensive aging and offers earthy oak and tobacco aromas with dried cherry flavors and plenty of tannin.

Pinot Noir $ A classy and inexpensive wine revealing vanilla and leather aromas with flavors of dried cherries and bell peppers backed with plenty of acidity and a lovely farewell.

Zinfandel $ A crisp red with jammy strawberry and raspberry flavors. This is a pleasing sipper.

WHERE TO BUY: WINERY, WINE SHOPS, GROCERY STORES

240 Vineyard Lane, Roseburg, OR 97470; 541-673-3709. Open daily.

HIP CHICKS DO WINE

PORTLAND   ESTABLISHED 1999

Depending on just how hip you are, this may be the most unusual and/or most fun winery in Oregon. Renee Neely and Laurie Lewis are the two chicks who make wine for the fun of it. Their unusual name, enjoyable label, and approachable wines are winning fans tired of too much pretension in their Pinot Noirs. The writing on the cork might just sum it up perfectly: "Yummy down on this."

BEST BETS

Pinot Noir $ An unassuming and tasty red showing off classic varietal notes with ripe cherry and berry aromas and flavors and just a hint of dark chocolate on the finish. Built for immediate enjoyment, age this on the way home, then enjoy it with pasta, chicken, or beef.

WHERE TO BUY: WINERY, WINE SHOPS

4510 S.E. 23rd Ave., Portland, OR 97202; 503-753-6374; www.hip chicks dowine.com. Open Thursday-Sunday or by appointment.

HONEYWOOD WINERY

WILLAMETTE VALLEY   ESTABLISHED 1934

Oregon's oldest winery makes perhaps the largest number of wines produced by any operation in the Northwest, with nearly forty different kinds. A third are from classic European grape varieties such as Pinot Noir, Chardonnay, and Gewürztraminer, while the rest are produced from fruit, including blackberry, rhubarb, peach, honey, and cranberry, as well as non-vinifera grapes such as Niagara.

BEST BETS

Gewurztraminer $ With classic aromas of perfumy grapefruit and orange, this is a slightly sweet, smooth, and tasty wine. Delicious on its own or serve with Chinese food.

Maréchal Foch $$ A big, thick red wine with black fruit and tobacco notes and rich tannins. Foch can make a lovely wine, and this is a good example.

Blackberry $ Wonderful varietal aromas and sweet, syrupy flavors. A tasty wine that would go well with (or on) vanilla ice cream.

Niagara $ With the grapy flavor and smell of white Concord juice (with a kick), this is a sweet, tasty wine that would match well with Sunday brunch, especially as an introductory wine.

WHERE TO BUY: WINERY, WINE SHOPS, GROCERY STORES

1350 Hines St. S.E., Salem, OR 97302; 503-362-4111; www.honey woodwinery.com. Open daily.

HOOD RIVER VINEYARDS

COLUMBIA GORGE   ESTABLISHED 1981

Bernie and Anne Lerch have revitalized an older Columbia Gorge winery and are great advocates of the Hood River region as a viticulture area. The Lerches produce a huge array of wines from their estate and nearby vineyards, including Merlot, Zinfandel, Nebbiolo, Gewürztraminer, and Cabernet Sauvignon. The winery makes a number of Port-style wines from grapes as well as fruits and also produces pear ciders and sherries.

BEST BETS

Zinfandel Port $ One of the Northwest's best Ports, this beauty's grapes come from an eighty-year-old vineyard near The Dalles, Oregon. This sipper is rich with flavors of berries, chocolate, spice, licorice, and more. This is a don't-miss if you love Port.

Merlot $ Chocolate and fruit dominate the aromas of this affordable Merlot. Lush and flavorful through the midpalate, this wine offers ripe flavors and a long finish.

Zinfandel $$ These grapes, too, are from old vines in The Dalles and result in a wine with nice spice, tobacco, and cherry notes, and rich flavors of currants, licorice, and black cherries.

Marionberry Port $ From Hood River fruit, this is a dandy sipper that shows off blackberry and raspberry flavors backed up with hints of chocolate. A grand way to end a meal.

WHERE TO BUY: WINERY, WINE SHOPS, GROCERY STORES

4693 Westwood Drive, Hood River, OR 97031; 541-386-3772. Seasonal hours.

IDYLWOOD WINERY

WILLAMETTE VALLEY   ESTABLISHED 1998

Longtime software developer and amateur winemaker Tony Nemeth moved to the Willamette Valley in the late 1980s and launched Idylwood Winery a decade later. His efforts focus on several styles of Pinot Noir, a Pinot Gris, and a dessert wine blend called Silver Magnolia.

BEST BETS

Founder's Reserve Pinot Noir $$ A lively and jammy wine showing off bright berries, oak spice, and violets. A richly structured wine to pair with lamb, beef, or fowl.

Chardonnay $ A bright and straightforward white that displays ripe orchard and tropical fruit with a creamy midpalate. A good match for chicken or shellfish.

WHERE TO BUY: WINERY, WINE SHOPS

11517 S.E. Hwy. 212, Clackamas, OR 97015; 503-657-6055; www.idylwoodwines.com. Open by appointment.

IRIS HILL WINERY

WILLAMETTE VALLEY   ESTABLISHED 2001

Pamela Frye and Richard Boyles are natives of Eugene, Oregon, who came back to the southern Willamette Valley after stints in Seattle and Germany. In the early '90s, they began planting forty-four acres of wine grapes in the Lorane Valley and now make small lots of wine from their estate fruit. The winery is named for the wild Douglas iris that grow around the vineyard.

BEST BETS

Pinot Gris $ A lighter-styled white with aromas and flavors of orchard fruit and sweet spices and a delicate herbal undertone. Enjoy with cheeses or pasta.

Pinot Noir $$ This up-front, fruit-driven red provides fresh flavors of raspberries and cherries. Enjoy with fowl or seafood.

Chardonnay $ Ripe pears and pineapples dominate the aroma and flavor profiles of this bright and delicious white wine. Pair with shellfish, chicken, or fresh pasta.

WHERE TO BUY: WINERY, WINE SHOPS

P.O. Box 137, Lorane, OR 97451; 541-345-1617; www.iris-hill.com. Open by appointment.

J. CHRISTOPHER WINES

PORTLAND   ESTABLISHED 2000

Former Cameron Winery employee Jay Somers has ventured out on his own with J. Christopher. In addition to Pinot Noir, he crafts Riesling and Sauvignon Blanc.

BEST BETS

Charlie's Vineyard Pinot Noir $$ Showing off bright berry and light oak aromas, this luscious red offers concentrated fruit flavors with layers of complex spices and velvety, approachable tannins. A delicious wine to enjoy with delicate meat dishes.

WHERE TO BUY: WINERY, WINE SHOPS

3823 S.E. Washington St., Portland, OR 97214; 503-231-5094. Open by appointment.

J. K. CARRIERE

YAMHILL COUNTY   ESTABLISHED 1999

Jim Prosser's entire focus is to make great Oregon Pinot Noir. Therefore, he makes nothing else. He buys grapes from top vineyards in Yamhill County and crafts small amounts of high-end Pinot Noir. Don't expect to find the word "reserve" on the label, as Prosser feels his best efforts should go into every bottle.

BEST BETS

Pinot Noir $$$ A deep, rich, penetrating red showing off aromas and flavors of moist earth, berries, cola, pie cherries, and spices. Excellent tannin management makes this a wine to drink now or put away for a few years.

WHERE TO BUY: WINERY, WINE SHOPS

30205 Benjamin Road, Newberg, OR 97132; 503-554-0721; www.jkcarriere.com. Open Memorial Day and Thanksgiving weekends or by appointment.

JOHN MICHAEL CHAMPAGNE CELLARS

APPLEGATE VALLEY   ESTABLISHED 1995

Michael Giovanni Giudici came north from California to find a quiet place to make sparkling wines. He settled on the idyllic Applegate Valley, where he now makes about five hundred fifty cases annually of sparkling and still wines.

BEST BETS

Blanc de Blanc $$ This blend of Pinot Blanc, Pinot Gris, and Chardonnay offers rich apple and cake aromas and flavors with a touch of sweetness. A big, delicious sparkler.

Blanc de Noir $$ Made from Pinot Noir and Zinfandel, this opens with lovely strawberry and pleasant yeast aromas with a rich, tasty mouth feel.

WHERE TO BUY: WINERY, WINE SHOPS

1425 Humbug Creek Road, Applegate, OR 97530; 541-846-0810. Open by appointment.

KEN WRIGHT CELLARS

YAMHILL COUNTY   ESTABLISHED 1994

Ken Wright knows the value of hard work, especially when it comes to producing world-class Pinot Noir. As much as anyone in the New World, Wright is pioneering ways to ripen this fickle grape in a marginal grape-growing climate and craft it into some of the best Pinot Noir you're likely to find. It all begins in the vineyard with by-the-acre contracts so he can control crop levels and ensure ripeness at harvest. He's fanatical about canopy management and crop thinning, as well as sorting the best grapes after they're harvested.

The California native moved to Oregon after he realized this was the best place in the country to fulfill his passion for making Pinot Noir. He began Panther Creek Cellars in 1986, then sold it in 1994. He also was Domaine Serene's first winemaker, making its award-winning wines from 1990 to 1998.

In addition to Pinot Noir, Wright makes Chardonnay from Washington's Celilo Vineyard and two Oregon vineyards and Pinot Blanc from Freedom Hill Vineyard. He's also looking to add hot-climate varieties from the vineyards of Eastern Washington and Southern Oregon under a separate label.

BEST BETS

Pinot Noir $$$$ Depending upon the quality of any particular vintage, Wright will release anywhere from one to twelve separate Pinot Noirs. In the superb 1999 vintage, he released twelve single-vineyard Pinots. Those wines that don't go into a single-vineyard designation will show up in his Willamette Valley bottling. Each vineyard site expresses something different, so Wright's Pinots can be everything from petite and lovely to big and bold. Regardless, from vintage to vintage, Ken Wright Cellars Pinot Noirs will be among the best you'll find.

Chardonnay $$ Produced with the same care as his Pinot Noirs, Wright will release up to three vineyard-designated Chardonnays from two Oregon vineyards and one Columbia Gorge site. Each shows off its site's characteristics and all are rich and intense with fruit and mild oak treatment.

WHERE TO BUY: WINERY, WINE SHOPS

338 W. Main St., Carlton, OR 97111; 503-852-7070; www.kenwright cellars.com. Open Memorial Day and Thanksgiving weekends.

KING ESTATE

WILLAMETTE VALLEY   ESTABLISHED 1992

King Estate is Oregon's most visible winery, thanks to broad distribution across the United States, and it is also the state wine industry's most tireless supporter. King Estate excels with all its wines, especially its Pinot Gris, which consistently is among the nation's best. The estate looks like a Tuscan hill town from the approach and may be as grand as any in Oregon. In addition to the winery, King Estate has a second label, Lorane Valley, and a vine nursery, which supplies plants to many of Oregon's new vineyards.

BEST BETS

Reserve Pinot Gris $$ Simply one of the best Pinot Gris you'll find, this is perfectly balanced with huge tropical and citrus fruit, crisp acidity, and a lingering, complex finish.

Pinot Gris $ This is no slouch, either, as it offers bright, floral aromas and ripe, complex fruit and sweet spice flavors. Great acidity makes this a shellfish-friendly wine.

Pinot Noir $$ A bright, food-friendly red with classic violet and cherry aromas and bold berry and cedar flavors. Try this with firm cheeses, beef, or game.

Chardonnay $ Well balanced and food friendly, King Estate's winemakers didn't get carried away with too much oak here. The bright citrus flavors with hints of butter make this a good match for halibut in an herbed butter sauce.

WHERE TO BUY: WINERY, WINE SHOPS, GROCERY STORES

80854 Territorial Road, Eugene, OR 97405; 541-942-9874; www.kingestate.com. Seasonal hours.

KRAMER VINEYARDS

YAMHILL COUNTY   ESTABLISHED 1989

This winery, which began with production of a few fruit wines, is now one of the most popular in Yamhill County. Under the watch of winemaker Trudy Kramer, Kramer Vineyards produces an array of wines from classic Pinot Noir and Pinot Gris to Müller-Thurgau and wine from a rare grape called Carmine, as well as a Merlot and Syrah from Washington grapes. When visiting the winery, be sure to track down the suit of armor.

BEST BETS

Müller-Thurgau $ This is one of the most-planted varieties in Germany, and the northern Willamette Valley's cooler climate is a good match for this grape, which produces a delicious off-dry white that works well with shellfish or Asian-inspired cuisine.

Pinot Noir $$–$$$ Kramer makes no fewer than four styles of Pinot Noir. Perhaps the favorite is Rebecca's Reserve, a succulent and seductive red with subtle earthy and fruity aromas, ripe berry flavors with hints of vanilla and spice, and a long, silky finish.

Merlot $$ A big wine showing off lots of oak and blackberry fruit, this is nicely balanced with good acidity, approachable tannins, and a smooth finish. A good match for Cornish game hen, stews, or pizza.

Kimberly's Reserve Pinot Gris $$ A fresh and fruity white with crisp acidity and a creamy mouth feel from oak aging. A perfect fit with lightly buttered scallops.

WHERE TO BUY: WINERY, WINE SHOPS, GROCERY STORES

26830 N.W. Olson Road, Gaston, OR 97119; 503-662-4545; www.kramerwine.com. Seasonal hours.

KRISTIN HILL WINERY

YAMHILL COUNTY   ESTABLISHED 1990

Check your pretensions at the door. Eric and Linda Aberg of Kristin Hill Winery have no need for snobbish wine. This doesn't mean they aren't serious about their efforts to produce good-quality Methode Champenoise sparkling wines as well as a number of still wines, but with names like Fizzy Lizzie, Magic Moments, and Generic Eric, the Abergs are more interested in mainstream customers than in those seeking out hundred-dollar Pinots.

BEST BETS

Fizzy Lizzy $ A fun, consumer-friendly bubbly with cherry concentrate added, the aromas might remind you of a cherry milkshake, and the flavors are bright and delicious. A good wine for casual parties or weddings.

Jordan's Joy Blanc de Noir $$ A delicious sparkler with classic yeast and strawberry aromas and a rich, lively midpalate. Will pair well with many dishes, but start with oysters.

Müller-Thurgau $ With hints of honey, oranges, and baked apples and a good dose of residual sugar, this is a pleasant summer sipper.

Magic Moments Brut $$ Toasty aromas come with cake and chopped hazelnut nuances and a rich mouth feel. Share this as an aperitif.

WHERE TO BUY: WINERY, WINE SHOPS

3330 S.E. Amity-Dayton Hwy., Amity, OR 97101; 503-835-0850. Seasonal hours.

LARÊTE WINES

PORTLAND   ESTABLISHED 1998

A boutique producer of high-quality wines, LaBête hit the Oregon wine scene with the vaunted 1998 vintage. In addition to Pinot Noir, the winery crafts Chardonnay, Aligoté, Pinot Gris, and Gamay Noir. In the future, look for Melón and Pinot Blanc.

BEST BETS

Temperance Hill/Corral Creek Vineyard Pinot Noir $$$ A classic Pinot Noir with aromas and flavors of violets, moist earth, cherries, berries, and sweet spices. A rich, deep, and flavorful wine to pair with an elegant meal.

WHERE TO BUY: WINERY, WINE SHOPS

8026 S.W. 10th Ave., Portland, OR 97219; 503-977-1493. Open by appointment.

LA GARZA CELLARS

UMPQUA VALLEY   ESTABLISHED 1975

With some of Oregon's oldest vineyards (planted in 1968 and 1971), La Garza focuses on Cabernet Sauvignon, Riesling, and Pinot Gris. The winery also has a restaurant, the Gourmet Kitchen, which is open during tourist season.

BEST BETS

Cabernet Sauvignon $$ A luscious red showing aromas and flavors of fresh leather, sweet pipe tobacco, and black currants. A delicious Cab to pair with beef in a mushroom sauce.

Reserve Cabernet Sauvignon $$ A big, smoky red showing aromas of elegant black currants, black cherries, and cedar with hints of bittersweet chocolate and a smooth finish.

Rosado de la Casa $ This dry white Cabernet Sauvignon is a serious rosé offering bright strawberry and cranberry aromas and flavors with hints of chopped hazelnuts. Plenty of acidity and a touch of sweetness makes this a good pairing with turkey or pork.

WHERE TO BUY: WINERY, WINE SHOPS, GROCERY STORES

491 Winery Lane, Roseburg, OR 97470; 541-679-9654; www.lagarza.com. Seasonal hours.

LANGE WINERY

YAMHILL COUNTY   ESTABLISHED 1987

High in the hills above the town of Dundee is nestled this family oper-
ation focusing on Pinot Gris and Pinot Noir. Lange, one of Oregon's
first Gris producers, crafts two styles of the state's signature white wine
and no fewer than six different Pinot Noirs. The concentration is on
quality from vineyard to glass, and Lange's efforts pay off with out-
standing wines.

BEST BETS

Pinot Gris $ Deliciously fresh, crisp, and fruit-filled, this white wine
has a rich mouth feel and spiciness, giving it great food-matching
potential. Try with shellfish, veal, or roast pork.

Reserve Chardonnay $$ Light oak treatment allows the orchard and
tropical fruit to shine in this rich, round, and lightly spicy wine.
Salmon or pasta would match well.

Reserve Pinot Noir $$ An elegant red with berry aromas, earthy and
spicy flavors, and a smooth mouth feel.

Three Hills Cuvée Pinot Noir $$$$ Hugely complex with cherry, vanilla,
espresso, cedar, and chocolate nuances and beautifully balanced
with rich, round silkiness. A real treat.

WHERE TO BUY: WINERY, WINE SHOPS, GROCERY STORES

18880 N.E. Buena Vista Drive, Dundee, OR 97115; 503-538-6476;
www.langewinery.com. Open Wednesday-Monday.

LAUREL RIDGE WINERY

YAMHILL COUNTY   ESTABLISHED 1986

This longtime producer has moved from a century-old farmhouse in
the North Willamette Valley to fashionable Yamhill County. Laurel
Ridge is best known for its classic sparkling wines and rich Ports, but it
also makes a variety of other wines, including Pinot Noir, Sauvignon
Blanc, Chardonnay, and Zinfandel.

BEST BETS

Tawny Port $$ A delicious red dessert wine crafted from Pinot Noir,
this shows luscious raisin and plum aromas and flavors. Smooth
through the finish, this will pair well with Stilton or a roaring fire
on a rainy winter night.

Pinotage $ This blend of Pinot Noir and Zinfandel is a crowd pleaser
and one of Laurel Ridge's most popular wines. A fruit-driven red
showing bright berry aromas and flavors, this will pair well with
pizza, beef stew, or a cheeseburger.

Brut $$ A classic bubbly and perennially one of the Northwest's best,
this is a dry, delicious sparkler showing caramel and cake

aromas and flavors with rich apple and pear notes through the well-structured palate.

WHERE TO BUY: WINERY, WINE SHOPS, GROCERY STORES

13301 N.E. Kuehne Road, Carlton, OR 97111; 503-852-7050. Open daily.

LEMELSON VINEYARDS

YAMHILL COUNTY   ESTABLISHED 1999

Eric Lemelson is a man driven to be the best. The owner and viticul turalist for Lemelson Vineyards and his winemaker, Thomas Bachelder, are turning heads with their young winery in the heart of Oregon wine country. And they're setting themselves up for success with their state-of-the-art winery and estate vineyards. The early efforts are massive Pinot Noirs with great depth and character and rich, exotic whites, wines to get excited about.

BEST BETS

Jerome Reserve Pinot Noir $$$ A muscular red showing huge amounts of drink-me-now character, including coffee, chocolate, cedar, and plum. A lip-smacking wine with penetrating flavors and tremendous balance. A sure match for prime rib or spicy lamb.

Tikka's Run Pinot Gris $$ Provocative aromas of tropical fruit and mineral notes lead to a big, creamy mouth feel with great acidity to back up all the fruit. A giant of a wine; pair this with pork or halibut.

Stermer Vineyard Pinot Noir $$$ Mesmerizing violet and berry aromas give way to an elegant, brooding wine filled with elements of black fruit, moist earth, vanilla, and oak spice. Pair with lamb or beef.

Riesling $$ A bright, approachable wine with wonderfully fragrant fruit aromas and rich, long, pleasing flavors.

WHERE TO BUY: WINERY, WINE SHOPS

12020 N.E. Stag Hollow Road, Carlton, OR 07111; 503-852-6619; www.lemelsonvineyards.com. Open Memorial Day and Thanksgiving weekends and by appointment.

LION VALLEY VINEYARDS

WILLAMETTE VALLEY   ESTABLISHED 1997

Owner/winemaker David Levinthal expresses his passion for Burgundian-style wines through the many styles of Pinot Noir and Chardonnay he produces at Lion Valley Vineyards. With fruit primarily from his densely planted estate vineyard west of Portland as well as grapes from such top vineyards as Shea, Lion Valley's wines show grace, elegance, and balance thanks to gentle care and limited use of new French oak.

BEST BETS

Reserve Pinot Noir $$ A classic Pinot Noir with cherry and dusty earth aromas and bright berry and red currant flavors. A rich, powerful, and velvety wine.

Chardonnay $$ This unfiltered wine shows off oak, butter, and vanilla from barrel fermentation and rich orchard fruit flavors. Try this with prawns or grilled white fish.

Pinot Gris $ Telltale pineapple and tropical aromas and a creamy mouth feel make this a real treat. A versatile and food-friendly wine that will match well with crab or baked oysters.

WHERE TO BUY: WINERY, WINE SHOPS, GROCERY STORES

35040 S.W. Unger Road, Cornelius, OR 97113; 503-628-5458; www.lionvalley.com. Open weekends.

MARSHANNE LANDING

UMPQUA VALLEY   ESTABLISHED 2001

Greg Cramer is a relative newcomer to the Oregon wine industry and has chosen the fertile Umpqua Valley to plant grapes and make wines. His attention to detail shows in his first offerings.

BEST BETS

Chardonnay $$ Elegant butter and pear aromas with hints of oak spice and ripe apples. The extravagant creamy mouth feel opens up flavors of butter rum and orchard fruit that lead to a long, luscious finish.

Merlot $$ Showing off toasty American oak, this racy red offers fresh black cherry and plum flavors with well-balanced tannins and integrated oak. A tasty wine for beef or lamb.

WHERE TO BUY: WINERY, WINE SHOPS

381 Hogan Road, Oakland, OR 97462; 541-459-8497. Call for hours.

MARQUAM HILL VINEYARDS

WILLAMETTE VALLEY   ESTABLISHED 1989

The parents of Willamette Valley Vineyards winemaker Joe Dobbes have created their own paradise in the Cascade Mountain foothills, where they have planted twenty acres of Pinot Noir, Chardonnay, Müller-Thurgau, Pinot Gris, Riesling, and Gewürztraminer. The winery property includes a lake and thirty acres of forests, so be sure to bring your picnic basket.

BEST BETS

Pinot Noir $$ A bright, fruit-driven red with berry and cherry flavors and a lingering finish. A good match with lamb or beef.

Pinot Gris $ Bright and tropical with a wonderful mouth feel. A pleasing sipper that pairs well with seafood.

Gewürztraminer $ A delicate and tasty wine that offers classic grapefruit and other citrus aromas and smooth fruit and honey flavors. Good acidity backs up the hints of residual sugar.

WHERE TO BUY: WINERY, WINE SHOPS, GROCERY STORES

35803 S. Hwy. 213, Molalla, OR 97038; 503-829-6677. Seasonal hours.

MONTINORE VINEYARDS

WILLAMETTE VALLEY   ESTABLISHED 1987

This huge estate in the northern Willamette Valley produces tasty and occasionally great wines from estate fruit. The vineyards, about two decades old, take up some two hundred sixty of the estate's five hundred eighty-five acres. Though the focus is on Pinot Noir, Montinore also crafts Riesling, Pinot Gris, Gewürztraminer, Chardonnay, and Müller-Thurgau. The name, by the way, is short for "Montana in Oregon" because of the owners' love for Big Sky Country.

BEST BETS

Parson's Ridge Pinot Noir $$ An incredible red that provides wonderfully structured aromas and flavors of spices, berries, and hints of earthiness. Well-managed tannins make this approachable in its youth. Pair with steak, lamb, or veal.

Pierce's Elbow Pinot Noir $$ A fruit-driven wine that shows off new oak, spices, vanilla, and ripe cherries. Enjoy with lamb or risotto.

Pinot Noir $ Montinore's low-end Pinot Noir is spectacular with earth and berry aromas and flavors, a strawberry jam midpalate, and approachable tannins. Enjoy with pork tenderloin or fish with a heavy sauce.

Gewürztraminer $ A lovely example of top-notch Oregon Gewürztraminer, this provides floral and citrus aromas and aggressive fruit flavors. Surprisingly good acidity makes this perfect for turkey, chicken, or lightly spiced dishes.

WHERE TO BUY: WINERY, WINE SHOPS, GROCERY STORES

3663 S.W. Dilley Road, Forest Grove, OR 97116; www.montinore.com. Seasonal hours.

MOUNTAIN VIEW WINERY

CENTRAL OREGON   ESTABLISHED 1991

High in the Central Oregon desert, Al and Rita Debons make small lots of handcrafted wines from Oregon and Washington grapes. They have a simple approach to winemaking: Take what the grape will give. The result is unpretentious wines that are tasty and straightforward.

BEST BETS

Syrah $ A delicious wine at a great price, this spicy, meaty red is rich with robust flavors and herbal undertones.

Cab–Merlot $ Perfect for spaghetti night, this is a tasty wine with perfumy, berry notes and just-right flavors and balance.

Merlot $ A big wine with rich berry aromas, hints of vanilla from oak aging, and smooth red berry flavors. Serve with a fine meal.

Pinot Gris $ Up-front citrus and orchard fruit give this good food-matching potential. Try this with prawns or salmon.

WHERE TO BUY: WINERY, WINE SHOPS

61905 Gosney Lane, Bend, OR 97702; 541-388-8339. Open by appointment.

MYSTIC WINES

WILLAMETTE VALLEY   ESTABLISHED 1992

After spending several years making wines in Northern California, Rick Mafit and his family headed north to make Merlot, Cabernet Sauvignon, and Syrah. The winery is in Salem, and the grapes are grown in The Dalles, on the Oregon side of the Columbia Gorge. The result is big, ripe red wines showing delicious characteristics.

BEST BETS

Cabernet Sauvignon $$ A long, rich, lush red with berry and vanilla aromas and creamy plum and blackberry flavors. A good wine to enjoy with a rare steak.

Merlot $$ Showing plenty of dark berry and oak aromas, this ripe red wine offers complex flavors of chocolate, cedar, herbs, and bright fruit. A tasty wine to enjoy with beef or venison.

Syrah $$ A jammy, up-front wine loaded with blackberry and plum aromas and flavors with espresso and bittersweet chocolate on the finish. A sensual and delicious example of the variety.

WHERE TO BUY: WINERY, WINE SHOPS

3995 Deepwood Lane N.W., Salem, OR 97304; 503-581-2769; www.mysticwine.com. Open by appointment.

NEHALEM BAY WINERY

OREGON COAST   ESTABLISHED 1974

For more than a quarter-century, Nehalem Bay Winery has been having fun along the Oregon Coast. The folks at Nehalem Bay take the stuffiness out of wine touring with their various festivals and fresh, fruit-driven wines.

BEST BETS

Riesling $ A fresh, delicious white with bright orchard fruit, good sweetness, and ample acidity. A good match with Tex-Mex or curried dishes.

Gewürztraminer $ Classic grapefruit and spiciness give way to sweet, smooth, soft flavors and a delicious finish. A fun summer sipper.

Pinot Noir $$ An unpretentious red with dusty cherry and earthy aromas and bright, fresh berry flavors with light tannins. A good everyday wine.

Niagara $ This North American grape is rarely used to make fine wine on the West Coast. It makes a breezy, grapy, tasty wine with plenty of sweetness.

WHERE TO BUY: WINERY

34965 Hwy. 53, Nehalem, OR 97131; 503-368-9463; www.nehalem baywinery.com. Open daily.

OAK GROVE ORCHARDS WINERY

WILLAMETTE VALLEY   ESTABLISHED 1987

Owner/winemaker Carl Stevens focuses on various varieties and styles of the Muscat grape, including Muscat of Alexandria, Golden Muscat, and Early Muscat, which reputedly was developed in Oregon. He also makes wines from Concord grapes and various fruits.

BEST BETS

Muscat of Alexandria $ With aromas and flavors of licorice and a floral aspect, this smooth, sweet wine has good balance and a lovely finish.

Golden Muscat Reserve $ Crafted in the style of an ice wine, this sweet sipper is smooth and rich without being cloying. Serve with cheesecake or gorgonzola.

Early Muscat $ An off-dry wine that shows off the wonderful floral and spice aromas of the variety. This is a smooth, tasty wine.

WHERE TO BUY: WINERY, WINE SHOPS, GROCERY STORES

6090 Crowley Road, Rickreall, OR 97371; 503-364-7052. Open Tuesday–Sunday.

OAK KNOLL WINERY

PORTLAND AREA   ESTABLISHED 1970

Oregon's third-oldest winery, Oak Knoll, quietly goes about its business making award-winning and consumer-friendly wines in Hillsboro. Started by Ron and Marj Vuylsteke and now managed by son Steve, Oak Knoll doesn't grow its own fruit but instead relies on long-term relationships with a variety of growers. In addition to the wines listed here, look for Chardonnay, Merlot, and Frambrosia, a sweet fruit wine.

BEST BETS

Pinot Noir $ Oak Knoll makes a few different styles of Oregon's famous red wine, and the winery's hallmark is consistently high quality from vintage to vintage. It provides earthy, cherry, raspberry, and violet aromas with rich, throaty berry, vanilla, and sweet spice flavors. Enjoy this with salmon or sirloin.

Pinot Gris $ This oak-free wine shows off wonderful fruit with a creamy midpalate and a crisp backbone. Pair this with grilled white fish, pasta in a cream sauce, or mild cheeses.

Riesling $ A lovely white with classic orchard fruit, honey, and spices. This crisp, off-dry wine would go wonderfully with Thai, Indian, or Tex-Mex.

Niagara $ This North American grape variety produces a simple, delicious wine that will remind you of white grape juice with a kick. It's a fresh, fruity, up-front brunch wine.

WHERE TO BUY: WINERY, WINE SHOPS, GROCERY STORES

29700 S.W. Burkhalter Road, Hillsboro, OR 97123; 503-648-8198; www.oakknollwinery.com. Open daily.

OWEN ROE

YAMHILL COUNTY   ESTABLISHED 2000

Winemaker David O'Reilly (a partner in the Newberg winery Sineann) and Jerry Owen make tiny amounts of highly sought-after wines of distinction using grapes from the Willamette, Columbia, Yakima, and Walla Walla Valleys. In addition to the wines reviewed here, look for Chardonnay, Cabernet Franc, Pinot Noir, and an ice wine.

BEST BETS

Zinfandel $$ A long, smooth wine showing off berry, pipe tobacco, and cherry aromas and flavors. Enjoy this with a zesty pasta dish.

Abbott's Table Red $$ A six-grape blend that includes Zinfandel, Syrah, and Merlot, this offers perfumy berry and vanilla aromas and rich, jammy, up-front fruit flavors. Well-managed tannins make this approachable now.

WHERE TO BUY: WINERY, WINE SHOPS

P.O. Box 10, Newberg, OR 97132; 503-678-5058; www.owenroe.com. Not open to the public.

PALOTAI

UMPQUA VALLEY   ESTABLISHED 2001

Gabor Palotai moved to the United States in 1983 and came to Oregon in 1999 to grow grapes and make wine, just as his family did in his native Hungary. His first offerings are small releases of Chardonnay and Pinot Noir, and he plans to make a Dolcetto and a Bordeaux-style blend in the future.

BEST BETS

Chardonnay $ Rich aromas of butterscotch and hints of oranges lead to lush, round flavors of citrus backed up with a creamy mouth feel. A lovely handcrafted wine that will pair with a fat salmon steak.

WHERE TO BUY: WINERY

272 Capital Lane, Roseburg, OR 97470; 541-464-0032. Open by appointment.

PANTHER CREEK CELLARS

YAMHILL COUNTY   ESTABLISHED 1986

Panther Creek earned its reputation as a top Pinot Noir producer thanks to the efforts of then-owner Ken Wright. After Wright sold the property in 1994 to start Ken Wright Cellars, Panther Creek continued to be one of the most respected producers in star studded Yamhill County. In addition to offering no fewer than a half-dozen Pinot Noirs depending on vintage, Panther Creek makes Pinot Gris, Melón, Chardonnay, and a sparkling wine.

BEST BETS

Freedom Hill Vineyard Pinot Noir $$$$ Richly structured and showing plenty of plum, black cherry, and berry fruit, this elegant red pairs well with lamb or duck.

Knight's Gambit Vineyard Pinot Noir $$$$$ This stylish red opens with complex aromas of ripe cherries, mint, earth, and violets and a velvety mouth feel revealing long, luscious flavors such as those of dark fruit, sweet spices, and vanilla. A wine to savor with veal or lamb.

WHERE TO BUY: WINERY, WINE SHOPS

455 N. Irvine St., McMinnville, OR 97128; 503-472-8080; www.panthercreekcellars.com. Open Memorial Day and Thanksgiving weekends and by appointment.

PASCHAL WINERY

ROGUE VALLEY   ESTABLISHED 1998

One of the youngsters in the Rogue Valley, Paschal Winery is drawing attention with its top-rated wines, including powerful Cabs and

Chardonnays, bright Pinot Gris and Pinot Blanc, and elegant Pinot Noir. In its short history Paschal has produced nothing but high-quality wines from its estate vineyards, which were planted in 1989.

BEST BETS

Estate Pinot Noir $$ A great wine at a reasonable price, this Pinot Noir is an extravagant wine showing silky aromas with hints of vanilla from oak aging and juicy, fruit-forward cherry and berry flavors with a seductive finish. Pair with lamb or sirloin.

Chardonnay $$ Well balanced with plenty of citrus and tropical fruit showing through moderate oak treatment, this is a white with great depth of flavor and a delightful mouth feel. A perfect match for salmon, mussels, or oysters.

Cabernet Sauvignon $$ A big, smoky Cab showing off vanilla and fruit aromas and big, jammy flavors on the midpalate. A flavorful wine that would pair well with beef dishes, lasagna, lamb, and venison.

Pinot Blanc $$ Pinot Blanc is an underappreciated white variety that can shine with the proper treatment in the vineyard and cellar. This is a great example with butterscotch and tropical notes, crisp acidity, and pleasant mouth weight. A good match for pork or shellfish.

WHERE TO BUY: WINERY, WINE SHOPS

1122 Suncrest Road, Talent, OR 97540; 541-535-7957; www.paschal winery.com. Open Tuesday–Sunday.

PATRICIA GREEN CELLARS

YAMHILL COUNTY   ESTABLISHED 2000

If you want to understand Oregon Pinot Noir, consider starting with Patricia Green Cellars. Patricia Green and Jim Anderson made Torii Mor a cult winery among Pinot lovers, and they purchased the former Autumn Wind Winery and its surrounding vineyards in 2000 to create Patricia Green Cellars. They continue to work with the top grapes in the Willamette Valley and craft no fewer than ten different Pinot Noirs, each showing off nuances from specific sites or blends. The hallmark of Patricia Green Cellars wines is their expressive fruit that doesn't let oak become more than a minor component. The wines, though among the best the state has to offer, are more than reasonably priced.

BEST BETS

Notorious $$$ A blend of the winery's two best barrels each year. This means there are fewer than fifty cases of this elegant Pinot Noir with dark fruit, rich spice, and sensual, penetrating, and dreamy layers of complexity.

Balcombe Vineyard Pinot Noir $$ Classic aromatics tease the senses and lead to bright, pure fruit flavors with silky tannins and a long farewell.

Shea Vineyard Pinot Noir $$ Black cherries, violets, and light earth high-light the aromas from this great vineyard. The flavors show off bright intensity with plenty of backbone and a lengthy finish.

Estate Vineyard (Block 32) Pinot Noir $$ An exciting and sexy wine that shows off aromas of jasmine, sweet spices, and moist earth that lead to a medley of focused wild berry flavors and rich structure.

WHERE TO BUY: WINERY, WINE SHOPS

15225 N.E. North Valley Road, Newberg, OR 97132; 503-554-0821. Open Memorial Day and Thanksgiving weekends or by appointment.

PATTON VALLEY VINEYARD

WILLAMETTE VALLEY   ESTABLISHED 1999

When founders Monte Pitt and Dave Chen decided they wanted to craft fine Pinot Noir, they chose Oregon's Willamette Valley over California. That decision is paying off because the young winery's early releases are showing tremendous depth and character.

BEST BETS

Pinot Noir $$ An exquisite and subtle nose leads to abundantly rich berry flavors with undertones of sweet spiciness. Drink now or hold for a half-decade.

WHERE TO BUY: WINERY, WINE SHOPS, GROCERY STORES

9449 Old Hwy. 47, Gaston, OR 97119; 503-985-3445; www.patton valley.com. Open Memorial Day weekend or by appointment.

PENNER-ASH WINE CELLARS

YAMHILL COUNTY   ESTABLISHED 1998

Former longtime Rex Hill Vineyards winemaker Lynn Penner-Ash and her husband, Ron, launched their winery with a minuscule amount during the vaunted 1998 vintage. She added Syrah from Southern Oregon to her repertoire in 2000.

BEST BETS

Pinot Noir $$$$ Richer and more muscular in style than the wines she crafted for Rex Hill Vineyards, Penner-Ash's Pinot is loaded with rich cherry and blackberry aromas and flavors, with complex layers of coffee and mocha and a long, fruit-driven finish.

WHERE TO BUY: WINERY, WINE SHOPS

P.O. Box 1207, Newberg, OR 97132; 503-554-5545; www.pennerash.com. Open by appointment.

PHEASANT COURT WINERY

WILLAMETTE VALLEY   ESTABLISHED 2001

One of Oregon's smallest wineries is Pheasant Court, which produces just a few hundred cases a year. The first effort is a tasty Pinot Gris. Also look for Pinot Noir, Chardonnay, and Maréchal Foch.

BEST BETS

Pinot Gris $ A fruit-laden white loaded with tropical and citrus aromas and flavors and laced with sweet, seductive spices. This zesty wine will pair well with chicken or barbecued shrimp.

WHERE TO BUY: WINERY, WINE SHOPS, GROCERY STORES

1731 Pheasant Court, Philomath, OR 97370; 541-740-5832; www.pheasantcourtwinery.com. Open by appointment.

PONZI VINEYARDS

WILLAMETTE VALLEY   ESTABLISHED 1974

The Ponzi family has been an Oregon wine pioneer ever since establishing its vineyard in 1970. Since then the family, which has been instrumental in putting Oregon Pinot Noir on the world wine map, opened a wine bar in Yamhill County, opened a wonderful bistro next door, and even launched the state's first microbrewery (BridgePort, now under different ownership). While Dick and Nancy Ponzi still are deeply involved in the winery, their children have taken over much of the operation as the second generation thrives in Oregon's booming wine industry.

BEST BETS

Pinot Blanc $$ A bright, rich wine loaded with creamy tropical and orchard fruit. This is a fresh and delicious example that embodies all that is good about Oregon Pinot Blanc. A sure match for shellfish, cod, and Asian-inspired dishes.

Reserve Pinot Noir $$$$ A deep, brooding red loaded with berry, chocolate, cola, cedar, and earthy notes with herbal and espresso underpinnings and solid tannins. Pair this with a good steak.

Pinot Noir $$ A bright, fresh red that shows off straightforward cherry and raspberry aromas and flavors with a smooth, silky mouth feel and finish. An elegant wine to pair with veal, turkey, or even salmon.

Arneis $$ This rare variety shows off exotic aromas of bananas and spices with a rich, creamy palate and nuances of peaches and chopped walnuts. Enjoy this with pasta in a cream sauce.

WHERE TO BUY: WINERY, WINE SHOPS, GROCERY STORES

14665 S.W. Winery Lane, Beaverton, OR 97007; 503-628-1227; www.ponziwines.com. Open daily.

PRIVÉ VINEYARD

YAMHILL COUNTY   ESTABLISHED 2001

Tina and Mark Hammond have launched their tiny winery, with about two hundred fifty cases of premium Pinot Noir annually. With Tina as winemaker and Mark as vineyard manager, the Hammonds use estate fruit from a vineyard planted in 1981, primarily Müller-Thurgau that was grafted over to Pinot Noir in 1999. They produce two Pinot Noirs, one from the North Block (Le Nord) and one from the South Block (Le Sud).

BEST BETS

Le Nord $$$ A bright, approachable wine with fresh cherry, raspberry, violet, and lavender aromas and flavors with a creamy vanilla mid-palate. A good match with salmon.

Le Sud $$$ A dark, rich wine with distinctive black fruit, ripe tannins, and a long, delicious finish. Try this with sirloin or lamb.

WHERE TO BUY: WINERY

28155 N.E. Bell Road, Newberg, OR 97132; 503-554-0464; www.privevineyard.com. Open Memorial Day and Thanksgiving weekends.

RANSOM CELLARS

WILLAMETTE VALLEY   ESTABLISHED 2000

Ransom Cellars is the creation of Tad Seestedt, who owns and operates Ransom Spirits, a distillery in the southern Willamette Valley. The wines are approachable in quality and in price.

BEST BETS

Pinot Gris $ Wonderful orchard and tropical fruit aromas give way to ripe fruit flavors, plenty of acidity, and a long finish. A tasty Gris that will pair well with chicken, salmon, or shellfish.

Cuvée Reunion Pinot Noir $ With warm, approachable aromas of black cherries and vanilla, this tasty and nicely priced red offers bright, rich berry and cherry flavors, refreshing acidity, and a good finish. Priced for everyday enjoyment, it's a wine to serve with pasta, turkey, or pork tenderloin.

WHERE TO BUY: WINERY, WINE SHOPS

1025E N.W. Ninth St., Corvallis, OR 97339; 541-738-1565; www.ransomspirits.com. Call for hours.

REDHAWK VINEYARD

WILLAMETTE VALLEY   ESTABLISHED 1989

Tom Robinson isn't into making wine a complex and unapproachable beverage. Rather, he'd prefer to have a little fun with it, which is why his wines have gained notoriety for what's on the label rather than what's in the bottle. His most famous is a Pinot Noir called Grateful Red, but he also has a rosé called Punk Floyd, a red blend called Donner Party ("Good Friends, Good Food"), a white wine called Great White, and a couple of political statements with Ruby Ridge and Waco Red. Redhawk's wines are meant to be enjoyed with a smile.

BEST BETS

Grateful Red $ This Pinot Noir is a straightforward and enjoyable red with bright cherry and berry flavors. A tasty and inexpensive wine that will assure discussion.

Reserve Chardonnay $ A delicious wine with aromas of butter rum and candied apples and creamy flavors of intense fruit. Enjoy with scallops or grilled halibut.

Pinot Gris $ Pleasing aromas and flavors of kiwis and dried pineapples and luscious flavors of apples and pears. A good, inexpensive example of Oregon Pinot Gris.

Donner Party Red $ A blend of Pinot Noir and Merlot, this shows off cherry, vanilla, and caramel aromas and deep cherry, berry, and creamy vanilla flavors. A delicious wine, especially for the price.

WHERE TO BUY: WINERY, WINE SHOPS, GROCERY STORES

2995 Michigan City Lane N.W., Salem, OR 97304; 503-362-1596; www.redhawkwine.com. Open daily spring to fall and weekdays in winter.

REX HILL VINEYARDS

YAMHILL COUNTY   ESTABLISHED 1983

Rex Hill Vineyards is one of Oregon's largest and most vibrant wineries. Led by owners Paul Hart and Jan Jacobsen, the winery and its vineyard firm, Oregon Grape Management Company, own or control nearly 300 acres of vineyards in the Willamette Valley. In the mid-1990s, Rex Hill shifted its focus to acreage contracts so it could have greater control of the quality of its grapes. This has resulted in outstanding wines amid its array of more than twenty bottlings, including as many as ten different Pinot Noirs per vintage.

BEST BETS

Pinot Noir $$ Rex Hill's flagship Pinot Noir is an elegant, approachable red with smooth, ripe berries, velvety tannins, and layers of earth and tobacco nuances.

Reserve Pinot Noir $$$$ The best of Rex Hill's vineyard-designated Pinots go into the Reserve, and this strategy pays off with a rich, complex wine with petite berry and violet aromas and ripe fruit showing off sweet oak nuances.

Vineyard-designated Pinot Noirs $$$$ Rex Hill produces wines from a number of top vineyards, including Maresh, Jacob-Hart, Seven Springs, and Croft. Each shows off the qualities of the site, clone, and care in the cellar, and all can be highly recommended.

Reserve Pinot Gris $$ Rex Hill began producing Pinot Gris in 1987 and makes no fewer than three styles. This, its top tier, is a bold, food-friendly white loaded with fruit flavors and mineral undertones.

Kings Ridge Pinot Noir $ Rex Hill's Kings Ridge wines are defined by their quality, approachability, and affordability. This Pinot holds its own amid its higher-priced siblings with earthy, black fruit aromas, touches of vanilla, a round mouth feel, and a medium finish.

WHERE TO BUY: WINERY, WINE SHOPS, GROCERY STORES

30835 N. Hwy. 99W, Newberg, OR 97132; 503-538-0666; www.rex hill.com. Open daily.

SASS WINERY

WILLAMETTE VALLEY   ESTABLISHED 1995

Owner and winemaker Jerry Sass focuses on small lots of Pinot Gris and Pinot Noir from his small Willamette Valley vineyards. Sass has been working in the Oregon wine industry since the late 1980s and is focused on gentle winemaking and sustainable agriculture practices.

BEST BETS

Pinot Gris $ A fruit bowl of aromas and flavors led by pineapple, melon, apple, and citrus. With its full, creamy mouth feel, this pairs well with scallops, oysters, or crab.

Pinot Noir $$ A ripe, concentrated wine showing aromas and flavors of violets, cherries, vanilla bean, and sweet spices. A graceful wine to serve with lamb.

WHERE TO BUY: WINERY, WINE SHOPS

P.O. Box 13662, Salem, OR 97309; 503-391-9991. Open by appointment.

SECRET HOUSE VINEYARDS

WILLAMETTE VALLEY   ESTABLISHED 1991

Allegedly named for a bordello that occupied the site long ago, Secret House is tucked in the southern Willamette Valley. The vineyards, planted in the early '70s, contain Pinot Noir, Riesling, and Chardonnay, and the winery also sources grapes from the nearby Umqua Valley.

BEST BETS

Pinot Gris $ Loaded with exotic spices, citrus, and tropical fruit, this is a delectable example of Oregon Pinot Gris. Pair it with mussels, salmon, or chicken.

Cabernet Sauvignon $$ A rich, deep, and rare Cab for a Willamette Valley winery (though the grapes are from the Umqua), this is a big, chewy wine showing off classic dark fruit, cedar, chocolate, vanilla, and more. Leave it in the cellar or enjoy now with a thick steak.

Riesling $ This white shows off citrus and orchard aromas and flavors and is backed up with a bit of residual sugar and good acidity. Enjoy with spicy dishes, such as chorizo.

Red Silk $$ This red sparkler shows off savory cherry and raspberry fruit with enough residual sugar to make it perfect for brunch or celebration.

WHERE TO BUY: WINERY, WINE SHOPS, GROCERY STORES

88324 Vineyard Lane, Veneta, OR 97487; 541-935-3774; www.secret housewinery.com. Open daily.

SHAFER VINEYARD CELLARS

WILLAMETTE VALLEY   ESTABLISHED 1981

With vineyards first planted in the early '70s, Harvey and Miki Shafer make modest amounts of wines from estate grapes. The Shafers produce a great number of wines, including two Chardonnays, three Pinot Noirs, a Pinot Gris, a Sauvignon Blanc, five Rieslings, a Gewürztraminer, and a Müller-Thurgau. The wines are tasty and affordable.

BEST BETS

Vintner's Cuvée Chardonnay $ A tasty and inexpensive Chardonnay that shows off more fruit than oak. Aromas of spice and citrus lead to clean, uninhibited flavors that pair well with chicken or seafood.

Gewürztraminer $ A classic Gewürztraminer with floral, grapefruit, and nutmeg aromas with smooth, clean, tasty flavors, just a hint of sweetness, and a gentle farewell. A tasty sipper or pair with turkey.

Riesling $ Delicate fruit aromas lead to flavors of light honey dripped over fresh apples. Try with crab, pork, or a cheese plate.

Vintner's Cuvée Pinot Noir $ Crafted in a refreshingly fruity style, this offers aromas of cherries and bacon fat with smooth berry flavors. Age it on the way home and enjoy with everyday cuisine.

WHERE TO BUY: WINERY, WINE SHOPS, GROCERY STORES

6200 N.W. Gales Creek Road, Forest Grove, OR 97116; 503-357-6604; www.shafervineyardcellars.com. Open daily.

SHALLON WINERY

OREGON COAST   ESTABLISHED 1978

As the boys on Monty Python's Flying Circus *would say, "And now for something completely different." That's what Paul van der Veldt is doing at his small winery in downtown Astoria. Van der Veldt is a character who makes wine his own way—and doesn't mind telling you about it. He produces little grape-based wine, with most of his creations made from fruit, whey and, yes, chocolate. Visit Shallon with an open mind and at least an hour, and you'll enjoy the experience greatly.*

BEST BETS

Chocolate-Orange $$ This whey-based wine (using whey from Tillamook) is a wonder of the wine world. It's as thick as a sauce and uses some of the world's finest chocolates.

Lemon Meringue $$ Another whey wine that is meant to remind you of a lemon meringue pie.

Cran-Du-Lait $ A cranberry and whey wine that is a pleasing summer sipper or could be enjoyed at the Thanksgiving table.

WHERE TO BUY: WINERY

1598 Duane St., Astoria, OR 97103; 503-325-5978; www.shallon.com. Open daily including holidays.

SHEA WINE CELLARS

YAMHILL COUNTY   ESTABLISHED 1996

Dick Shea owns and operates what is perhaps Oregon's most famous vineyard, and some of the state's top Pinot Noir producers make Shea Vineyard-designated wines. Shea is using a few of his grapes to make Pinot Noir under his own label and in 2002 he hired a full-time winemaker and has plans for a winery in Yamhill County.

BEST BETS

Estate Pinot Noir $$$ A blockbuster red with dense, sweet blackberry and blueberry aromas and flavors. Pair this wine with prime rib.

Estate Pinot Noir, Block 32 $$$ A black, earthy wine with hints of jasmine and wild berry aromas and flavors. A full-bodied, focused wine with big tannins that are well balanced with plenty of fruit and acidity for good cellar potential.

WHERE TO BUY: WINERY, WINE SHOPS

4304 S.W. Strathwell Lane, Portland, OR 97221; 503-241-6527. Not open to the public.

SILVAN RIDGE / HINMAN VINEYARDS

WILLAMETTE VALLEY   ESTABLISHED 1979

Hinman Vineyards was one of the state's early wineries. In the early '90s the winery launched a reserve line, Silvan Ridge, which has emerged as the operation's flagship label. Silvan Ridge gets grapes from throughout Western Oregon and produces consistently good to great wines. Its Semi-sparkling Early Muscat is one of the state's most popular wines.

BEST BETS

Semi-sparkling Early Muscat $ A fast favorite because of its classic floral and fruit aromas and rich, ripe, sweet pear and orange flavors. This is a hugely delicious wine with lots of sweetness, and it is perfect for brunches and picnics.

Viognier $$ This white wine bursts with tropical notes and is loaded with aromas and flavors of pineapples, bananas, and toasted coconuts. Great acidity leads to a long, food-friendly finish. A delicious example of the variety.

Merlot $$ From Southern Oregon fruit, this opens with bright cherry and herbal overtones and is smooth and supple on the palate with flavors of black cherries and vanilla. A good everyday Merlot to enjoy with pasta or most meat dishes.

Chardonnay $ This bright, fruit-driven white shows a nice balance of toastiness from barrel fermentation and aging. It's a clean, delicious wine with mouth-filling flavors.

WHERE TO BUY: WINERY, WINE SHOPS, GROCERY STORES

27012 Briggs Hill Road, Eugene, OR 97405; 541-345-1945; www. silvanridge.com. Open daily.

SINEANN

YAMHILL COUNTY   ESTABLISHED 1994

One of Oregon's most talked-about wineries is Sineann, headed by owner and winemaker Peter Rosback. Sineann is unusual in Oregon because it embraces both warm-climate grapes from east of the Cascades as well as cool-climate grapes from the Willamette Valley. Sineann is making some of Oregon's most robust wines, and they should be highly sought after. In addition to the wines reviewed here, Sineann also makes a number of whites.

BEST BETS

Reed and Reynolds Vineyard Pinot Noir $$$ An exquisite red showing off complex aromas of spice, earth, sage, and berries and a silky mouth feel. Enjoy with braised lamb.

Cabernet Sauvignon Block One $$$ From famed Champoux Vineyard in Washington's Horse Heaven Hills, this is a dark and elegant wine with deep, intense flavors of blackberries, smoky oak, cherries, and sweet spices. Rich tannins give this plenty of structure. Age or pair with rare beef.

Old Vine Zinfandel $$$ The source of the grapes is a century-old vineyard near The Dalles, Oregon, and the result is a dense and intense wine showing off deep berry and plum flavors with black pepper and rich tannins.

Hillside Vineyard Merlot $$$ Exquisite aromas lead to rich, silky flavors including creamy vanilla, blackberries, and sweet spices. An approachable red to pair with lamb or pasta.

WHERE TO BUY: WINERY, WINE SHOPS

15000 N.E. Springbrook Road, Newberg, OR 97132; 503-341-2698; www.sineann.com. Open by appointment.

SOKOL BLOSSER WINERY

YAMHILL COUNTY   ESTABLISHED 1977

One of Oregon's wine pioneers continues to be a trendsetter by moving toward lower-yield, higher-quality estate grapes and away from Chardonnay (the last vintage was 1999). Organic practices and sustainable viticulture play key roles in Sokol Blosser's commitment to quality.

BEST BETS

Pinot Gris $$ Loaded with fruit aromas and flavors with a creamy midpalate and a crisp, refreshing finish. A year-round favorite that matches well with fresh regional cuisine.

Evolution $ This blend of no fewer than nine varieties is a wonderful picnic or brunch wine that is a popular summer sipper. Grapes include Gewürztraminer, Semillon, Pinot Gris, Riesling, Müller-Thurgau, Chardonnay, Pinot Blanc, Muscat, and Madeleine Sylvaner.

Pinot Noir $$ An approachable and bright red with telltale cherry and berry aromas, light cedar, and smooth, supple tannins.

Twelve Row Block Pinot Noir $$$$$ Selected from a small area of the estate vineyard up the hill from the tasting room, this elegant yet powerful Pinot Noir is rich in supple black fruit with medium tannins, and has a long, intense finish. A spendy collector wine.

WHERE TO BUY: WINERY, WINE SHOPS, GROCERY STORES

5000 Sokol Blosser Lane, Dundee, OR 97115; 503-864-2282; www.sokolblosser.com. Open daily.

SOLÉNA

YAMHILL COUNTY   ESTABLISHED 1999

What's a Bordeaux-trained winemaker to do when he's in the heart of Oregon Pinot Noir country? Start his own label, of course. That's what Laurent Montalieu, formerly of WillaKenzie Estate, did in the early '90s when he launched La Merleausine. After marrying Danielle Andrus, whose family started Archery Summit, the couple created Soléna, a winery dedicated to Bordeaux-style wines and Zinfandel from Washington and Southern Oregon. The wines are powerful, spectacular, and age-worthy and should be highly sought after.

BEST BETS

Klipsun Vineyard Cabernet Sauvignon $$ A big wine that will blossom and mature with patience in the cellar. This shows a restrained nose in its youth but also reveals some of the deep, rich flavors that take a bit to come around. The balance of fruit, acidity, and tannin give this wine long-term potential.

WHERE TO BUY: WINERY, WINE SHOPS

213 Pine St., Carlton, OR 97111; 503-852-0082. Open weekends and by appointment.

SPRINGHILL CELLARS

WILLAMETTE VALLEY   ESTABLISHED 1988

A small producer of high-end Pinot Noir, Springhill Cellars also crafts fine Pinot Gris, Riesling, and a dry rosé. Led by winemaker Mike McLain, the winery works with fruit coming primarily from estate vineyards between Salem and Corvallis.

BEST BETS

Pinot Noir $$ This velvety wine offers earth and cherry aromas and supple flavors. The smooth tannins make this approachable and food friendly. Try it with sirloin, salmon, or veal.

WHERE TO BUY: WINERY, WINE SHOPS

Springhill Cellars, 2920 N.W. Scenic Drive, Albany, OR 97321; 541-928-1009; www.springhillcellars.com. Open Memorial Day and Thanksgiving weekends and by appointment.

ST. INNOCENT WINERY

WILLAMETTE VALLEY   ESTABLISHED 1988

Winemaker Mark Vlossak makes wines of great distinction in the Eola Hills. Vlossak crafts no fewer than five Pinot Noirs, three Pinot Gris, two Chardonnays, a Pinot Blanc, and a sparkling wine.

BEST BETS

Shea Vineyard Pinot Gris $$ This flamboyant white offers huge aromas and flavors such as orange oil, apples, and citrus. It's a big wine and will pair nicely with spicy dishes.

Freedom Hill Vineyard Chardonnay $$ A richly structured white that opens with citrus, butter, and nutmeg aromas and fruit flavors amid a creamy midpalate. A huge wine with long flavors and plenty of acidity, this will match up with scallops or pasta in a cream sauce.

Temperance Hill Vineyard Pinot Noir $$ Earthy mushroom notes mingle with ripe cherry and vanilla aromas, and there's a velvety smooth midpalate with bright fruit backed up with plenty of acidity. Pair this with grilled flank steak.

Seven Springs Vineyard Pinot Noir $$$ An elegant and approachable red showing off classic earth and dusty cherries on the nose and bright, tart fruit with supple tannins and a medium finish. Try this with a steak smothered in a mushroom sauce.

WHERE TO BUY: WINERY, WINE SHOPS

1360 Tandem Ave. N.E., Salem, OR 97303; 503-378-1526; www.st innocentwine.com. Open weekends, Memorial Day and Thanksgiving weekends, or by appointment.

ST. JOSEF'S WINERY

WILLAMETTE VALLEY   ESTABLISHED 1983

Josef Fleishmann emigrated from Europe and began to make wines in Oregon in the late 1970s. Today, St. Josef's Winery produces a wide variety of wines, including Pinot Noir, Merlot, and Cabernet Sauvignon. The wines are modestly priced and are built for everyday enjoyment.

BEST BETS

L'Esprit Gewürztraminer $ Aromatics of honey, spice, and apricots give way to sweet fruit flavors. A crisp, rich wine, this is a pleasant sipper.

Riesling $ Classic aromas of fresh apples and petrol lead to tart, delicious fruit flavors. A good wine to pair with pork, halibut, or chicken.

Chardonnay $ Orchard and citrus fruit mingle on the nose with exotic spices, leading to fresh apple and pear flavors and a creamy mouth feel. Pair with chicken or salmon.

WHERE TO BUY: WINERY, WINE SHOPS, GROCERY STORES

28836 S. Barlow Road, Canby, OR 97013; 503-651-3190. Seasonal hours.

STAG HOLLOW WINES AND VINEYARDS

YAMHILL COUNTY   ESTABLISHED 1994

This small winery in the heart of venerable Yamhill County focuses on high-quality Pinot Noir and Chardonnay, with vineyards and wines handled with great care. Owners Mark Huff and Jill Zarnowitz also dabble in Italian-style wines, including the rarely grown Dolcetto and some white blends.

BEST BETS

Vendance Selection Pinot Noir $$$ A splendid, spicy red showing off silky flavors of blackberries, vanilla, sweet spice, and chocolate with complex undertones of black pepper, sage, and cola. Cellar this for a few years or enjoy now with venison or lamb.

Cuvée Pinot Noir $$ This bright, rich red offers strawberry and herbal notes with dark, dense flavors and cleansing acidity. Pair with pork, beef, or pasta.

Tre Secco $ A dry blend of Chardonnay, Muscat Ottonel, and Early Muscat, this is wildly aromatic and flavorful with notes of white flowers, grapefruit, and more. Enjoy with chicken.

Tre Dolco $ A sweet blend of Chardonnay, Muscat Ottonel, and Early Muscat, this is loaded with honey, spice, and perfume aromas and flavors of orange blossoms, anise, and apricots. Enjoy as an after-dinner sipper.

WHERE TO BUY: WINERY, WINE SHOPS

7930 N.E. Blackburn Road, Yamhill, OR 97148; 503-662-5609; www.staghollow.com. Open Memorial Day and Thanksgiving weekends or by appointment.

STANGELAND VINEYARDS AND WINERY

WILLAMETTE VALLEY   ESTABLISHED 1991

With a quarter-century and more of grape growing under their belts, Larry and Kinsey Miller have been crafting quality wines for more than a decade. Their focus is on Pinot Noir, Chardonnay, and Pinot Gris, and they also make Gewürztraminer. The Millers are friendly folks whose motto is, "There are no strangers at Stangeland."

BEST BETS

Winemaker's Reserve Pinot Noir $$$$ A delicate red with perfume, violet, and wonderful elegance on the aromas and smooth, rich cherry and pepper flavors. Velvety tannins and a silky finish make this a wonderful wine.

Martha's Vineyard II Pinot Noir $$ Soon to be renamed "Miller's Vine-yard" because of sensitive Californians who don't want it confused with the famed Napa vineyards, this luscious Pinot opens with violet and earth aromas, smooth cherry and berry flavors, and solid tannins.

Pinot Gris $ Perfumy pineapples give way to a fruit-driven wine with a good balance of flavor and acidity that will match well with lobster, crab, or prawns.

Chardonnay $ Rich butter aromas pair well with orchard and tropical aromas and flavors. A food-friendly wine that will match up with pasta in a clam sauce.

WHERE TO BUY: WINERY, WINE SHOPS

8500 Hopewell Road N.W., Salem, OR 97304; 503-581-0355; www.stangelandwinery.com. Seasonal hours.

STARR WINERY

YAMHILL COUNTY   ESTABLISHED 1991

Former wine shop owner Rachel Starr now crafts rich and penetrating wines of distinction. In addition to Pinot Noir, she also makes Chardonnay and Pinot Gris.

BEST BETS

Pinot Noir, Bert's Blend $$ Opening with subtle and seductive aromas, this fruit-filled Pinot invites further exploration with its layered berry and cherry flavors and velvety mouth feel. A wonderful choice with beef or Cornish game hen.

WHERE TO BUY: WINERY, WINE SHOPS

Starr Winery, 31590 N.E. Schadd Road, Newberg, OR 97132; 503-538-3467. Open by appointment.

STEVENSON BARRIE

YAMHILL COUNTY   ESTABLISHED 1999

Mark Stevenson, winemaker for Panther Creek Cellars, and Scott Barrie teamed up to launch Stevenson Barrie, concentrating on Pinot Noir from vaunted Shea Vineyard. They use no new oak in order to ensure that their wines express the fruit rather than the wood the wines are aged in.

BEST BETS

Shea Vineyard Pinot Noir $$ An expressive red that opens with earth and berry aromas and dense, penetrating flavors of black cherries and spices with approachable tannins. Enjoy this with beef or lamb.

WHERE TO BUY: WINE SHOPS

455 N. Irvine St., McMinnville, OR 97128 (at Panther Creek Cellars); 503-472-8080.

STONE WOLF VINEYARDS/MYSTIC MOUNTAIN VINEYARD

WILLAMETTE VALLEY   ESTABLISHED 1996

With vineyards in the Eola Hills (Stone Wolf) and Coast Range (Mystic Mountain), this operation runs two labels producing delicious and food-friendly wines. Wine lovers will find much to enjoy here, including a refreshing embrace of Müller-Thurgau, an early ripening white that shows quite well in Oregon.

BEST BETS

Stone Wolf Legend Reserve Pinot Noir $$ A big, tasty red with classic earth and bell pepper aromas and black cherry flavors. Pair this with pork or beef.

Stone Wolf Müller-Thurgau $ This clean, crisp, slightly sweet white shows off its Riesling roots with apple and citrus aromas and flavors. A tasty sipper or enjoy it with chicken or pasta.

Stone Wolf Pinot Gris $ A fruit-driven white displaying zesty aromas and flavors of oranges and apples and a pleasant mineral quality. Just a hint of sweetness on the finish. Pair this with shellfish, salmon, chicken, or pork.

Mystic Mountain Chardonnay $ A lovely and luscious white showing off aromas of rose water and light orange oil with approachable flavors of apples and citrus. Enjoy with halibut or chicken.

WHERE TO BUY: WINERY, WINE SHOPS, GROCERY STORES

22470 S.W. Bernette Road, McMinnville, OR 97128; 503-434-9025; www.stonewolfvineyards.com. Open Memorial Day and Thanksgiving weekends.

STONECROFT CELLARS

WILLAMETTE VALLEY   ESTABLISHED 1998

Winemaker Bryan Croft came to Oregon in the mid-1990s from Napa Valley to make wine for Flynn Vineyards, which also makes wine for a handful of other Oregon wineries. During the celebrated 1998 vintage, he started his own small label, which has been highly regarded.

BEST BETS

Pinot Noir $$ A bright, jazzy wine with raspberry and vanilla aromas and rich flavors of cherries, raspberries, and spice. A delicious and fruity wine to enjoy with salmon or light beef dishes.

Reserve Pinot Noir $$ A dark, earthy wine with dusty cherry and oak spice aromas, and deep, rich, smooth flavors of plums and blueberries. Enjoy with beef in a mushroom sauce.

WHERE TO BUY: WINERY, WINE SHOPS

P.O. Box 592, Dallas, OR 97338; 877-933-9463; www.stonecroft cellars.com. Call for appointment.

TEMPEST VINEYARDS

YAMHILL COUNTY   ESTABLISHED 1988

Tempest produces small amounts of handcrafted Pinot Noir, Chardon-
nay, and aperitif wines. The family-run operation believes in minimal
and gentle handling of the wines.

BEST BETS

Pinot Noir $$ A bright and tasty red showing off strawberry jam,
vanilla, and berry aromas and flavors. Smooth and approachable,
this should pair well with chicken, turkey, or pork.

WHERE TO BUY: WINERY, WINE SHOPS

6000 Karla's Road, Amity, OR 97101; 503-835-2600. Open Memorial
Day and Thanksgiving weekends.

TORII MOR WINERY

YAMHILL COUNTY   ESTABLISHED 1993

Torii Mor gained Pinot Noir cult status with Patricia Green and Jim
Anderson teaming together on the winemaking. After they left to
launch Patricia Green Cellars, Torii Mor's wines were made by Joe
Dobbes of Willamette Valley Vineyards. The wines continue to be con-
sistently delicious and are highly sought after by fans and collectors. In
addition to Pinot Noir, Torii Mor also crafts Pinot Blanc, Chardon-
nay, and Pinot Gris.

BEST BETS

Pinot Noir $$ An outstanding effort with classic complexity from aromas through the finish. Berries, earth, violets, and spice highlight
this delicious wine.

Reserve Pinot Noir $$$ A giant red displaying fresh berry and cherry
aromas up front and explosive flavors through the palate that lead
to a velvety finish.

Olson Vineyard Pinot Noir $$$$ A concentrated, penetrating wine with
great complexity of earth, spice, berry, and tobacco notes. Pair with
lamb or beef.

Pinot Gris $$ A zippy white showing off wonderful orange aromas
with tropical fruit flavors. A crisp mouth feel gives this firm back-
bone and makes for a good match with scallops, pasta, or pork.

WHERE TO BUY: WINERY, WINE SHOPS

18325 N.E. Fairview Drive, Dundee, OR 97115; 503-538-2279;
www.toriimorwinery.com. Open Friday–Saturday and by appointment.

TROON VINEYARDS

ROGUE VALLEY   ESTABLISHED 1993

Longtime grape grower Dick Troon launched his winery in the early '90s and has gained a regional following for his Cabernet Sauvignon, Zinfandel, and Chardonnay. His operation isn't open to the public, but his wines can be found for sale in the Grants Pass area.

BEST BETS

Cabernet Sauvignon $$ A pleasing wine showing good varietal character with aromas and flavors of black currants, blueberries, black pepper, and more. A good wine to pair with beef or lasagna.

WHERE TO BUY: WINE SHOPS

1475 Kubli Road, Grants Pass, OR 97526; 503-846-6562. Not open to the public.

TYEE WINE CELLARS

WILLAMETTE VALLEY   ESTABLISHED 1985

Ask around Oregon about who makes great Gewürztraminer, and the answer often will be, "Tyee." The winery is the collaboration of Dave and Margy Buchanan, winemaker Barney Watson, and Nola Mosier. In addition to Gewürztraminer, Tyee also produces highly praised Pinot Noir, Pinot Gris, Pinot Blanc, and Chardonnay.

BEST BETS

Dry Gewürztraminer $ A wonderful white wine made in a traditional Alsace style with grapefruit and nutmeg aromas and big, crisp, dry citrus and spice flavors. A classic that will go well with barbecued shrimp or pasta in a cream sauce.

Pinot Noir $$ A European-style red with leather and spice aromas complementing complex flavors of ripe cherries and penetrating black fruit. A choice wine for robust meat dishes.

Pinot Gris $ This crisp white opens with a touch of toastiness mingling with pear and apple aromas and flavors. A clean, tasty wine to enjoy with shellfish or salmon.

Pinot Blanc $ A light, lovely wine showing off aromas of exotic orange oil and apple and citrus flavors. Enjoy this delicate wine with shellfish or mild cheeses.

WHERE TO BUY: WINERY, WINE SHOPS, GROCERY STORES

26335 Greenberry Road, Corvallis, OR 97333; 541-753-8754; www.tyeewine.com. Open weekends April–December or by appointment.

VALLEY VIEW WINERY

APPLEGATE VALLEY   ESTABLISHED 1978

The Wisnovsky family has been growing grapes in Southern Oregon for three decades. Fiercely proud of the lush Rogue Valley, Valley View is a marketing and quality leader. In vintages that warrant it, Valley View grants reserve status to some of its bottles, called Anna Maria on the label, indicating to consumers that they are getting the winery's best.

BEST BETS

Anna Maria Merlot, Quail Run Vineyard $$ This long, complex wine offers bright fruit, cedar, and spice aromas and flavors. It's expertly balanced with acidity and tannin, ensuring good aging potential and food pairing possibilities.

Anna Maria Meritage $$$ A classy blend of Merlot, Cabernet Franc, and Cabernet Sauvignon with sweet oak, mocha, and cherry aromas and rich, mouth-filling flavors of coffee, dark chocolate, and blackberries. Serve this with the finest cuts of beef.

Cotes du Rogue $ You gotta love the name nearly as much as the wine, which is a blend of Syrah and Zinfandel. It's a bright, spicy red built for easy drinking and priced for everyday consumption. Pair with artichoke and feta pizza.

Anna Maria Chardonnay $ A showpiece Chardonnay that will be perfect with hors d'oeuvres, this big, buttery white wine shows off smoky, butterscotch flavors and aromas.

WHERE TO BUY: WINERY, WINE SHOPS, GROCERY STORES

1000 Upper Applegate Road, Jacksonville, OR 97530; 541-899-8468; www.valleyviewwinery.com. Winery tasting room open daily. Downtown Jacksonville tasting room closed Sundays.

VAN DUZER VINEYARDS

WILLAMETTE VALLEY   ESTABLISHED 1989

This winery with a distinctive label is making plenty of noise with its high quality, thanks to new owners and a new attitude. Carl and Marilynn Thoma purchased the winery and vineyard in the late '90s and have made a commitment to quality that is showing in the wines. The wildly colorful label, by the way, depicts Zephyra, the goddess of Van Duzer's western wind.

BEST BETS

Barrel Select Pinot Noir $$ A spicy red wine showing cherry and nutmeg aromas with thick, chewy flavors of berries, vanilla, and peppercorns. Enjoy this with lamb or beef.

Flagpole Block Pinot Noir $$$ A classy red with aromas and flavors of violets, cherries, and cedar. Medium-bodied with tangy fruit on the finish. Enjoy with venison, veal, lasagna, or duck.

Chardonnay $$ A delicious white showing a fine balance of oak and fruit. It provides plenty of citrus and pear flavors with undertones of vanilla and butter components. A perfect wine to pair with chicken or shellfish.

WHERE TO BUY: WINERY, WINE SHOPS

11875 Smithfield Road, Dallas, OR 97338; 503-623-6420; www. vanduzer.com. Seasonal hours.

VIENTO WINES

YAMHILL COUNTY   ESTABLISHED 1999

Oregon winemaking veteran Rich Cushman launched Viento with the idea of selecting grapes from top Washington and Oregon vineyards. His early efforts show great promise, including limited bottlings of Viognier, Riesling, Sangiovese, Pinot Noir, and Syrah. Viento, Spanish for "wind," reflects Cushman's affection for the winds that howl through the Columbia Gorge, where he grew up.

BEST BETS

Sangiovese $$ Earthy aromas and big cherry and plum flavors. This is a jammy and richly structured red that pairs well with steak, lamb, and spicy pasta dishes. Grapes are from the Walla Walla Valley.

Sangiovese Rosé $ A delicious and serious effort with bright cherry and strawberry aromas and flavors. This is perfect for a summer picnic.

Riesling $ From Columbia Gorge grapes, this steely, minerally wine is well balanced with orchard fruits and sweet spices. The slight sweetness is expertly backed up with good acidity that makes this a good match with Asian-inspired dishes, chicken, or Tex-Mex.

WHERE TO BUY: WINERY, WINE SHOPS

P.O. Box 1403, McMinnville, OR 97128; 503-434-9587. Open by appointment.

WALNUT CITY WINEWORKS

YAMHILL COUNTY   ESTABLISHED 2000

Operating out of an old walnut processing plant, Walnut City Wineworks is a boutique operation run by three partners. The winery buys from several vineyards, including Del Rio in the Rogue Valley, which has a reputation for growing grapes that produce bold reds. The partners are vineyard managers by day, so they plan to keep the operation small.

BEST BETS

Cabernet Sauvignon $$ With grapes from Del Rio Vineyard in the Rogue Valley, this provides herbal and plum aromas with flavors of thick coffee, chocolate, and black, jammy fruit. A yummy wine.

Pinot Noir $$ Opening with aromas of tangy raspberries, rose water, violets, and hints of vanilla and continuing with clean, rich flavors of raspberries and cherries.

Pinot Gris $ A bright, crisp, approachable white with aromas of lemons, apples, and vanilla and clean, rich flavors of floral and tropical fruit. Bring on the oysters.

WHERE TO BUY: WINERY, WINE SHOPS

475 N.E. 17th St., McMinnville, OR 97128; 503-472-3215; www. walnutcitywineworks.com. Open by appointment.

WEISINGER'S OF ASHLAND

ROGUE VALLEY   ESTABLISHED 1988

The father-and-son team of John and Eric Weisinger are producing some of Southern Oregon's finest wines. Just north of the California border, the Weisingers take advantage of the warm climate to craft delicate whites and bold reds, including a blend called Petite Pompadour that should not be overlooked by fans of Bordeaux-style wines. Visitors should inquire about the B&B amid the estate vineyards.

BEST BETS

Petite Pompadour $$ A blend of Cabernet Sauvignon, Merlot, Cabernet Franc, and Malbec, this is a muscular wine that will pair well with a thick steak now or reward several years of aging in the cellar. It's loaded with fruit and is nicely balanced with oak undertones and bold tannins. Not for the meek!

Gewürztraminer $ One of the finest dry Gewürztraminers you'll likely come across, this opens with floral notes mingling with grapefruit, cloves, and apples. A treat that will show well with turkey.

Chardonnay $ This fruit bomb is loaded with lemons, apples, and pears laced with hints of vanilla and toast from oak aging. A great match for salmon.

Mescolare $$ A blend of Pinot Noir, Nebbiolo, and Cabernet Sauvignon, this may remind you of the house wine at your favorite hole-in-the-wall Italian restaurant. Serve this with a thick slab of lasagna.

WHERE TO BUY: WINERY, WINE SHOPS, GROCERY STORES

3150 Siskiyou Blvd., Ashland, OR 97520; 541-488-5989; www.weisingers.com. Seasonal hours.

WESTREY WINE COMPANY

YAMHILL COUNTY   ESTABLISHED 1993

Two philosophy graduates-turned-winemakers, Amy Wesselman and David Autrey, create highly regarded Pinot Noir, Chardonnay, and Pinot Gris in the heart of Yamhill County. They produce several vine-

yard-designated Pinot Noirs and have planted an estate vineyard to extend quality control over their wines.

BEST BETS

Pinot Noir $$ A rich and zippy red showing off toasty cherry aromas and cherry, oak, and peppercorn flavors. Try this with a pepper steak or lamb grilled with rosemary.

WHERE TO BUY: WINERY, WINE SHOPS

1065 N.E. Alpine St., McMinnville, OR 97218; 503-224-7360. Open by appointment.

WETHERELL VINEYARDS

UMPQUA VALLEY   ESTABLISHED 1999

The Wetherell family supplies grapes to several Oregon wineries and has been farming in the region for decades. With the help of Eola Hills Wine Cellars, it now makes seven thousand cases of white Zinfandel from its twenty-two acres of Zin, one of the largest such vineyards in the Pacific Northwest.

BEST BETS

White Zinfandel $ With its rhubarb and berry aromas and strawberry flavors, this is a crisp, tasty wine with good acidity to back up the residual sugar.

WHERE TO BUY: GROCERY STORES

577 Mode Road, Umpqua, OR 97486; 541-459-4222. Not open to the public.

WILLAKENZIE ESTATE

YAMHILL COUNTY   ESTABLISHED 1995

The often-confusing French term terroir *makes perfect sense at Willa-Kenzie Estate, near the town of Yamhill. That's not just because the owners and winemaker are French—though that helps—but because everything here is about the wine grapes and how they interact with the soil and climate. WillaKenzie focuses on four members of the Pinot family: Noir, Meunier, Blanc, and Gris. Additionally, WillaKenzie crafts small lots of Gamay Noir and Chardonnay.*

In addition to its gentle handling of wines, WillaKenzie preaches sustainable agriculture. To build the winery and plant a hundred and five acres of grapes, only three trees were cut down, and a twenty-acre site perfect for grape growing has been left alone because the owners would just as soon leave the trees untouched.

BEST BETS

Pinot Blanc $$ Break out the shellfish for this beautifully balanced white wine that is rich in fresh orchard fruit aromas and flavors and a round, spicy mouth feel.

Pinot Gris $$ Tropical and citrus aromas invite the consumer to venture forth and enjoy the crisp apple and pear flavors. The delicious mouth feel and spiciness make this a nice match with grilled salmon or curry.

Pierre Léon Pinot Noir $$$ A blend of nine Pinot Noir clones creates this dark, complex, robust red with earthy, black fruit aromas and flavors with solid tannins that smooth out quickly for a supple finish.

Aliette Pinot Noir $$$ This seductive Pinot opens with sultry floral and bright berry fruit aromas and rich, long, layered flavors. Perhaps WillaKenzie's most brilliant wine.

WHERE TO BUY: WINERY, WINE SHOPS, GROCERY STORES.

19143 N.E. Laughlin Road, Yamhill, OR 97148; 503-662-3280; www.willakenzie.com. Open seasonally.

WILLAMETTE VALLEY VINEYARDS / TUALATIN ESTATE / GRIFFIN CREEK

WILLAMETTE VALLEY   ESTABLISHED 1989

One of Oregon's largest producers makes a dizzying array of wines under no fewer than three labels. This publicly traded winery produces wines of good quality at a wide range of prices. Though Willamette Valley Vineyards focuses on making top-notch Pinot Noirs under the Willamette Valley Vineyards and Tualatin Estate labels, it also has the flexibility to work with Bordeaux and Rhône varieties in the Griffin Creek line, using fruit from the warm Rogue Valley in Southern Oregon. Beginning with the 1997 and 1998 vintages, winemaker Joe Dobbes gently turned the company toward quality over quantity before leaving to start his own winery. This shift in focus shows more with each successive release and is finding favor with critics and consumers alike.

BEST BETS

Willamette Valley Vineyards Freedom Hill Vineyard Pinot Noir $$$ Just one of at least eight different bottlings of Pinot Noir that Dobbes crafts each year, this is an expressive and delicate wine that shows off bright cherry and raspberry fruit, cloves, hints of oak, and good tannins for a long, full finish.

Tualatin Estate Pinot Noir $$ Typically, this wine develops a bit more slowly in the bottle, but patience will reveal a powerful yet elegant wine showing off cherries, black olives, and supple tannins.

Griffin Creek Viognier $$ An explosive white wine rich with tropical and citrus aromas and flavors and a long finish. This is a real charmer that will pair well with shellfish.

Tualatin Estate Semi-Sparkling Muscat $ A perennial favorite, this is a sweet sipper loaded with honeysuckle and citrus aromas and flavors. Perfect for beginners as well as wine veterans, enjoy this on picnics or by itself in the hot tub.

8800 Enchanted Way S.E., Turner, OR 97392; 800-344-9463; www.wvv.com. Open daily.

WINE COUNTRY FARM CELLARS

YAMHILL COUNTY   ESTABLISHED 1994

Tucked in the hills above Highway 99W on the same road as Domaines Drouhin and Serene is Wine Country Farm, a winery and bed and breakfast. The B&B was built more than eighty years ago, and the estate vineyard is a quarter-century old. Small lots of five wines are produced, with most sold to visitors, guests, and wedding parties.

BEST BETS

Riesling $ Classic varietal aromas and flavors of green apples and orchard fruits, with a little sweetness and plenty of acidity to back it up. This is a smooth and tasty sipper to match with pasta, chicken, or Asian-inspired cuisine.

Chardonnay $ Richly structured, this fruit-forward, approachable white provides a hint of butter from oak aging and tropical, pear, and apple flavors.

Pinot Gris $ A versatile, food-friendly wine with good flavors, including those of apples and pears.

WHERE TO BUY: WINERY

6855 Breyman Orchard Road, Dayton, OR 97111; 503-864-3446; www.winecountryfarm.com. Open seasonally.

WINTER'S HILL VINEYARD

YAMHILL COUNTY   ESTABLISHED 1998

Winter's Hill wines have been a delight since their first release. Peter and Emily Gladhart are producing Pinot Noir and Pinot Gris that exhibit grace and evoke pleasure. The vineyard was planted in 1991, and the family focuses on Oregon's two favorite varieties.

BEST BETS

Pinot Noir $$ A tremendous wine (and great value amid higher-priced Oregon Pinot Noirs) laced with spicy oak and approachable fruit, this is a complex, layered wine that will pair well with veal, pork, or sirloin.

Pinot Gris $ Another huge favorite, this crisp, delicious white is rich with tropical and orchard fruit aromas and flavors and has layers of complexity. This would be a great match with salmon, pasta in a white sauce, pork, or mussels.

WHERE TO BUY: WINERY, WINE SHOPS

Antique Mall 943, Hwy. 99W, Lafayette, OR 97127; 503-864-4610; www.wintershillwine.com. Open weekends.

WITNESS TREE VINEYARD

WILLAMETTE VALLEY   ESTABLISHED 1987

Named for an ancient oak that served as a land surveyor's mark in the 1850s, Witness Tree is a producer of great distinction. Relying only on its forty-nine acres of estate vineyards, Witness Tree has great control—Mother Nature permitting—over the grapes it uses. The results are good to stunning Pinot Noir and Chardonnay.

BEST BETS

Vintage Select Pinot Noir $$$ A rich, toasty wine with bold dark fruit aromas and long, elegant flavors backed up with ripe tannins. A classy wine that you can expect to be one of the best each vintage.

Pinot Noir $$ Inviting fruit aromas mingle with subtle vanilla and bright, elegant, and smooth flavors. A well-balanced wine that pairs well with lamb or smoked salmon.

Vintage Select Chardonnay $$ This big, buttery wine offers mouth-filling flavors. It's a flashy, showpiece Chardonnay that pairs well with appetizers.

Chardonnay $ This lightly toasted wine shows off hints of butter and citrus aromas and pleasing flavors of apples and pineapples. A soft, approachable wine to enjoy with fowl or linguine in a cream sauce.

WHERE TO BUY: WINERY, WINE SHOPS, GROCERY STORES

7111 Spring Valley Road N.W., Salem, OR 97304; 503-585-7874; www.witnesstreevineyard.com. Seasonal hours.

YAMHILL VALLEY VINEYARDS

YAMHILL COUNTY   ESTABLISHED 1983

In its two decades of making fine Oregon wines, Yamhill Valley Vineyards has gained much praise for its Pinot Noir. In fact, its first vintage was the top wine in a famous Oregon-versus-Burgundy judging in 1985. The winery continues to focus on quality, primarily with three grapes: Pinot Noir, Pinot Gris, and Pinot Blanc. And like the wines, the Yamhill Valley prices are approachable.

BEST BETS

Pinot Blanc $ Opening with floral and melon aromas, this bright, fresh wine offers lush honeydew, cantaloupe, and pear flavors and and is backed up with well-balanced acidity. Try it with chicken in a cream sauce or grilled halibut.

Reserve Pinot Noir $$ A luscious, penetrating red, this opens with bright fruit aromas with underlying spice and moist earth components. Thick strawberry jam flavors waltz with your taste buds to a long, satisfying finish.

Pinot Gris $$ Aromas of rose water, orange oil, and apples give way to crisp, clean fruit flavors. A great match for cold chicken, mussels, or salmon.

Riesling $ Classic fruit aromas invite further exploration, which leads to flavors of sweet apples and cleansing acidity. A wonderful summer sipper.

WHERE TO BUY: WINERY, WINE SHOPS, GROCERY STORES

16250 S.W. Oldsville Road, McMinnville, OR 97128; 503-843-3100; www.yamhill.com. Open seasonally.

YOUNGBERG HILL VINEYARD

YAMHILL COUNTY   ESTABLISHED 1996

Offering one of the most stunning views and romantic places in Northwest wine country, Youngberg Hill Vineyard caters to those looking for delicious wine as well as a weekend getaway. The winery, vineyards, and B&B are run by the tireless Tasha and Kevin Byrd. The vineyards were planted in 1989 and are showing maturity in the bottle.

BEST BETS

Pinot Noir, Vino Mas $$$ A bold, classy red with earth and pepper notes amid aromas of cherries and raspberries. On the palate, loads of fruit and sweet spice are backed up with ripe tannins and hints of vanilla from aging in neutral barrels. Pair with lamb.

Pinot Noir $$ A bright, elegant wine with fruit-driven aromas and flavors, medium tannins, and a tangy finish. A delicious red for sirloin, spicy pasta, or even salmon.

Vino Blanco $ This blend of several white grapes opens with hints of flint and apple aromas and fresh orchard fruit flavors. Made off-dry, this is a fun, breezy wine to be sipped at the end of a summer day.

WHERE TO BUY: WINERY, WINE SHOPS

10660 S.W. Youngberg Hill Road, McMinnville, OR 97128; 503-472-2727; www.youngberghill.com. Open Memorial Day and Thanksgiving weekends or by appointment.

ZELKO

YAMHILL COUNTY   ESTABLISHED 2000

John and Kathy Zelko moved to Oregon in the early 1980s and got involved helping at various wineries in the Willamette Valley. In the mid-1990s they bought property in the Eola Hills and began to plant Pinot Noir. Their early efforts are nothing short of spectacular as they produce Pinot Noirs of great elegance and distinction.

BEST BETS

Pinot Noir $$$ From first whiff through the luscious finish, this is an exquisite wine. It opens with lovely cream and berry aromas that lead to rich, silky cherry and bright berry fruit. Vanilla and sweet spice are undertones in this velvety and seductive wine.

WHERE TO BUY: WINERY

Zelko, 31590 N.E. Schaad Road, Newberg, OR 97132; 503-528-0704; Open by appointment.

BRITISH COLUMBIA WINES & WINERIES

Perhaps the most exciting wine region to watch in the Pacific Northwest is British Columbia. Canada's westernmost province had a long history of making poor wine, but in the late 1980s, growers pulled out their hybrid grapevines and replanted using classic European varieties. This bold move allowed B.C. growers and winemakers to start fresh, and the results have been nothing short of amazing.

Already well known for its crisp white wines, British Columbia is starting to make its mark with reds. But its most famous and successful style is ice wine, a specialty dessert wine made when grapes are frozen on the vine a month or more after the traditional harvest is finished.

British Columbia's most important wine-producing region is the vast Okanagan Valley in the province's interior. The Okanagan stretches about 100 miles north from the U.S. border. The southern Okanagan is the only desert in Canada. One-third of the entire province's vineyards are in this twenty-mile-long section, which receives more light intensity and heat than the Napa and Sonoma Valleys.

The Okanagan includes a series of lakes, which are moderating influences that help create several interesting microclimates up and down the valley. Farther north, toward the city of Kelowna, temperatures are a little cooler, offering good conditions for growing Pinot Noir and Chardonnay. And several out-of-the-mainstream grapes are grown, including Auxerrois and Ehrenfelser, with the latter a great variety for ice wine.

British Columbia Appellations

Okanagan Valley. About four hours east of Vancouver, this valley is home to most of the province's vineyards and wineries. The southern end is capable of growing high-quality Bordeaux varieties. The Okanagan also is where British Columbia's ice wines are produced.

Similkameen Valley. This small, warm valley west of the Okanagan is a source of grapes for a number of Okanagan wineries.

Fraser Valley. This fertile valley in the Lower Mainland is similar in climate to Washington's Puget Sound appellation. Cool-climate grapes are grown for the handful of wineries in the valley.

Vancouver Island. A small troupe of vintners populates the huge island west of Vancouver. The winemakers are fiercely proud of their island-grown grapes and rarely rely on fruit from the Okanagan Valley.

British Columbia Subappellations and Regions of Interest

Black Sage Bench. Perhaps the most important stretch of land in Canada for growing classic Bordeaux grape varieties is the Black Sage Bench. The west-facing area just north of the U.S. border already is planted to at least a third of British Columbia's total vineyard acreage, and it is in the country's only desert.

South Okanagan Valley. In the last ice age, a glacier that helped carve out the Okanagan Valley stopped at a huge outcropping called MacIntire Bluff (you can still see where the glacier scraped against it). Everything south of the bluff is sandy glacial soil and is perfect for growing wine grapes. The South Okanagan includes the Black Sage Bench.

Naramata Bench. A region on the east side of Okanagan Lake just north of the city of Penticton, this growing area is filled with vineyards, orchards, and other agricultural offerings and has a growing legion of wine-loving fans.

Key British Columbia Vineyards

Outside of estate vineyards, British Columbia winemakers don't tend to label vineyard-designated wines. The few that do are from the Black Sage Bench, including Black Sage Vineyard and Burrowing Owl Vineyard.

ALDERLEA VINEYARDS

VANCOUVER ISLAND   ESTABLISHED 1997

Just north of the "City of Totems," Alderlea Vineyards is fiercely dedicated to producing high-quality wines from its estate vineyards. Roger Dosman manages the vines and crafts the wines. His efforts prove that Vancouver Island, especially the beautiful Cowichan Valley north of Victoria, can produce delicious, classy wines.

BEST BETS

Pinot Gris $ Opening with exotic orange zest and tropical aromas, this big, round wine is loaded with flavors of pears, pineapples, oranges, and apples. Enjoy this with halibut, ahi, or scallops.

Bacchus $ This important German variety grows well at Alderlea and produces a steely wine showing off aromas and flavors including green apples, white flowers, and pineapples. It offers well-balanced acidity that makes it a perfect match for shellfish, especially crab and mussels.

Clarinet $$ If you've turned up your nose at Maréchal Foch in the past, give this a try. It's a smooth, delicious wine that takes advantage of everything good about the variety (including blackberries in vanilla cream and black cherries) and none of the bad. Enjoy this with beef or pasta.

WHERE TO BUY: WINERY, WINE SHOPS

1751 Stamps Road, Duncan, B.C. V9L 5W2, 250-746-7122. Open Thursday–Sunday.

BENCHLAND VINEYARDS

OKANAGAN VALLEY   ESTABLISHED 1999

In a region filled with grape varieties not often found elsewhere, Benchland Vineyards stands out with its German-style wines. A Pinot Noir called Spätburgunder, a blush called Weissherbst, and a Pinot Blanc called Weisshurgunder lead the way for Zweigelt, a bright red grape rare in the New World. If you aren't interested in experimenting, Benchland also offers such standards as Chardonnay, Riesling, Merlot, and Cabernet Sauvignon.

BEST BETS

Zweigelt $ A young, tasty red that shows pie cherry aromas and rich, bright fruit with touches of herbs. Match with savory or rich meat dishes.

Spätburgunder $ This approachable Pinot Noir is a bright, enjoyable wine with cherry and raspberry fruit and silky tannins.

Riesling $ Aromas of orchard fruit with hints of honey and crisp acidity. Pork, chicken, and firm cheeses would be good matches.

Weissherbst $ A Pinot Noir Rosé built for brunches, picnics, and summer sipping. A bright, refreshing wine that will be enjoyed by newer wine lovers.

WHERE TO BUY: WINERY

170 Upper Bench Road S., Penticton, B.C. V2A 8T1; 250-770-1733. Open seasonally.

BLACK HILLS ESTATE WINERY

OKANAGAN VALLEY   ESTABLISHED 1999

Concentrating on small amounts of Bordeaux-style wines, Black Hills is well situated on the venerable Black Sage Bench in British Columbia's southern Okanagan Valley. A Quonset hut that creates a romantic, cave-like feel serves as the winery's tasting room and production facility. The surrounding twenty-six acres are planted to Cabernet Sauvignon, Merlot, Cabernet Franc, Chardonnay, Pinot Noir, and Sauvignon Blanc, most of which is sold to other wineries.

BEST BETS

Nota Bene $$ This Bordeaux blend that is primarily Merlot shows off toasty oak and leather aromas and is loaded with black cherries, chocolate, cassis, and an herbal stamp characteristic of this region.

Sequentia $$ A late-harvest Sauvignon Blanc ripe with spicy orange zest and honey aromas with flavors of fresh apricots. Good acidity balances delicious sugars.

WHERE TO BUY: WINERY, WINE SHOPS

30880 Black Sage Road, Oliver, B.C. V0H 1T0; 250-498-0666; www.blackhillswinery.com. Open seasonally.

BLASTED CHURCH VINEYARDS

OKANAGAN VALLEY   ESTABLISHED 1998

If you had to nominate one place in the Okanagan Valley as the most beautiful, Blasted Church Vineyards wouldn't be a bad bet. It sits on the lightly traveled east side of Skaha Lake north of Okanagan Falls on a gentle, west-facing slope that gets all the advantages of the warm afternoon sun. The vineyards were planted in the early 1980s and, under new ownership, are likely to produce superior fruit. The winery originally was known as Prpich Hills Vineyard, but it changed its name in 2002 to pay homage to a historic church that was dynamited off its foundation and moved to nearby Okanagan Falls.

BEST BETS

Lemberger $ A rare variety outside of Washington, this native of Austria produces jammy, fruit-driven red wines with bright berries and black pepper notes. Delicious for everyday enjoyment with meatloaf or thick hamburgers.

Chasselas–Optima $ This fresh, ripe summer sipper is loaded with bright tropical fruit and is a delightful sipper to finish a summer day with a smile.

Rosé $ A blend of Pinot Noir and Chardonnay, this seriously delicious blush is loaded with fresh flavors and just enough sweetness to make it a perfect picnic wine.

WHERE TO BUY: WINERY, WINE SHOPS

378 Parsons Road, Okanagan Falls, B.C. V0H 1R0; 250-497-1125. Open daily.

BLUE GROUSE VINEYARDS AND WINERY

VANCOUVER ISLAND   ESTABLISHED 1989

One of the first modern-day island wineries, Blue Grouse is dedicated to producing wines with grapes from its ten-acre vineyard. Hans Kiltz and his son Richard make a number of cool-climate wines in the temperate Cowichan Valley.

BEST BETS

Le Classique $ A blend of Ortega and Bacchus, this white wine is a long, delicious one with floral, orange, and spice aromas and apple and ripe pear flavors. It's a big, tasty wine with just a touch of sweetness. Enjoy with crab or chicken.

Pinot Gris $ This tasty, food-friendly wine offers up such aromas and flavors as dried pineapple, lemon, and kiwi. It has plenty of acidity for matching with scallops or halibut.

WHERE TO BUY: WINERY, WINE SHOPS

4365 Blue Grouse Road, Duncan, B.C. V9L 6M3; 250-743-3834; www.bluegrousevineyards.com. Seasonal hours.

BLUE MOUNTAIN VINEYARDS

OKANAGAN VALLEY   ESTABLISHED 1991

This is one of the Northwest's hidden treasures. Nestled in the hills south of Okanagan Falls, Blue Mountain is home to sixty-five beautiful acres of European wine grapes grown since 1971. Ian Mavety and his family have built a wonderful Italian-style villa in which to craft some of the Northwest's best wines.

BEST BETS

Pinot Noir $$ This suave red wine is an absolute delight and one of the best-crafted Pinot Noirs in the Northwest. Classic cherry aromas greet the person fortunate enough to hold a glass. Its raspberry and cherry flavors are smooth yet rich, velvety yet huge, delicate yet long. A great wine.

Pinot Blanc $ This finely crafted white wine is richly aromatic, with the fragrance of fresh apples, pears, and citrus fruit. This beauty demands oysters, scallops, shrimp, or other shellfish.

Chardonnay $$ If you've grown weary of oak-driven Chardonnays, this will help you appreciate the variety again. Light butter and tropical fruit aromas don't give away this wine's huge tropical flavors of pineapples, bananas, and kiwis. This wine typically gets about 50 percent barrel fermentation, which shows up in the round creaminess backing up all the fruit and acidity.

Pinot Gris $$ A nice balance of crisp fruit and creamy roundness makes this a seafood-friendly wine. Apples and lemons highlight this bright, tasty wine.

WHERE TO BUY: WINERY, WINE SHOPS, RESTAURANTS

Allendale Road, Okanagan Falls, B.C. V0H 1R0; 250-497-8244; www.bluemountainwinery.com. Open by appointment.

BURROWING OWL VINEYARDS

OKANAGAN VALLEY   ESTABLISHED 1999

Sitting on one of the best stretches of wine grape growing soil in the Pacific Northwest, Burrowing Owl is well situated for success. Its nearly 300 acres of vineyards on the highly regarded Black Sage Bench give it excellent fruit sources, and its modern facility is built to handle the wine gently. Burrowing Owl's wines have been well received from the winery's infancy, making it one of the most highly sought-after wines in the province.

BEST BETS

Cabernet Sauvignon $$ A blockbuster wine with black fruit, bittersweet chocolate, rich boldness, and herbal undertones.

Chardonnay $$ Bright and clean with deliciously lush tropical and citrus flavors with hints of butter. Match with seafood or chicken.

Merlot $$ Bright cherry with a full mouth feel in a supple, approachable red.

Pinot Noir $ Creamy vanilla and intense cherry aromas meld to earthy complexities. A delicate, spicy wine.

WHERE TO BUY: WINERY, WINE SHOPS

100 Burrowing Owl Place, Oliver, B.C. V0H 1T0; 877-493-0620; www.bovwine.com. Seasonal hours.

CALONA VINEYARDS

OKANAGAN VALLEY   ESTABLISHED 1932

The charismatic Howard Soon leads one of the Okanagan's largest and oldest wineries. The winemaker affectionately refers to Calona as the "Gallo of the north" because of the large amounts of wine it produces, and he's fiercely proud of the high-quality varietal wines made for the Private Reserve, Artist Series, Sandhill, and Copper Moon lines.

BEST BETS

Sandhill Cabernet Franc $ Smooth from start to finish with rich, bright fruit and telltale herbal notes. A delicious, approachable, food-friendly wine.

Artist Series Pinot Gris $ A rich and fruit-driven white with a creamy mouth feel from sur lie aging. Perfect with seafood or pasta in a cream sauce.

Artist Series Sovereign Opal $ This unusual white variety produces a bright, racy, spicy, fruit-driven wine that is a great summer sipper or brunch wine.

Sandhill Pinot Blanc $ With ripe orchard fruit and vanilla aromas and flavors backed up by solid acidity, this is another food-friendly wine that would match well with lobster, cod, or chicken.

1125 Richter St., Kelowna, B.C. V1Y 2K6; 250-762-3332; www.calona.kelowna.com. Open daily.

CALLIOPE VINTNERS

OKANAGAN VALLEY   ESTABLISHED 2000

Calliope is the creation of two experienced Okanagan Valley winemakers, Ross and Cherie Mirko. In addition to consulting for a number of other valley wineries, they are crafting these wines, which are classy and delicious.

BEST BETS

Semillon–Sauvignon Blanc $ A classic white Bordeaux-style blend that shows off fig, grass, and melon notes amid the rich mouth feel. A graceful and delicious wine to pair with pasta or chicken.

Gewürztraminer $ An intensely delicious and spicy wine that shows an abundance of varietal characteristics. Pair this with turkey, pasta, or Thai dishes.

Cabernet Sauvignon $$ A long, wonderful wine with rich berry and vanilla aromas and smooth, luscious flavors. A great wine. Pair with lamb or beef.

Merlot–Cab $ A big, delicious, up-front wine showing off bright berry and oak aromas and long, chewy fruit and spice flavors. Enjoy with everyday cuisines, such as lasagna, meatloaf, or cheeses.

WHERE TO BUY: WINERY, WINE SHOPS

1060 Poplar Grove Rd. (at Poplar Grove Winery), Penticton, B.C. V2A 8T6; 250-494-7213; www.calliopewines.com. Open by appointment.

CARRIAGE HOUSE WINES

OKANAGAN VALLEY   ESTABLISHED 1995

This small family operation on the Black Sage Bench in the southern Okanagan Valley focuses on Kerner, a little-known grape that can produce white wines of considerable quality. Carriage House also makes small amounts of Chardonnay, Pinot Noir, and Merlot.

BEST BETS

Kerner $ With Gewürztraminer-like grapefruit and spiciness, this slightly sweeter wine is loaded with fresh tropical fruit flavors and would match well with spicier curries or Asian-inspired cuisine.

Kerner Dry $ Though bone dry, this wine is rich with tropical flavors and a crisp mouth feel.

Ebonage Blanc $ A blend of Kerner and Chardonnay that is bright, crisp, and clean. Enjoy with a variety of seafood.

32764 Black Sage Road, Oliver, B.C. V0H 1T0; 250-498-8818. Seasonal hours.

CEDARCREEK ESTATE WINERY

OKANAGAN VALLEY   ESTABLISHED 1986

CedarCreek is one of the Okanagan Valley's most progressive wineries. With a gravity-flow facility, the winemaking team handles the grapes and wines gently, and the result is some of the valley's best bottlings on a consistent basis. It's a first-class operation with a large number of wines, with its Merlot, Pinot Noir, and Pinot Gris of particular interest.

BEST BETS

Platinum Reserve Pinot Noir $$ An exceptional wine that will hold its own in any company. Powerful cherry, chocolate, and leather aromas with rich, deep fruit flavors and spicy French oak nuances. Deep and complex through the finish.

Pinot Gris $ One of the best in the Northwest. The grapes for this complex white are from the southern Okanagan Valley and little-known Similkameen Valley. Rich vanilla and nectarine aromas are just the start of this layered and beautiful wine.

Platinum Reserve Merlot $$ Bright fruit, rich tannins, and great length give this well-structured red a place among the Okanagan Valley's best Bordeaux-style reds. Beautiful balance gives this a lot of cellar potential, or serve young with a thick, rare steak.

WHERE TO BUY: WINERY, WINE SHOPS

5445 Lakeshore Road, Kelowna, B.C. V1W 4S5; 250-764-8866; www.cedarcreek.bc.ca. Open daily.

CHALET ESTATE VINEYARD

VANCOUVER ISLAND   ESTABLISHED 2000

This winery north of Victoria specializes in small quantities of wines from island vineyards. Like many Vancouver Island wines, some of the varieties are out of the mainstream, but don't let that scare you off. The wines are bright and approachable and tend to pair well with regional cuisine, especially seafood. Also look for Chalet Estate's Chardonnay, Cabernet Franc, and Pinot Noir from Okanagan Valley grapes.

BEST BETS

Bacchus $ Loaded with bright, fresh fruit aromas and flavors, this is an approachable and flavorful wine with a bit of sweetness and good acidity to match with crab or chicken.

Ortega $ This tasty white opens with aromas and flavors of citrus fruit. It's a medium-bodied wine with a fruit-driven mouth feel and a bit of sweetness. Enjoy this with grilled halibut or mild cheeses.

11195 Chalet Road, North Saanich, B.C. V8L 5M1; 250-656-2552; www.chaletestatevineyard.ca. Open Tuesday–Sunday.

CHATEAU WOLFF

VANCOUVER ISLAND   ESTABLISHED 1997

Harry von Wolff is passionate about his wines. He takes special care from vineyard to bottle to use no pesticides in his organic vineyards and to personally manage everything by hand, including bottling, corking, and labeling. And if you're sensitive to sulpites, Chateau Wolff adds none to its unfined and unfiltered products.

BEST BETS

Viva! $ Under Wolff's Nanaimo Vineyards label, this late-harvest Bacchus is loaded with aromas and flavors of honey, hazelnuts, sweet spices, and tangerines. Enjoy it by itself as an after-dinner sipper or serve with table grapes and apple slices.

Grand Reserve Pinot Noir $ An elegant red with dusty cherry and chocolate aromas, bright berry flavors, and a silky finish. Try it with sirloin.

Grand Rouge $ A ripe, lush red dessert wine, this is a blend of Dornfelder, Pinot Noir, Bacchus, Siegerrebe, Viognier, and Sylvaner. It's rich with overripe plums and black cherries, has a luscious mouth feel, and will pair well with Stilton or barbecued ribs.

WHERE TO BUY: WINERY, WINE SHOPS

2534 Maxey Road, Nanaimo, B.C. V9S 5V6; 250-753-9669. Open weekends and by appointment.

CHERRY POINT VINEYARDS

VANCOUVER ISLAND   ESTABLISHED 1994

Located in the lush Cowichan Valley, Cherry Point Vineyards is the creation of Wayne and Helena Ulrich, who began planting their vineyards in 1990 and were licensed as a winery in 1994. As part of their dedication to developing the island as a grape-growing region, they have dedicated an acre to no fewer than thirty-two wine grape varieties to see what will do best in this climate.

BEST BETS

Pinot Blanc–Auxerrois $ This delicious white blend offers some Riesling-like aromas with classic petrol and apple, followed by big, long flavors of spiced apples. It's an edgy wine with plenty of food-friendly acidity. Enjoy with chicken, pasta, or turkey.

Blanc de Noir $ This rosé offers pleasing aromas and flavors of strawberries and cherries with plenty of structure backing them up. This is the perfect picnic wine, so enjoy it with a ham sandwich.

Agria $ This relatively unknown red grape is crafted into a delicious wine with spicy black plum and cherry aromas and flavors. It's a smooth, impressive effort that pairs well with beef, lamb, or pasta.

Valley Sunset $ A blend of Pinot Noir, Castel, and Agria, this is a big wine with dark, penetrating aromas and flavors. It offers nuances of black cherries, plums, and freshly cracked black pepper. Try this with a roast.

WHERE TO BUY: WINERY, WINE SHOPS

840 Cherry Point Road, Cobble Hill, B.C. V0R 1L0; 250-743-1272; www.cherrypointvineyards.com. Open daily.

DOMAINE COMBRET

OKANAGAN VALLEY   ESTABLISHED 1993

Olivier Combret knows a little something about winemaking. He should, since he's the tenth generation of winemakers in his family, dating back to 1638. Hailing from Provence, France, Combret moved to British Columbia in 1992 to open his winery on an estate with Chardonnay vineyards more than three decades old. He makes a wide variety of wines, often letting them age in the bottle for a few years before release. "Wines deserve to age," he says.

BEST BETS

Saint Vincent Chardonnay $$ With nutty, toasty aromas, this richly structured wine offers a level of elegance that would match well with escargot or veal.

Reserve Riesling $ Classic petrol and mineral aromas lead to clean, rich flavors of poached pears. Should enhance with age.

Rosé $ It takes a deft touch to make a rosé this good. Crafted with Cabernet Franc grapes, this offers inviting strawberry aromas and flavors and would match well with ham or barbecued chicken.

Saint Vincent Cabernet Franc $$ Captivating aromas, including blackberries, currants, cloves, and pencil shavings. Delicate fruit flavors are backed up with perfectly balanced tannins. Imagine this with venison or a pepper steak.

WHERE TO BUY: WINERY, WINE SHOPS

32057 Road 13, Oliver, B.C. V0H 1T0; 250-498-6966; www.combret wine.com. Open by appointment.

DOMAINE DE CHABERTON ESTATE WINERY

FRASER VALLEY   ESTABLISHED 1991

Claude and Inge Violet have brought more than 350 years of wine-making history with them to British Columbia's Lower Mainland and have applied it to their efforts at Domaine de Chaberton. Claude is a ninth-generation winemaker from Paris who spent his early years in the Swiss and Spanish wine industries before he and his wife, Inge, moved to Langley, a community south of Vancouver. They make a variety of wines from estate and Okanagan Valley grapes and are perhaps best known for their two styles of Bacchus, a grape that is a cross between Silvaner, Riesling, and Müller-Thurgau.

BEST BETS

Bacchus $ A delightful sipper, this crisp, off-dry white is rich in apricot and sweet spice aromas and flavors. Enjoy on its own or pair with shellfish or chicken.

Madeleine Sylvaner $ This cool-climate grape might remind you of Riesling with its fresh apple and pear aromas and flavors. It's finished off-dry and will match well with mussels, grilled chicken, or pork.

Gamay Noir $ We don't see this fresh, fruit-driven variety enough in the Northwest, and this red's bright berry flavors and tangy fruit are perfect for barbecued ribs.

Gewürztraminer $ Gewürz doesn't get much better than this, with its distinctive perfumy, grapefruity aromas and classic fruit flavors with a surprisingly crisp finish. Enjoy with Thai dishes, Asian-inspired duck, or curried turkey.

WHERE TO BUY: WINERY, WINE SHOPS, GROCERY STORES

1064 216th St., Langley, B.C. V2Z 1R3; 604-530-1736; www.domainedechaberton.com. Open daily.

ELEPHANT ISLAND WINERY

OKANAGAN VALLEY   ESTABLISHED 2001

Even if you scoff at fruit wines, don't overlook Elephant Island Orchard Wines on British Columbia's Naramata Bench. Owners Del and Miranda Halladay take their efforts very seriously, including hand-sorting fruit and hiring a Bordeaux-trained winemaker. The Okanagan Valley's only non-grape winery produces no fewer than seven wines, from dry table wines to sweeter and Port-style after-dinner delights.

BEST BETS

Apricot $ This dessert wine has a fascinating aroma that is true to its origins. Plenty of acid backs up the 12 percent residual sugar, and the lovely stone fruit flavors lead to a smooth, delicious finish.

Bartlett Pear $ This bone-dry wine is bright, smooth, and fruit-driven. Its tart, acidic backbone makes it a great match with chicken.

Cherry $ In addition to the telltale cherry aromas, anise and other complexities come through. Tasty and round, this would match well with turkey or other poultry.

Crab Apple $ This apple with little commercial use makes a delicious wine. Round and viscous, it has enough residual sugar (4 percent) to make it a tasty hot-tub sipper.

WHERE TO BUY: WINERY

2730 Aikens Loop, Naramata, B.C. V0H 1N0; 250-496-5522. www.elephantislandwine.com. Seasonal hours.

FAIRVIEW CELLARS

OKANAGAN VALLEY   ESTABLISHED 1999

This small winery focuses on Bordeaux-style wines that are highly regarded by wine shop owners and restaurateurs in the Lower Mainland and Okanagan Valley. The wines come from the six acres of vineyards alongside the Fairview Golf Course south of the wine village of Oliver. Owner Bill Eggert's focus is on good-quality reds at great values.

BEST BETS

Bear's Meritage $$ A blend of Cabernet Sauvignon, Merlot, and Cabernet Franc, this has rich, approachable fruit that shows off its oak aging.

Cabernet Franc $ A consumer favorite with herbal and cherry aromas and good bright flavors.

Cab–Merlot $ This blend of two classic grapes is rich with cherries, blackberries, and smooth tannins.

WHERE TO BUY: WINERY, WINE SHOPS

13147 334th Ave., Oliver, B.C. V0H 1T0; 250-498-2211. Open Tuesday–Saturday.

GEHRINGER BROTHERS ESTATE WINERY

OKANAGAN VALLEY   ESTABLISHED 1985

German-trained Walter and Gordon Gehringer planted their vineyards in 1981 and established their winery just north of the U.S. border in the mid-1980s with the idea of crafting steely wines, including Riesling, Auxerrois, Ehrenfelser, Schönburger, Pinot Noir, and ice wines. In the late '90s, the Gehringers added their Dry Rock Vineyards label, which gave them a vehicle to make bigger, more concentrated wines. Gehringer Brothers is one of the Okanagan's finest and most consistent producers.

BEST BETS

Dry Rock Vineyards Chardonnay $ Loaded with tropical and citrus fruit aromas and flavors, this shows off mere hints of its oak aging. This is a perfect example of a food-friendly Chardonnay. Pair it with shellfish, salmon, or chicken.

Cabernet Franc Ice Wine $$$ A somewhat rare red ice wine, this offers generous amounts of raspberry, cherry, banana, rhubarb, and chocolate nuances. Solid acidity backs up the ample sugar. Serve as dessert with a cheese plate.

Dry Rock Vineyards Cab–Merlot $ Priced for everyday enjoyment, this delicious red blend opens with bright and opulent fruit aromas and flavors and finishes long and smooth. A perfect match for pasta, stews, or casseroles.

Optimum Pinot Noir $ This reserve wine is a full bodied red with big, jammy strawberry and raspberry flavors and a velvety finish. Pair with sirloin.

WHERE TO BUY: WINERY, WINE SHOPS

Road 8, RR1, Site 23, Comp 4, Oliver, B.C. V0H 1T0; 250-498-3537. Seasonal hours.

GERSIGHEL WINEBERG

OKANAGAN VALLEY   ESTABLISHED 1994

The first winery over the U.S. border in British Columbia's Okanagan Valley is Gersighel Wineberg, a small producer focusing on Riesling, Gewürztraminer, Pinot Blanc, and blends.

BEST BETS

Riesling $ Ripe apples and a touch of sweetness are backed up with good acidity. Serve with cheese, cold cuts, or curried dishes.

Pinot Blanc $ Another food-friendly wine with floral aromas, spicy fruit flavors, and good acidity. Perfect with pork, crab, or oysters.

Gewürztraminer $ Good varietal characteristics, including grapefruit and tropical nuances and a bit of sweetness. A good brunch wine.

WHERE TO BUY: WINERY

29690 Hwy. 97, Oliver, B.C. V0H 1T0; 250-495-3319. Seasonal hours.

GLENTERRA VINEYARDS

VANCOUVER ISLAND   ESTABLISHED 1999

John Kelly and Ruth Luxton run their four-acre vineyard and craft the wines of this small operation in Vancouver Island's Cowichan Valley. Nearly all of their fruit comes from the island, and a small percentage is purchased from the Okanagan Valley.

BEST BETS

Vivace $ A blend of no fewer than ten grape varieties, this zesty white wine is filled with aromas and flavors of apples, oranges, pears, and nectarines. It's a smooth, clean wine with plenty of shellfish-friendly acidity.

Pinot Noir $ An animated red with well-integrated oak, pleasing black cherry and chocolate flavors, and good mouth weight. Pair with salmon or sirloin.

WHERE TO BUY: WINERY, WINE SHOPS

3897 Cobble Hill Road, Cobble Hill, B.C. V0R 1L0; 250-743-2330. Open daily.

GODFREY-BROWNELL VINEYARDS

VANCOUVER ISLAND   ESTABLISHED 1997

Dave Godfrey is crafting wines from his estate vineyard in the Cowichan Valley, as well as from grapes he purchases from the Similkameen Valley in the province's interior. He is focused on making small quantities of high-quality wine and is experimenting with growing several different varieties on the island, including Lemberger, Dornfelder, and maybe even Cabernet Sauvignon.

BEST BETS

Chardonnay $ This elegant and delicious wine offers citrus, butter, and vanilla bean aromas and rich, round, creamy flavors from French oak aging. A good match for scallops, salmon, or pasta in a clam sauce.

Pinot Noir $$ Made with Similkameen Valley grapes, this is a bright and lovely wine with cherry and vanilla aromas and smooth berry flavors. The velvety mouth feel gives this a gentle and enjoyable farewell.

WHERE TO BUY: WINERY, WINE SHOPS

4911 Marshall Road, Duncan, B.C. V9L 6T3; 250-748-4889; www.gbvineyards.com. Open daily.

GOLDEN MILE CELLARS

OKANAGAN VALLEY   ESTABLISHED 1997

If you're coming north across the border from Washington, one of the first wineries you'll encounter is Golden Mile Cellars. And if you happen to turn up the road for a visit, you won't soon forget the occasion because the operation is housed in a castle, complete with a knight in armor watching over the vineyard. Inside, the friendly owners will serve crisp white wines, as well as rich, smooth reds. The setting is popular for picnics and weddings.

BEST BETS

Bacchus $ The god of wine would be pleased with this effort, a flinty white with crisp apple and tangerine flavors and a tasty, food-friendly finish. Shellfish would be perfect with this.

Riesling $ This rich, viscous wine is loaded with ripe pear and apple nuances and long flavors. A real pleaser.

Pinot Noir $ This bright, unassuming wine offers tasty berry flavors with hints of earth and pepper. A match for pork or, perhaps, salmon.

Kernet $ If you want to compare apples and oranges, this is the wine for you because that's the flavor profile of this crisp, sweeter wine. A tasty summer sipper.

WHERE TO BUY: WINERY, WINE SHOPS

12343 316A Ave., Road 13, Oliver, B.C. V0H 1T0; 250-498-8330. Seasonal hours.

GRAY MONK CELLARS

OKANAGAN VALLEY   ESTABLISHED 1982

Former hair stylists George and Trudy Heiss came west from Edmonton to plant their vineyard overlooking beautiful Okanagan Lake in the early 1970s. A decade later they launched Gray Monk Cellars, specializing in crisp dry white and dessert wines. The winery is named after the white Pinot Gris grape, which is called Gray Monk in the couple's native Germany and Austria.

BEST BETS

Siegerrebe $ This difficult-to-say but easy-to-drink white is more typically grown in Washington's Puget Sound appellation. However, this central Okanagan Valley version is a terrific wine with delicate yet powerful aromas and generous flavors of sweet oranges and green apples. Serve with mild cheeses.

Pinot Gris $ A crisp white loaded with fresh citrus and tropical fruit aromas and sweet spice flavors. Eminently food-friendly.

Cabernet Franc $ A tasty red with all the aromas and flavors of Cabernet Sauvignon without the big tannins. Enjoy with pepper steak or pasta with a red sauce.

Ehrenfelser $ This early-ripening German variety shows well in the Okanagan Valley, especially farther north in the central valley. Gray Monk's version is highlighted by loads of fruit flavors, including apples, oranges, pineapples, and kiwis. A bright sipper to enjoy with shellfish or cheese.

WHERE TO BUY: WINERY, WINE SHOPS

1055 Camp Road, Okanagan Centre, B.C. V2V 2H4; 250-766-3168; www.graymonk.com. Open daily.

HAINLE VINEYARDS ESTATE WINERY

OKANAGAN VALLEY   ESTABLISHED 1985

Winery founder Walter Hainle was the first to make a true ice wine (with grapes frozen on the vine rather than in a fridge) in Canada when he made a batch for himself in 1973, and he made the country's first commercial ice wine a half-decade later. His son, Tilman, continues his father's innovative ways, producing moderate amounts of primarily dry wines using minimalist methods in the vineyard and cellar, including organic practices and a gravity-flow facility. An ownership change occurred in 2002, with Tilman staying on to run the vineyard and winery.

BEST BETS

Gewürztraminer $ An expressive and richly aromatic wine with surprisingly solid acidity and classic flavors.

Kerner $ Loaded with tropical notes, including toasted coconut, apricot, mango, and fresh flavors, this would match well with Asian cuisine or stinky cheeses.

Cabernet Franc $$ Bright fruit flavors with hints of milk chocolate amid the jammy mouth feel. Smooth through the finish.

Riesling Ice Wine $$$$ Canada's first ice wine producer actually makes very little (if any) each year. When it does, you can count on a heavenly treat of aromas and flavors that might remind you of baklava with its nuances of buckwheat honey, pastries, and nuttiness.

WHERE TO BUY: WINERY, WINE SHOPS

5355 Trepanier Bench Road, Peachland, B.C. V0H 1X0; 250-767-2525; www.hainle.com. Open daily.

HAWTHORNE MOUNTAIN VINEYARDS

OKANAGAN VALLEY   ESTABLISHED 1995

In a valley that offers one spectacular view after another, Hawthorne Mountain Vineyards has one of the best. The winery is only a few minutes off Highway 97, yet the steep drive will give you a feeling of getting away from it all in a hurry. The winery crafts no fewer than a dozen wines, with its spectacular dessert wines standing out from the crowd.

BEST BETS

Ehrenfelser Ice Wine $$$$ If you want one of the world's best dessert wines, this is it. From first whiff, you'll be in love with this wine's ample cardamom-infused pears, peaches, and honey. The lusty flavors include rich apples, dried fruit, tropical notes, and sweet spices. And the tremendous sweetness is backed up with a surprising amount of acid. Drink this sitting down or risk your knees buckling.

Oraniensteiner Ice Wine $$$$ The intensity of this rare dessert wine is incredible. Loaded with complex layers of fresh and dried fruits, it's backed with an exceptionally well-balanced mix of sugar and acid.

Lemberger $$ A rare wine anywhere, especially in Canada, this quaffable red has plenty going on, including flavors of cherries, blackberries, vanilla, and raspberries. You can't beat this with meat-loaf, ham, turkey, or thick hamburgers.

WHERE TO BUY; WINERY, WINE SHOPS, GROCERY STORES

Green Lake Road, Okanagan Falls, B.C. V0H 1R0; 250-497-8267; www.hmvineyard.com. Open daily.

HESTER CREEK ESTATE WINERY

OKANAGAN VALLEY   ESTABLISHED 1996

Hester Creek has been producing some of the province's most exciting wines. Winemaker Frank Supernak rehabilitated the estate vineyards and cellar. In 2002, Supernak left Hester Creek for another valley winery before tragically passing away during the 2002 harvest, and the challenge now at Hester Creek is to maintain the level of quality he established.

BEST BETS

Chardonnay–Semillon $ An incredibly delicious blend of two favorite varieties, this shows gobs of fruit, including peaches, pears, citrus, and fresh figs. This is, undoubtedly, one of the best white blends in the Pacific Northwest. And at this price, buy by the case.

Pinot Gris $ Consistently one of the top Pinot Gris in the Northwest, Hester Creek's also is one of its best bargains. Incredibly complex and showing off the best of the variety, it's a great match with seafood, chicken, pasta in a cream sauce, and pork.

Late Harvest Trebbiano $$ A rare, perhaps unique, wine for the Pacific Northwest, this dessert wine has a delicious balance of sugar and acidity with rich flavors of butterscotch, orchard fruit, and more.

Pinot Blanc Ice Wine $$$ This nectar of the gods is loaded with sultry aromas of apricots, honey, spice, and poached pears and huge, rich flavors of stone fruit and hints of plum brandy.

WHERE TO BUY: WINERY, WINE SHOPS

13163 326th St., Oliver, B.C. V0H 1T0; 250-498-4435; www.hester creek.com. Seasonal hours.

HILLSIDE ESTATE WINERY

OKANAGAN VALLEY   ESTABLISHED 1989

One of British Columbia's original small "farmgate" wineries, Hillside went through a major face-lift in the mid-1990s with new ownership and a state-of-the-art building. In addition to its tasty wines and friendly staff, it's also home to a bistro that is open spring through fall.

BEST BETS

Gewürztraminer $ A classy wine with aromas and flavors of fresh grapefruit and hints of rose water. Its long flavors help make this a good match with Thai cuisine.

Syrah $$ A rare wine for B.C., this red is ripe with plum and chocolate aromas and flavors and has a medium finish. Try this with lamb.

Cabernet Franc $ Black currants and blackberries greet the nose, and bright cherry and berry flavors make this a good match with pepper-encrusted steaks.

WHERE TO BUY: WINERY, WINE SHOPS

1350 Naramata Road, Penticton, B.C. V2A 8T6; 250-493-6274; www.hillsideestate.com. Seasonal hours.

HOUSE OF ROSE WINERY

OKANAGAN VALLEY   ESTABLISHED 1982

Vern Rose and his family make a variety of wines at value prices in their winery just outside Kelowna, the Okanagan Valley's largest city. House of Rose is far from the mainstream, focusing on hybrid grapes such as Okanagan Riesling and Maréchal Foch. The wines tend to be somewhat sweet and quaffable, and are popular among locals and visitors alike.

BEST BETS

Perle of Zala $ This Hungarian grape produces Riesling-like qualities with pleasant petrol and green apple aromas and plenty of acidity. A slightly sweet wine that woud match well with Asian-inspired dishes and would be a fun brunch wine.

Maréchal Foch $ Dark fruit, including blueberries and black cherries, highlight this tasty red wine. Some oak treatment rounds out this soft, flavorful wine.

Winter Wine Rosé $$ This blend of various grapes offers up floral and rose water aromas. Good fruit flavors and plenty of acid back up some nice sweetness.

WHERE TO BUY: WINERY, WINE SHOPS

2270 Garner Road, Kelowna, B.C. V1P 1E2; 250-765-0802. Open daily.

INNISKILLIN OKANAGAN VINEYARDS

OKANAGAN VALLEY   ESTABLISHED 1994

Though it tends to take a backseat to its older and larger sibling, Inniskillin in Ontario, Inniskillin Okanagan is no slouch. This southern Okanagan Valley property produces highly regarded Pinot Noir, Cabernet Franc, and a red blend, as well as delicate white wines and succulent ice wines from Riesling and Ehrenfelser. Like several of British Columbia's top wineries, Inniskillin Okanagan is owned by the large Vincor company.

BEST BETS

Dark Horse Vineyard Cabernet Franc $ One of the Northwest's top Cab Francs (and its most affordable), this is a rich red showing a graceful balance of dark fruit and oak with vanilla bean and spice elements. Pair with lamb chops or lasagna.

Dark Horse Vineyard Pinot Noir $ Loaded with classic strawberry jam aromas and flavors with delicate and complex layers of flavor. Enjoy with pork, turkey, or a rich salmon.

Reserve Chardonnay $ A zesty wine showing citrus and tropical fruit with toasty oak undertones. Enjoy with halibut or chicken.

Riesling Ice Wine $$$ A richly structured and sweet dessert wine with honey and apricot notes amid floral undertones. Plenty of acidity backs up the sugar and makes this an enjoyable sipper.

WHERE TO BUY: WINERY, WINE SHOPS

Road 11 W., RR1, Site 24, Comp 5, Oliver, B.C. V0H 1T0; 250-498-6663; www.inniskillin.com. Seasonal hours.

JACKSON-TRIGGS VINTNERS

OKANAGAN VALLEY   ESTABLISHED 1993

Jackson-Triggs Vintners is a brand created by wine giant Vincor, the world's fourth-largest wine company, which also owns Inniskillin Okanagan, Sumac Ridge Estate Winery, and Hawthorne Mountain Vineyards in the Okanagan Valley, among others. Behind the brilliance of winemaker Bruce Nicholson, Jackson-Triggs has emerged as a leader in high-quality Northwest wines. In fact, Jackson-Triggs is making so many wines that are turning heads in competitions in North America that it can easily be placed in a category of regional and quality leaders with Chateau Ste. Michelle. Each year, Jackson-Triggs can hang its hat—and dozens of medals—on its incredible Riesling ice wines. But it's also bringing home critical acclaim with most of its other wines, from Dry Rieslings and Chardonnays to serious Rosés to Merlots and Cabernet Sauvignons. Jackson-Triggs is as close to a "can't-miss" as there is in the Northwest.

BEST BETS

Riesling Ice Wine $$$ The quintessential dessert wine, every year, this rates at or near the top of British Columbia's venerable ice wines. It is richly sweet and thickly viscous, with abundant character and flavor, including honey, sweet spice, apricots, orange zest, and much more. This wine usually carries enough acidity to balance out the sugar and give sufficient backbone for the long haul.

Pinot Blanc $ This normally unassuming variety becomes a wonder in the hands of Bruce Nicholson. Loaded with citrus and heavenly aromas, this is one of the best Pinot Blancs you're likely to run across.

Cabernet Sauvignon $$ A ripe, delicious red showing rich fruit components and underlying herbal notes. Bright acidity makes this a food-friendly wine that will pair well with lasagna, pork, or turkey.

Blanc de Noir $ This serious rosé is seductively aromatic and filled with flavors of freshly picked strawberries and bright cherries. A good, dry rosé is difficult to find, but not at Jackson-Triggs.

WHERE TO BUY: WINERY, WINE SHOPS, GROCERY STORES

Hwy. 97, Oliver, B.C. V0H 1T0; 250-498-4981. Open daily.

KETTLE VALLEY WINERY

OKANAGAN VALLEY   ESTABLISHED 1992

Named after an old railroad that ran up and down the valley, Kettle Valley produces three thousand cases of wine from fifteen acres of vineyards on the Naramata Bench. Partners Bob Ferguson and Tim Watts began growing grapes in the mid-1980s and making wine in 1992. They make seven styles of wine. The reds are classy, concentrated, and age-worthy. The Crest Cabernet Sauvignon is made in small lots and should be highly sought after by serious wine lovers.

BEST BETS

Crest Cabernet Sauvignon $$ This classy red wine opens with delicious black currants, dark fruit, and a hint of cedar. It's a big, chewy wine with dense fruit flavors, dense tannins, and rich complexity. One of the best Cabs in the Pacific Northwest.

Gewürztraminer $ Delicious grapefruit, floral, and citrus aromas and flavors with good acidity and a nice touch of sweetness.

Old Main Red $$ This blend of Cabernet Sauvignon, Cabernet Franc, and Merlot offers rich, bright flavors of cherries and raspberries. A tasty, approachable wine that will match well with most beef cuts and pasta in red sauce.

WHERE TO BUY: WINERY, WINE SHOPS

2988 Hayman Road, Naramata, B.C. V0H 1T0; 250-496-5898. Seasonal hours.

LA FRENZ WINERY

OKANAGAN VALLEY   ESTABLISHED 2001

Aussie Jeff Martin is building a reputation for classic wines. The former Quails' Gate winemaker is growing Viognier, Merlot, and Syrah on six acres along the Naramata Bench. Additionally, he uses grapes from the venerable Black Sage Bench region in the southern Okanagan Valley. Martin's style of winemaking is "fruit in the front, complexity in the back."

BEST BETS

Semillon $ Expertly blended with Sauvignon Blanc, this white wine leads off with grassy and grapefruit aromas. Fruit flavors are nicely balanced with a mouth-filling creaminess from barrel aging.

Chardonnay $ Light butter and citrus aromas open up this delicious, multidimensional wine with white fruit, butter, and citrus flavors. This round, rich, subtle, complex wine finishes long and flavorful.

Cabernet Sauvignon $$ A big, chewy wine with great aromatics and flavors. Dark chocolate leads off with cherries, black fruit, cedar, and approachable tannins.

WHERE TO BUY: WINERY, WINE SHOPS

740 Naramata Road, Naramata, B.C. V2A 8T6; 250-492-6690. Open Monday–Saturday.

LAKE BREEZE VINEYARDS

OKANAGAN VALLEY   ESTABLISHED 1996

This former orchard on the Naramata Bench was planted to vineyards in the mid-1980s, and the winery opened a decade later. Now in its third ownership change, Lake Breeze's focus has been on Pinot Blanc, though it also produces a number of other good-quality wines.

BEST BETS

Pinot Blanc $ Lake Breeze's signature wine is rich with fruit, including melon and apple. Pair this with salmon or pasta in a clam sauce.

Ehrenfelser $ This perfumy, fruit-driven wine is made from a German grape that is a cross of Riesling and Sylvaner. The bright, slightly sweet wine makes a lovely summer sipper.

Cabernet Franc $ This is a classic with its dusty aromas of vanilla extract and plums, smooth, creamy flavors, supple tannins, and a delicious, steak-friendly finish.

Pinot Blanc Ice Wine $$ A thick honey of a wine with rich apricot aromas and flavors and wonderful spiciness—and just enough acidity to back up all the sweetness. Serve with cheesecake or poached pear stuffed with Stilton.

WHERE TO BUY: WINERY, WINE SHOPS

930 Sammet Road, Naramata, B.C. V0H 1N0; 250-496-5659. Seasonal hours.

LANG VINEYARDS

OKANAGAN VALLEY   ESTABLISHED 1990

Located on the eclectic Naramata Bench north of Penticton, Lang focuses on fruit-driven wines made without the aid of oak. Lang is a well known for its beautiful packaging as it is for its wines, whic range from crisp Rieslings and fruity Merlots to red and white ice wines and a unique maple syrup wine.

BEST BETS

Auxerrois $ A bright, fresh wine with cleansing acidity and good seafood-matching potential.

Riesling $ Classic European style with ripe apple and petrol aromas with good balance on the palate. Pair with picnic fare.

Canadian Maple Syrup Brut $$ A sparkling wine made with Canadian maple syrup, this offers smooth, honeyed aromas and flavors. It's not only delicious, it's a real conversation starter, as well.

Merlot Ice Wine $$ Strawberry aromas and flavors highlight this rare red ice wine. While the acidity doesn't quite keep up with the sugar, this is a bright wine loaded with flavor. Try this with French vanilla ice cream.

WHERE TO BUY: WINERY, WINE SHOPS

2493 Gammon Road, Naramata, B.C. V0H 1N0; 250-496-5987. Seasonal hours.

LARCH HILLS WINERY

OKANAGAN VALLEY   ESTABLISHED 1996

Located farther north than most could have imagined growing classic wine grapes, Larch Hills Winery produces cool-climate wines of great character. Not all of the varieties are in the mainstream, including Ortega, Siegerrebe, Madeleine Angevine, and Agria. Winery owners Hans and Hazel Nevrkla also purchase Pinot Noir, Gewürztraminer, and Merlot from farther south.

BEST BETS

Tamarack Rosé $ A blend of Pinot Noir and Madeleine Angevine, this is a tasty off-dry rosé with delicate aromas of strawberries, rhubarb, and dried pineapples, and smooth flavors. A nice sipper that also will pair well with turkey or cold chicken.

Ortega $ A delicious white that shows off herbal and pink grapefruit notes amid refreshingly crisp acidity. A sure match for a cheese and fruit plate or barbecued shrimp.

Gewürztraminer $ Aromatic with grapefruit and sweet spice aromas and smooth, dry, rich flavors of almonds. Plenty of acidity gives this good food-pairing potential.

Pinot Noir $ A smooth, easy-drinking red with pleasant sweet spice, black cherry, and red currant flavors. A good wine to pair with steak.

WHERE TO BUY: WINERY, WINE SHOPS

110 Timms Road, Salmon Arm, B.C. V1E 2P8; 250-832-0155; www.larchhillswinery.bc.ca. Seasonal hours.

MISSION HILL FAMILY ESTATE

OKANAGAN VALLEY   ESTABLISHED 1981

Architecturally speaking, Mission Hill must be the most spectacular winery in the Pacific Northwest. And under the tutelage of John Simes, the wines are among the best in British Columbia. At nearly 100,000 cases per year, Mission Hill is one of the province's largest producers. Simes makes a vast array of wines that are widely distributed, from dry whites and supple reds to rich ice wines. The winery is a stunning building that resembles an Italian hill-town.

BEST BETS

Sauvignon Blanc $ With its classic grass, pear, and apple flavors, this fruit-driven white is a crisp, food-friendly treat to match with scallops, salmon, pasta, pork, or chicken.

Reserve Shiraz $ One of the best buys for a Syrah that you'll find in the Northwest. This shows magnificently with mature black fruit aromas and deliciously racy and rich flavors.

Merlot $ An elegant and balanced wine with subtle, complex herbal and black fruit notes.

Reserve Chardonnay Ice Wine $$$ Even in its dessert form, this Chardonnay shows off varietal characteristics of butterscotch and citrus aromas and rich apple and tropical flavors.

WHERE TO BUY: WINERY, WINE SHOPS, GROCERY STORES

1730 Mission Hill Road, Westbank, B.C. V4T 2E4; 250-768-7611; www.missionhillwinery.com. Open daily.

MT. BOUCHERIE ESTATE WINERY

OKANAGAN VALLEY   ESTABLISHED 1999

The Gidda family, longtime Okanagan Valley grape growers, launched their winery on a great note, hiring Alan Marks, a well-respected winemaker who has worked on both sides of the border. His style is straightforward, as he allows the grapes to show their best without too much cellar interference. The results are clean, delicious, consistent wines.

BEST BETS

Gewürztraminer $ An outstanding example of the variety, with layers of luscious grapefruit and spice aromas and classic tropical and citrus flavors. As an added bonus, it enjoys good acidity, something not always possible south of the border in Washington.

Pinot Gris $ A top-rated white with delicious citrus and sweet spice aromas and a complex mixture of flavors keyed by crisp lemon. An extremely versatile food wine.

Pinot Noir $ Bright berry fruit aromas and lusciously jammy flavors make this approachable red a perfect foil for salmon or pork.

Mt. Boucherie Estate Winery, 829 Douglas Road, Kelowna, B.C. V1Z 1N9; 250-769-8803; www.mtboucherie.bc.ca. Open daily.

NEWTON RIDGE VINEYARDS

VANCOUVER ISLAND   ESTABLISHED 1998

This tiny producer twenty minutes out of Victoria focuses on small lots of Pinot Noir, Pinot Gris, Pinot Blanc, and Ortega from its three-acre estate vineyard and supplements its crop with a bit of purchased fruit from the Okanagan Valley. The vineyard, planted in the mid-1990s, is in a warm area on Vancouver Island. The wines are nearly impossible to find outside the winery, so savor them if you can find them.

BEST BETS

Pinot Noir $ Classic earthy, cherry aromas give way to tangy cherry flavors with good richness, velvety tannins, and a delicious finish. Enjoy with beef or lamb.

WHERE TO BUY: WINERY

1595 Newton Heights, Saanichton, B.C. V8M 1T6; 250-652-8810. Not open to the public.

NICHOL VINEYARD

OKANAGAN VALLEY   ESTABLISHED 1993

Alex and Kathleen Nichol enjoy an idyllic life on the Naramata Bench, a fifteen-mile stretch of terrain on the east bank of Okanagan Lake north of Penticton. Here they grow a handful of European wine grapes on their four and a half acres of estate vineyards, including St. Laurent, a relatively obscure red grape of France's Alsace region. The Nicholses were one of the first producers of Syrah in Canada, and it's a wine that continues to be one of their benchmarks.

BEST BETS

Syrah $$ Classic cherry and plum aromas and flavors, loaded with peppercorns and other spices. Surprisingly good acidity for this grape, probably because of the northerly clime.

Cabernet Franc $$ This dense, delicious wine is approachable and food-friendly in its youth. Smooth tannins meld nicely with the black fruit and herbal notes.

Pinot Noir $$ Pie cherries highlight this smooth, tasty, richly flavored wine that's silky on the midpalate with a pleasantly dusty edge on the finish.

WHERE TO BUY: WINERY, WINE SHOPS

1285 Smethurst Road, Naramata, B.C. V0H 1N0; 250-496-5962. Seasonal hours.

PARADISE RANCH WINES

Situated on a spectacular plateau on the north end of British Columbia's Naramata Bench north of Penticton, Paradise Ranch is a longtime vineyard that specializes in late-harvest and ice wines. Perhaps best known for its dramatic packaging, Paradise Ranch is gaining a reputation for quality dessert wines amid some of the world's great ice wines. In 2002 the vineyards were purchased by Mission Hill Family Estates.

BEST BETS

Late Harvest Merlot $$ Unfortified red dessert wines are somewhat rare, and this effort is delicious, with nuances of strawberries and cranberries, solid acidity, and a tasty finish.

Chardonnay Ice Wine $$$ A thick, honeyed wine with aromas and flavors of ripe pears and apples.

WHERE TO BUY: WINE SHOPS

Business office: Suite 901, 525 Seymour St., Vancouver, B.C. V6B 3H7; 604-683-6040; www.icewines.com. No tasting room.

PELLER ESTATES

Peller is part of the huge Andrés Wines, based in Ontario. Best known for low-end jug wines, Andrés produces premium wines under the Peller and Hillebrand names. The company's roots are with Andrew Peller, who founded a small winery in the early 1960s in British Columbia. The Peller Estate wines are tasty, affordable, and show off good varietal characteristics.

BEST BETS

Pinot Blanc $ A round, tasty wine with tropical aromas and flavors. Enjoy with chicken in a cream sauce.

Cool Climate White $ This white blend opens with fresh fruit aromas and flavors with a round mouth feel and a crisp finish. A good wine to pair with chicken, pasta, or shellfish.

Riesling $ Showing classic varietal tendencies, this provides delicate floral aromas, citrus flavors, and a good dose of sweetness. Pair with a cheese plate or Tex-Mex.

Merlot $ A fruit-driven red that provides jammy berry aromas and flavors with hints of violets and vanilla bean. Approachable throughout, enjoy this with everyday cuisine, such as meatloaf, casseroles, and pasta.

WHERE TO BUY: WINERY, WINE SHOPS, GROCERY STORES

2120 Vintner St., Port Moody, B.C. V3H 1W8; www.andreswines.com. Open by appointment.

PINOT REACH CELLARS

OKANAGAN VALLEY   ESTABLISHED 1997

Pinot Reach's name is a bit of a misnomer, as winemaker Roger Wong crafts a wide variety of wines, not just Pinot Noir. In fact, his Old Vines Riesling is one of the Northwest's best, and his Cabernet Sauvignon may be the most northerly planted in the world. Pinot Meunier, a traditional blending grape in France's famous Champagnes, also is a specialty.

BEST BETS

Old Vines Riesling $ A glorious wine with complex fruit and nut flavors with nice sweetness, plenty of bold acidity, and a lingering finish. Match with curries or savory dishes.

Gewürztraminer $ Touches of vanilla meld with crisp pear flavors and a soft finish. Serve with Thai cuisine or duck.

Pinot Meunier $ Naturally lighter bodied, with bright cherry and raspberry flavors and a smooth mouth feel. A tasty picnic or brunch wine.

Old Vines Riesling Brut $$ From vines planted in 1978, this is a sparkler to fall in love with. Apple and pear aromas with crisp peach, apple, and lemon flavors with beautiful bubbles. Tremendous food-matching potential, especially with pâté, oysters, and creamy cheeses.

WHERE TO BUY: WINERY, WINE SHOPS

1670 Dehart Road, Kelowna, B.C. V1W 4N6; 250-764-0078. www.pinotreach.com. Open Tuesday–Saturday.

POPLAR GROVE WINERY

OKANAGAN VALLEY   ESTABLISHED 1995

This winery on the Naramata Bench north of Penticton sits above the southern end of Okanagan Lake amid six and a half acres of wine grapes. Ian and Gitta Sutherland produce several wines, which are as delicious as the view they have of the valley. They also run a cheese-making operation.

BEST BETS

Cabernet Franc $$ One of the three important red Bordeaux varieties takes center stage in this delicious wine. Lovely aromas of black currants and herbal notes lead to dense, chewy black cherry flavors layered with pepper and surprisingly strong tannins.

Pinot Gris $ French oak aging shows up in this well-balanced white wine. Vanilla and butter flavors meld with citrus and apple to make a complex wine that cries out for seafood, herb-infused chicken, or pasta in clam sauce.

Gewürztraminer Ice Wine $$$ From a grape that is notoriously low in acidity, Poplar Grove has managed to craft a dessert wine with plenty of backbone. Gewürztraminer's telltale spiciness greets the nose and leads to flavors of nectarines, peaches, honey, and sweet spices.

WHERE TO BUY: WINERY, WINE SHOPS

1060 Poplar Grove Road, Penticton, B.C. V2A 8T6; 250-492-4575. Open seasonally.

QUAILS' GATE ESTATE WINERY

OKANAGAN VALLEY   ESTABLISHED 1989

With estate vineyards stretching down to the shores of Okanagan Lake, picturesque Quails' Gate is one of the valley's top producers. After reaching fifty-five thousand cases, Quails' Gate now is working to reduce vineyard yields to lower production and increase quality. Quails' Gate is one of the friendliest stops in the central Okanagan Valley, and its Old Vines Patio is a great place to stop for a meal.

BEST BETS

Riesling Ice Wine $$$ One of British Columbia's best, this intense ice wine opens with inviting aromas of tropical fruit, honey, and sweet baked apples. Its bold flavors include oranges, pineapples, and peaches. The 27 percent residual sugar is perfectly balanced with crisp acidity.

Limited Release Pinot Noir $ A Burgundian-style red with earthy raspberry and cherry aromas and dark fruit flavors. This full-bodied wine is a great match with lamb or pork.

Cab-Merlot $$ A delicious blend with plum and spice aromas and jammy black fruit and bittersweet chocolate tones.

Old Vines Foch $$ This red grape is a remnant of British Columbia's French hybrid days. One of the few hybrids that can produce truly delicious wine, Maréchal Foch is an intensely dark wine with black cherry and blueberry nuances with hints of leather and cedar.

WHERE TO BUY: WINERY, WINE SHOPS

3303 Boucherie Road, Kelowna, B.C. V1Z 2H3; 250-769-4451; www.quailsgate.com. Open daily.

RECLINE RIDGE VINEYARDS

OKANAGAN VALLEY   ESTABLISHED 1998

With vineyards planted in 1994, Mike and Sue Smith use estate grapes to make a wide variety of wines, including Maréchal Foch, Madeleine Sylvaner, and Agria. The winery and vineyard are in Tappen, a community well north of Kelowna and the Okanagan's main wine route.

BEST BETS

Ortega $ Clean and delicious pineapple aromas and flavors with a crisp finish. A fine pairing with pasta in a clam sauce or chicken.

Gewürztraminer $ A sweet, soft, fresh wine with citrus aromas and flavors. An enjoyable sipper.

WHERE TO BUY: WINERY, WINE SHOPS, GROCERY STORES

2640 Skimikin Road, Tappen, B.C. V0E 2X0; 250-835-2212; www.recline-ridge.bc.ca. Seasonal hours.

RED ROOSTER WINERY

OKANAGAN VALLEY   ESTABLISHED 1998

Nobody can accuse Beat and Prudence Mahrer of not having fun. Or not making world-class wine. The Swiss transplants are favorites in the central Okanagan among visitors and locals alike, and their delicious wines will make believers out of the most serious oenophile. In addition to making about the best Pinot Gris in the Pacific Northwest, Red Rooster crafts a rare Vin Santo, the holy wine of Tuscany.

BEST BETS

Pinot Gris $ Rich tropical and citrus fruit abound in this delightful and consistently superior white wine. It will match with a vast number of dishes, but start with crab legs.

Chardonnay $ Fermented in stainless steel, then aged for a short time in oak, this opens with aromas of peaches and cream. Crisp, round acidity is balanced perfectly with a creamy midpalate. A match for chicken in a cream sauce.

Merlot $ Opening with classic sweet spice, vanilla, and cherry aromas, this offers smooth, creamy flavors that would pair well with turkey and gravy.

Vin Santo $$ Made by pressing grapes that have dried to raisins on mats, this offers intriguing spice, honey, and almond aromas. It starts sweet, then finishes dry with nutty, dried-fruit flavors.

WHERE TO BUY: WINERY, WINE SHOPS

910 Debeck Road, Naramata, B.C. V0H 1N0; 250-496-4041; www.redroosterwinery.com. Seasonal hours.

SATURNA ISLAND VINEYARDS

VANCOUVER ISLAND   ESTABLISHED 1997

This young winery and estate vineyards are on Saturna Island, in British Columbia's Gulf Islands. The early releases were produced with grapes from the island as well as from the arid Okanagan and Similkameen Valleys. With sixty acres of estate vines coming into production, big things can be expected from Saturna Island.

BEST BETS

Pinot Gris $ A sassy white showing notes of honey, pears, and freshly crushed hazelnuts. A sweeter wine that will pair well with brunch or picnic fare.

Robyn Vineyard Chardonnay $ From estate grapes, this is loaded with fresh fruit flavors that mingle with light butter and vanilla bean notes. A rich, citrusy wine that would do well with pasta in a cream sauce or scallops.

Riesling $ With its classic petrol and apple aromas, this is a long and luscious wine with rich flavors and a fairly dry finish. Enjoy with shellfish, chicken, or even Asian-inspired dishes.

Cabernet Sauvignon $$ A tasty, approachable red showing off aromas and flavors of ripe plums, blackberries, and herbal notes. Solid tannins give this some cellar potential.

WHERE TO BUY: WINERY, WINE SHOPS

8 Quarry Road, Saturna Island, B.C. V0N 2Y0; 250-539-3521; www.saturnavineyards.com. Seasonal hours.

SCHERZINGER VINEYARDS

OKANAGAN VALLEY   ESTABLISHED 1995

This little winery in the hills near Summerland specializes in delicious estate-grown Gewürztraminer, with the white grape playing a part in no fewer than five of Scherzinger's wines. The style is fruit-forward, with the vineyards treated in an organic manner.

BEST BETS

Dry Gewürztraminer $ Showing spicy grapefruit aromas and citrus flavors, this also has hints of orange oil and just a touch of residual sugar to give greater balance.

Select Gewürztraminer $ A bit more sweetness (2 percent residual sugar) gives this a nice mouth feel to go along with the bright, spicy citrus and white fruit flavors.

Sweet Caroline $ An interesting blend of Gewürztraminer and Pinot Noir, it's spicy with flavors of red currants, citrus, and bright cherries.

Pinot Noir $ Tons of character show in this earthy red wine, with plums and tart cherries. A delicious, affordable wine.

Amy's Riesling $ A late-harvest white with classic apple and petrol aromas, with good sweetness and plenty of crisp acidity backing it up.

WHERE TO BUY: WINERY

7311 Fiske St., Summerland, B.C. V0H 1Z0; 250-494-8815. Seasonal hours.

SILVER SAGE WINERY

OKANAGAN VALLEY   ESTABLISHED 1999

Victor and Anna Manola escaped from Romania during the Cold War and settled in British Columbia, where they launched Silver Sage Winery, directing their attention to dessert wines. The signature wine is a Pinot Blanc ice wine with a chili pepper in it. During the 2002 harvest, Victor died in a winery accident along with friend and fellow winemaker Frank Supernak, formerly of Hester Creek Estate Winery.

BEST BETS

Pinot Blanc Spiced Wine $ Lovely apricot aromas lead to a hot and spicy wine with full, smooth flavors. A good wine to enjoy with seafood or fresh goat cheese.

Raspberry $ This fortified fruit wine is a delicious example, with pure fruit aromas and flavors and a smooth, rich finish. Enjoy on its own or over vanilla ice cream.

Blueberry $ Lovely blueberry aromas and flavors with long, smooth flavors and a rich mouth feel.

Merlot Ice Wine $ A deep, penetrating dessert wine with full-bodied flavors and a creamy midpalate. An enjoyable after-dinner sipper.

WHERE TO BUY: WINERY, WINE SHOPS

32032 87th St., Oliver, B.C. V0H 1T0; 250-498-0310; www.silver sagewinery.com. Open daily.

SLAMKA CELLARS

OKANAGAN VALLEY   ESTABLISHED 1994

Peter Slamka moved to British Columbia in the early '90s to build his winery amid quarter-century-old vines and today produces small amounts of reds and whites, with a focus on the little-known Auxerrois, a French white grape. In fact, he is believed to be the only producer of Auxerrois Ice Wine in the world.

BEST BETS

Pinot Auxerrois $ Toasty nose with rich orchard and tropical flavors throughout. Pair with seafood or chicken.

Pinot Noir $$ Classic earthy and raspberry aromas lead to a full-flavored red with berry and spice components.

Tapestry $ A white wine made of a blend of five grapes: Riesling, Auxerrois, Gewürztraminer, Siegerrebe, and Schönburger. A tasty wine for brunch, picnics, or sipping at the end of a summer day.

Auxerrois Ice Wine $$ A delicious and rare dessert wine with distinctive butterscotch, hazelnut, and alfalfa honey notes.

2815 Ourtoland Road, Kelowna, B.C. VIZ 2H5; 250-769-0404; www.slamka.bc.ca. Seasonal hours.

ST. HUBERTUS ESTATE WINERY

OKANAGAN VALLEY   ESTABLISHED 1992

The St. Hubertus estate has a lot of history behind it, as vines origi nally were planted in 1928. The Gebert brothers established the winery in the early '90s and make a number of wines under the St. Hubertus and Oak Bay Vineyard labels. Of special interest are the Pinot Meunier, a little-known grape primarily used to make classic Champagne, and Chasselas, a white grape of Swiss origin (like the owners) that can be crafted into a true delight.

BEST BETS

Chasselas $ Delicate aromas of rose water and orange peel and soft, elegant flavors of ripe pears and citrus. Try this with a cheese plate or perhaps with oysters.

Riesling $ Honey, light spice, and Golden Delicious apples dominate the aromas in this richly structured white. A penetrating wine to pair with Indian cuisine or fish with a heavy sauce.

Pinot Meunier $ Wonderfully spicy aromas provide notes of raspberry, cherry, and vanilla. This wine's bold flavors are surprising, and it's likely to pair well with pheasant, veal, or venison.

Pinot Blanc Ice Wine $$ Apricot and honey aromas lead to copious levels of fruit and sweetness on the palate. This viscous wine provides the acidity to back up the 30-plus percent of sugar, and this would work as a dessert unto itself or perhaps with a cheese and nut plate.

WHERE TO BUY: WINERY, WINE SHOPS

5225 Lakeshore Road, Kelowna, B.C. T1W 4J1; 250-764-7888; www.st-hubertus.bc.ca. Seasonal hours.

STAG'S HOLLOW WINERY & VINEYARD

OKANAGAN VALLEY   ESTABLISHED 1995

Nestled in the hills south of Okanagan Falls, Stag's Hollow is a well-established winery focusing on Chardonnay, Vidal, Merlot, and Pinot Noir. Delicious, focused wines that are consistent medal winners make Stag's Hollow a good bet.

BEST BETS

Vidal $ This is one of the winery's most popular wines and is one of the few dry vidals you're likely to find. Crisp and flavorful, the wine's lemon and other citrus flavors make it a nice match with seafood.

Merlot $$ Cherry aromas and flavors meld with vanilla and peppercorns in this rich, round, delicious wine. A youthful, bright wine that would be a good match with Italian-inspired cuisine.

Late-Harvest Vidal $ A good dessert wine with smooth, supple flavors of nectarines, peaches, and tropical fruit. Good acidity backs up the sweetness.

WHERE TO BUY: WINERY, WINE SHOPS

2237 Sun Valley Way, Okanagan Falls, B.C. V0H 1R0; 250-497-6162. Seasonal hours.

SUMAC RIDGE ESTATE WINERY

OKANAGAN VALLEY   ESTABLISHED 1970

Under the direction of Harry McWatters, Sumac Ridge has established itself as one of British Columbia's top producers. McWatters has been a tireless promoter of B.C. wines and has been a main reason for the region's rapid improvement in overall quality. In 2000, McWatters sold Sumac Ridge to Vincor International, one of North America's biggest wine producers. He remains as president of Sumac Ridge. The winery produces a huge array of wine styles and excels at all.

BEST BETS

Red Meritage $$ This Bordeaux-style blend's grapes come from the venerable Black Sage Bench, an area near the U.S. border that probably is the best spot in Canada for growing Cabernet Sauvignon, Merlot, and Cabernet Franc. This wine is rich with fruit and deep in complexity. It is steak-friendly in its youth or can be cellared for a half-decade or more.

Steller's Jay Brut $$ This delicious sparkling wine is named after the official provincial bird and is a classic Champagne-style beauty. The bubbles enliven the mouth, and the flavors of bright berries and cake meld perfectly.

Cabernet Franc $$ This minor grape in most areas of the wine world often takes center stage in the Okanagan. This wine is richly aromatic and flavorful with smooth, silky tannins.

Gewürztraminer $ This is a textbook example of an Alsatian-style white, full of aromas and flavors led by sweet spice, honey, and white flowers. A delicious wine that should be enjoyed within a year or two of release.

WHERE TO BUY: WINERY, WINE SHOPS

17403 Hwy. 97, Summerland, B.C. V0H 1Z0; 250-494-0451; www.sumacridge.com. Open daily.

SUMMERHILL ESTATE WINERY

OKANAGAN VALLEY   ESTABLISHED 1992

This is the story of a fellow who made his fortune in New York real estate, then moved to the interior of British Columbia to make wine in a pyramid. It's the story of Stephen Cipes and Summerhill Estate Winery. On the banks of Okanagan Lake, Summerhill owner Cipes believes in harnessing the power of the earth. His vineyards are organically maintained, and he ages his wines in a scaled-down replica of Egypt's Cheops Pyramid, carefully oriented toward true north. Cipes believes that storing his wines in the pyramid causes them to age differently and to increase in quality. Other Okanagan winemakers may shake their heads at his methods, but they can't deny the quality of his wines or his commitment to the region.

BEST BETS

Cipes Brut $$ A dry sparkling wine with delicious citrus and yeast aromas and flavor, this classy bubbly will match nicely with shellfish.

Reserve Gewürztraminer $$ Slightly sweet and delightful with citrus and apricot aromas and classic varietal spiciness. Excellent balance and a terrific match with Asian-influenced cuisine. A bit spendier than most Gewürztraminers.

Ehrenfelser Dry $$ This variety, not often found outside of British Columbia, is a delicious white wine grape developed in the 1920s. It's one of Cipes's favourites. Gorgeous floral and fruit aromas on the nose that would lead one to believe it has some residual sugar. But on the palate, it is dry, soft, and flavorful, with enough acid to give it a generous finish.

Pinot Noir Ice Wine $$$$ One of the rarest and most expensive wines you'll find in the Okanagan Valley, and also one of its best. Richly sweet and exotic with plenty of acid to balance the sugar and offer nice aging potential.

WHERE TO BUY: WINERY, WINE SHOPS

17403 Chute Lake Road, Kelowna, B.C. V1W 4M3; 250-764-8000; www.summerhill.bc.ca. Open daily.

THORNHAVEN ESTATES WINERY

OKANAGAN VALLEY   ESTABLISHED 1999

The Fraser family has built a Santa Fe–style winery in the central Okanagan Valley and is focusing on small, handcrafted lots of fruit-driven reds and whites from the winery's nine acres of estate vineyards. Veteran winemaker Christine Leroux is crafting the first vintages as winery partner Alex Fraser gains cellar experience. The winery plans to introduce a Gewürztraminer.

BEST BETS

Pinot Meunier $ This traditional sparkling-wine grape also makes a wonderful varietal still wine, and Thornhaven's is a bright, spicy, lighter-bodied red with abundant strawberry and cherry flavors. Great for picnics or with turkey.

Sauvignon Blanc–Chardonnay $ This is known as a "field blend" because these two great white varieties were planted together inadvertently and thus are harvested, fermented, and bottled together, too. It's a delicious combination that shows off the herbal, grassy, and tropical fruit nuances of each variety.

Pinot Noir $ This clean, delicious red offers varietal characteristics, including cherry, earth, and vanilla.

WHERE TO BUY: WINERY, WINE SHOPS

6816 Andrew Ave., Summerland, B.C. V0H 1Z0; 250-494-7778; www.thornhaven.com. Seasonal hours.

TINHORN CREEK VINEYARDS

OKANAGAN VALLEY   ESTABLISHED 1994

In 1999, Tinhorn Creek entered the Tri-Cities Wine Festival in Eastern Washington, annually one of the top judgings of Northwest wines. It came into the heart of Merlot country and won the only gold medal for Merlot that year. This fact speaks volumes about Tinhorn Creek Vineyards, where native Californian Sandra Oldfield is winemaker and part owner. The winery's grapes come from estate vineyards on both sides of the southern Okanagan Valley.

BEST BETS

Merlot $$ Perhaps Tinhorn Creek's best wine and consistently a medal winner and top Merlot in the Pacific Northwest. Bright and fruity up front, this food-friendly red wine has Merlot's hallmark cherry and pepper flavors. Better vintages will age nicely for a half-decade or more.

Gewürztraminer $ Famed wine writer Dan Berger calls Tinhorn's Gewürztraminer one of the best he's tasted in the New World. This stunner embraces the nose with its telltale honey and cardamom aromas. It is loaded with fruit flavors, including grapefruit, lemon, and apple, and has plenty of acid to back up the fruit. Delicious with raw oysters, crab, sushi, or Thai cuisine, or alone as an aperitif. This is a don't-miss.

Pinot Noir $ A bit lighter in style than Pinot Noirs found in Western Oregon, this tasty Pinot is approachable in its youth and is a nice match with salmon and other fish.

Kerner Ice Wine $$$ Always a favorite among consumers and professional judges, this rare ice wine is seductive and luscious with tremendous flavor year in and year out.

WHERE TO BUY: WINERY, WINE SHOPS

32830 Tinhorn Creek Road, Oliver, British Columbia, V0H 1T0; 250 498-3743; www.tinhorncreek.com. Open daily.

TOWNSHIP 7 VINEYARDS AND WINERY

FRASER VALLEY   ESTABLISHED 1999

After nearly a decade of experience in the Okanagan Valley, Corey and Gwen Coleman opened Township 7 in the fertile Fraser Valley south of Vancouver. With grapes from the Okanagan, they are hand-crafting small amounts of Merlot and Chardonnay, as well as a sparkling wine called Seven Stars. They also plan to make Sauvignon Blanc and Cabernet Sauvignon.

BEST BETS

Chardonnay $ Showing off American oak aging, this solid Chardonnay is rich with smoky toast, butter, and crisp, fresh tropical and white fruit flavors.

Merlot $$ Bright, rich, smooth, and approachable, this delicious red is built to be enjoyed in its youth.

WHERE TO BUY: WINERY

21152 16th Ave., Langley, B.C. V2Z 1K3; 604-532-1766; www.township7.com. Seasonal hours.

VENTURI-SCHULZE VINEYARDS

VANCOUVER ISLAND   ESTABLISHED 1993

Giordano and Marilyn Venturi produce their wines from estate-grown organic vineyards. The family manages about twenty acres in the fertile Cowichan Valley north of Victoria. Giordano grew up in the Modena region of Italy, the home of classic balsamic vinegar, and the winery produces a minute amount of this highly valued condiment.

BEST BETS

Brut Naturel $$ A sparkling wine made from Pinot Noir that shows strawberries and raspberries amid a background of yeasty nuttiness. A dry wine that has so much fruit, you'll swear it has a bit of sweetness.

Madeleine Sylvaner $ Loaded with fresh, spicy apricots and apples and plenty of crisp acidity. Savor this with halibut or chicken.

Ortega $ A complex white offering dried tropical-fruit aromas with a slightly smoky background and long flavors of ripe apples and no shortage of acidity. Try this with pasta in a clam sauce or with salmon.

Brandenburg No. 3 $$ A luscious treat, this sweet amber wine is named for Bach's third Brandenburg concerto. It provides nutty, tawny, sherry-like aromas with smooth flavors of golden raisins and honeyed fruit. A rare treasure to sip around the holidays.

WHERE TO BUY: WINERY, WINE SHOPS

4235 Trans Canada Hwy., Cobble Hill, B.C. V0R 1L0; 250-743-5630; www.venturischulze.com. Open by appointment.

VICTORIA ESTATE WINERY

VANCOUVER ISLAND   ESTABLISHED 2000

This new winery north of Victoria produces wine using grapes from Vancouver Island as well as from the Okanagan Valley in the province's interior. The first wines are worthy efforts and include a somewhat rare Madeleine Sylvaner and a Pinot Gris from the island, as well as a Riesling, Chardonnay, and Merlot from the hot, sunny southern Okanagan Valley.

BEST BETS

Madeleine Sylvaner $ This crisp white wine offers exotic aromas of sweet spices, honey, and apricots, along with flavors of ripe orchard fruit with well-balanced sweetness and acidity. This is a refreshing wine to match with halibut, scallops, or pasta in a cream sauce.

Merlot $ A big, delicious, age-worthy red with tons of berry, cherry, spice, and chocolate nuances, well-balanced tannins, and an elegant finish. Enjoy this with turkey or pasta.

Chardonnay $ Loaded with tropical and citrus aromas, this bright, rich white wine offers flavors of orange zest, dried pineapples, and a round mouth feel. Pair this with salmon or chicken.

Riesling $ A food-friendly white with plenty of orchard and citrus fruit from aroma through the finish, this will pair with Asian-inspired dishes as well as Mexican cuisine.

WHERE TO BUY: WINERY, WINE SHOPS

1445 Benvenuto Road, Brentwood Bay, B.C. V8M 1R3; 250-652-2671. Open daily.

VIGNETI ZANATTA

VANCOUVER ISLAND   ESTABLISHED 1992

Using only estate grapes, Vigneti Zanatta produces a number of wines, both still and sparkling. In addition to the vineyard and winery, Zanatta operates a country-style restaurant called Vinoteca.

BEST BETS

Ortega $ A delicious white showing complex honey and orange spice aromas with delicate, sophisticated flavors. Pair this scallops, sausage, or a cheese plate.

Damasco $ A unique wine made from fermenting Auxerrois juice on Ortega and Muscat skins The result is an off-dry white with smooth aromas and flavors of apples and oranges. A lovely sipper.

Allegria Brut $$ A sparkling wine made from Pinot Nero and Auxerrois, this provides aromas and flavors of strawberries with hints of yeast. A richly structured wine that will pair well with salmon or chicken.

Glenora Fantasia Brut $$ This hugely structured sparkler is loaded with berry and orchard fruit aromas and flavors. A fabulous bubbly.

WHERE TO BUY: WINERY, WINE SHOPS

5039 Marshall Road, Duncan, B.C. V9L 6S3; 250-748-2338; www.zanatta.ca. Seasonal hours.

WILD GOOSE VINEYARDS AND WINERY

OKANAGAN VALLEY   ESTABLISHED 1990

High in the hills south of Okanagan Falls, Wild Goose Vineyards and Winery crafts top quality wines that have won numerous awards in the operation's first decade of winemaking, which began some ten years after the vineyards were planted. The family-run operation is producing world-class whites and some delicious reds.

BEST BETS

Pinot Blanc $ A wonderfully balanced wine with lovely melon and orange nuances and clean, refreshing flavors.

Gewürztraminer $ A delicious German-style white with floral and grapefruit aromas and tasty citrus flavors. Good acidity makes this a great match for turkey or curried dishes.

Tawny Pipe $ Only a handful of Port-style wines are made in British Columbia; this one is from Maréchal Foch grapes. It's rich with black fruit, chocolate, and raisin qualities and smooth through the finish. A great wine for a cold, rainy night.

Riesling $ Classic European qualities, including apple and petrol aromas and long, rich flavors of orchard and citrus fruits. A wonderful sipper.

WHERE TO BUY: WINERY, WINE SHOPS

2145 Sun Valley Way, Okanagan Falls, B.C. V0H 1R0; 250-497-8919; www.wildgoosewinery.com. Seasonal hours.

IDAHO WINES & WINERIES

The Pacific Northwest's smallest wine-producing region is the Gem State. It's also the Northwest's oldest wine region, as pioneers who got off the Oregon Trail early set down roots quickly. Prohibition did a lot of damage to the fledgling industry, then objections to alcohol by some religious groups held it back until the 1970s, when Ste. Chapelle became a force. The Idaho wine industry is now growing at the same pace as in the rest of the Northwest, with significant vineyard plantings occurring in the fertile Snake River Valley west of Boise.

Idaho wine country is closely aligned with Washington. The climates are similar, and after particularly bad winters Washington vintners have turned to Idaho for much-needed grapes. The vineyards in the Snake River Valley are significantly higher than vineyards just about anywhere else in the world, usually at least 2,000 feet above sea level. They enjoy warm days and cool nights, perfect for Idaho's famous crisp white wines.

Idaho is well known for its agricultural research, including studies of wine grapes. Growers and researchers are making significant progress in learning which varieties will do well.

Idaho Appellations

At this time, Idaho has no official appellations. Wines using grapes originating from within the state will simply say Idaho on the label.

Idaho Subappellations and Regions of Interest

Snake River Valley. The region with most of the state's vineyards is west of Boise near the cities of Nampa and Caldwell.

Lewiston. The Lewiston area is one of the oldest grape-growing venues in the state. There is increased interest in producing grapes around this city where the Snake River enters Washington.

Key Idaho Vineyards

Vickers Vineyard. Kirby Vickers grows Chardonnay for his small winery and sells to a number of vintners, who often produce vineyard-designated wines. The grapes tend to be ripe and full-flavored with classic Chardonnay characteristics.

Arena Valley Vineyard. A beautiful vineyard west of Boise, Arena Valley supplies grapes to Ste. Chapelle, Sawtooth Winery, and Snake River Winery.

Skyline Vineyard. A large vineyard planted in the late '90s by Sawtooth Winery's Brad Pintler, this will gain in quality significance as the vines mature.

BITNER VINEYARDS

SNAKE RIVER VALLEY   ESTABLISHED 1981

Ron Bitner is an entomologist and grape grower west of Boise who focuses on Chardonnay, Cabernet Sauvignon, and Riesling in his fourteen-acre vineyard. Most of the grapes go to nearby Koenig Vineyards, which makes Bitner-designated wines under its label as well as small amounts under the Bitner Vineyards label.

BEST BETS

Chardonnay $$ Clean and crisp, this white is built to show off its fruit and, thus, matches well with shellfish, chicken, or pasta.

WHERE TO BUY: WINERY

16645 Plum Road, Caldwell, ID 83605; 208-454-0086. Not open to the public.

CAMAS WINERY

CENTRAL IDAHO   ESTABLISHED 1983

Camas owners Stu and Sue Scott describe their little operation in the college town of Moscow as a hobby run amok. They make a truly amazing array of wines (no fewer than twenty-five in all), including traditional reds and whites, sparklers, sweet wines, meads (honey wines), and fruit wines. They operate their winery with joy and a sense of humor, naming their wines Hog Heaven Red, Ewe Eye (also the initials of the University of Idaho), Domestic Goddess, and Palouse Gold. Though you won't find any stuffiness at Camas, you will find many seriously delicious wines.

BEST BETS

Champoux Vineyard Lemberger $ Luscious plum and blackberry aromas with underlying vanilla notes lead to smooth, ripe fruit and spice flavors with well-managed tannins and a delicious finish. Enjoy with duck, turkey, pasta, or thick hamburgers.

Raspberry Brut $$ With natural raspberry flavors added, this is a dry, fruit-filled bubbly with lovely raspberry and cherry aromas and a richly structured palate with ripe berry and cake flavors.

Tej $ A rare mead (in the New World) that uses Ethiopian hops, this provides exotically spiced aromas and rich, intriguing flavors. If you enjoy mead, rejoice; if you don't, give this a try.

Domestic Goddess $ A blend of Muscat Canelli and Riesling, this is a wildly aromatic white blend with good orchard fruit flavors backed up with plenty of sweetness and acidity. A tasty brunch or picnic wine.

WHERE TO BUY: WINERY, WINE SHOPS

110 S Main St., Moscow, ID 83843; 208-882-0214; www.camas winery.com. Open Tuesday–Saturday.

CARMELA WINERY

SNAKE RIVER VALLEY   ESTABLISHED 1988

Carmela is a true destination winery. In addition to its array of wines, it has an on-site resort and a nine-hole golf course winding through fifty acres of vineyards. In utterly gorgeous surroundings, Carmela makes several wines, which range from good to outstanding.

BEST BETS

Bodacious Meritage $$ A complex, classic Bordeaux blend of Cabernet Sauvignon, Merlot, and Cabernet Franc, this is rich in velvety fruit, supple tannins, and good acidity. Perfect for a thick steak.

Chardonnay $ A smoky white with citrus and tropical flavors and crisp acidity, just right for shellfish or pasta in a cream sauce.

Merlot $ An easy drinking red with jammy fruit, approachable tannins, and a food friendly approach.

WHERE TO BUY: WINERY, WINE SHOPS, GROCERY STORES

795 W. Madison Ave., Glenns Ferry, ID 83350; 208-366-2313; www.carmelawinery.com. Open daily.

HELLS CANYON WINERY

SNAKE RIVER VALLEY   ESTABLISHED 1984

Known as much for its beautiful labels as its distinctive wines, Hells Canyon Winery is a small, high-quality producer of serious Merlot, Chardonnay, and Cabernet Sauvignon. Owners Steve and Leslie Robertson enjoy a sense of elegance that seems far removed from their agricultural surroundings in southern Idaho. But make no mistake: They're hard-working, dawn-to-dusk folks whose estate vineyards are producing wines of great distinction.

BEST BETS

Reserve Merlot $$ A rich, complete red with layers of complexity and a big mouth feel—a wine that proves Idaho's wine-producing potential.

Reserve Cabernet Sauvignon $$ An enormous yet subtle wine with fruit-forward flavors but also layers of spice, vanilla, and other nuances.

Bird Dog White $ A pleasing, fruit-driven blend of Chardonnay and Sauvignon Blanc that offers refreshing flavors and a creamy mid-palate. A wine to enjoy with chicken, pasta, or seafood.

WHERE TO BUY: WINERY, WINE SHOPS

18835 Symms Road, Caldwell, ID 83605; 208-454-3300. Open weekends and by appointment.

INDIAN CREEK WINERY

SNAKE RIVER VALLEY   ESTABLISHED 1987

Bill and Mui Stowe run their small winery on Indian Creek between Boise and Caldwell. Bill is a retired Air Force major whose love for wine dates to time he spent in Europe in the 1960s. Taking advantage of his chemistry, business, and viticulture education, Bill crafts good to great wines from estate and nearby vineyards.

BEST BETS

Riesling $ A German-style white with outrageous aromas and flavors of citrus, honey, orange oil, rose water, and sweet spices. An outstanding effort that will pair well with shrimp, snapper, fresh goat cheeses, and pasta in a cream sauce.

Pinot Noir $ Soft, supple berry aromas and flavors make this a tasty, approachable wine to pair with sirloin, turkey, or pork tenderloin.

Cabernet Sauvignon $ An easy-drinking, affordable Cab that provides European-style herbal notes with blackberries, plums, and smooth tannins. Enjoy with everyday cuisine.

WHERE TO BUY: WINERY, WINE SHOPS, GROCERY STORES

1000 N. McDermott Road, Kuna, ID 93634; www.indiancreekwinery. com. Open Friday–Sunday.

KOENIG WINERY AND DISTILLERY

SNAKE RIVER VALLEY   ESTABLISHED 1995

Brothers Greg and Andy Koenig were inspired to launch their winery and distillery after living for three years in their father's hometown in Austria. The distillery produces grappas and eau de vies that are highly regarded by brandy lovers. The winery is producing award-winning wines, including Syrah, Cabernet Sauvignon, Chardonnay, and Semillon–Chardonnay.

BEST BETS

Bitner Vineyard Cabernet Sauvignon $$ Koenig makes two vineyard-designated Cabs, this one from Ron Bitner's vineyard, which was established in 1981. This is an elegant wine with flavors of black currants, berries, and bittersweet chocolate, a rich mouth feel, and a lingering finish.

Semillon–Chardonnay $ This blend, made popular in Australia, shows off the best of both varieties with hints of fig and spice aromas and lovely, bright apple and pear flavors. A crisp, salmon-friendly wine.

Merlot $$ An intense red with dark berry flavors, vanilla and cedar from oak aging, and a long, smooth mouth feel. This would match well with lamb, grilled chicken, or savory cheeses.

WHERE TO BUY: WINERY, WINE SHOPS

20928 Grape Lane, Caldwell, ID 83607; 208-455-8386; www.koenigvineyards.com. Seasonal hours.

PARMA RIDGE VINEYARDS

SNAKE RIVER VALLEY   ESTABLISHED 2000

Dick Dickstein began thinking about starting a winery in the early 1970s, but he waited until retirement to fulfill his dream. He began planting his vineyard in 1998, with the first crop coming in 2000. He plans to produce Chardonnay, Zinfandel, Syrah, Viognier, and Gewürztraminer.

BEST BETS

Mountain Spring Chardonnay $ This first effort shows a minerally edge with aromas and flavors of pears and citrus. Try this with grilled cod.

Gewürztraminer $ A complex white showing flinty, citrusy aromas and a creamy mouth feel with hints of oranges on the finish. Pair this with pork or pasta in a cream sauce.

WHERE TO BUY: WINERY, WINE SHOPS

24509 Rudd Road, Parma, ID 83660; 208-722-6885; www.parma ridge.com. Open by appointment.

PEND D'OREILLE WINERY

NORTHERN IDAHO   ESTABLISHED 1995

One of the Northwest's most exciting wineries also is one of the region's most off-the-beaten-path operations. Stephen Meyer makes delicious wines in the North Idaho community of Sandpoint, primarily with Washington grapes but also with fruit from the Snake River Valley west of Boise and some old vineyards near Lewiston. His style is fruit-forward and approachable; his resulting wines are graceful and stylish. Best of all, they're some of the best bargains in the Northwest.

BEST BETS

Bistro Rouge $ A Cab–Merlot blend that is fruit-driven and built for everyday consumption. It's a consistently outstanding wine that shows off the best of both varieties. Buy this early and often.

Bistro Blanc $ This Chardonnay is another winner in Pend d'Oreille's Bistro line. As elegant as the label, the wine shows off the best of the variety's fruit and is expertly structured with just enough oak to satisfy.

Syrah $$ This palate pleaser is loaded with concentrated black fruit and creamy aromas and flavors. A perfect wine to go with a thick steak.

Chardonnay $$ Meyer secures fruit from Idaho and Washington. His Idaho Chardonnays from Vickers Vineyard west of Boise are deliciously creamy with just the right amount of oak. He has begun to experiment with Chardonnay grapes from Clearwater Canyon Vineyard, a pre-Prohibition vineyard in the Lewiston area, producing wines with good potential.

WHERE TO BUY: WINERY, WINE SHOPS, GROCERY STORES

220 Cedar St., Sandpoint, ID 83864; 208-265-8545; www.powine.com. Open daily.

PHANTOM HILL

SOUTHERN IDAHO   ESTABLISHED 1997

Anthony Maratea crafts Chardonnay from Idaho grapes and Pinot Noir from Willamette Valley fruit. With help from former Archery Summit owner Gary Andrus, Maratea began making praiseworthy wines in the mid-1990s. The small amounts he makes generally go to restaurants and wine shops in the know.

BEST BETS

Pinot Noir $$ A silky, classy red showing off earth and vanilla aromas and ripe fruit, oak, and chocolate flavors. An elegant wine to pair with pheasant or duck.

Chardonnay $$ A richly structured white that provides great balance between oak and fruit, this should pair well with chicken in a cream sauce or with barbecued shrimp.

WHERE TO BUY: WINE SHOPS

270 Northwood Way, Unit 15, Ketchum, ID 83340; 250-726-0766. Not open to the public.

STE. CHAPELLE

SNAKE RIVER VALLEY   ESTABLISHED 1976

Idaho's largest and oldest winery is well known for high-quality white wines, especially its Rieslings and Chardonnays, and it also is gaining attention for its sparkling wines and reds. Its estate vineyards are at an elevation of about 2,700 feet, some of the highest in North America, and Ste. Chapelle buys grapes from vineyards throughout the Snake River Valley west of Boise. In 2001 the winery was purchased by Canandaigua Wine Company, one of the largest in North America, giving Ste. Chapelle a greater reach in North America.

BEST BETS

Dry Riesling $ Not only one of the best Rieslings you're likely to find, but also one of the best wine buys anywhere. This wine is loaded with classic Riesling aromas and delicate flavors of peaches and apples. Great acidity backs up the fruit.

Chardonnay $ This delicious white wine is loaded with aromas of lemon and tropical fruit and layers of fruit flavors, well balanced with crisp acidity and a long finish.

Spumante $ Crafted in a sweeter style, this delicious sparkler is rich in fruit and floral aromas and flavors and would work well as a dessert wine.

WHERE TO BUY: WINERY, WINE SHOPS, GROCERY STORES

19348 Lowell Road, Caldwell, ID 83605; 208-459-7222; www.stechapelle.com. Open daily.

SAWTOOTH WINERY

SNAKE RIVER VALLEY   ESTABLISHED 1988

Brad Pintler has grown up with the Idaho wine industry. The lifelong Nampa resident began Pintler Cellars in the late 1980s, then sold the winery to a Washington company a decade later, though he continues to run the operation. Pintler has built a reputation as a talented wine-maker and viticulturalist. He works with dozens of European grape varieties, looking for what works well in Idaho's dry climate, and he has planted 300 acres of vineyards on the slopes around the winery. Sawtooth's wines are delicious and value-priced, and its labels are as distinctive as any in the Northwest.

BEST BETS

Merlot $$ This spectacular red wine is loaded with vanilla and cedar aromas and bright, flavorful cherry flavors. It's rich and delicious to the end.

Chardonnay $ A classic white wine that's sure to please with toasty oak, lemon, dried pineapple, and a smattering of green olive. Buttery and soft, this will match nicely with shellfish or chicken.

Pinot Gris $ A pleasant white wine with dried pineapple aromas and flavors of fresh peaches and pears; a nicely balanced wine.

Cabernet Sauvignon $$ Smoky and rich, this complex red wine is loaded with blackberries and has a velvety mouth feel.

WHERE TO BUY: WINERY, WINE SHOPS, GROCERY STORES

13750 Surrey Lane, Nampa, ID 83686; 208-467-1200; www.sawtooth winery.com. Open Friday–Sunday.

SNAKE RIVER WINERY

SNAKE RIVER VALLEY   ESTABLISHED 2000

Scott and Susan DeSeelhorst purchased the venerable Arena Valley Vineyard in 1998 and conducted their first commercial crush two years later. The highly rated grapes are purchased by nearby Ste. Chapelle and Sawtooth wineries, and Snake River Winery's first releases are proving the greatness of the vineyard and site.

BEST BETS

Merlot $ A complex, robust wine showing a sensuality with its aromas of sweet oak spices, black cherries, and violets, then an explosion of big, jammy flavors and a luscious chocolate finish. Hubba, hubba!

Cabernet Sauvignon $ Showing off toasty oak, espresso notes, black currants, and a smoky, chocolaty finish. A fine wine to pair with a rare cut of beef, and a great value.

WHERE TO BUY: WINERY, WINE SHOPS

24013 Arena Valley Road, Parma, ID, 83660; 208-722-5858. Open by appointment.

VICKERS VINEYARD

SNAKE RIVER VALLEY   ESTABLISHED 1992

Kirby Vickers is passionate about Chardonnay, which is the focus of the vineyard he planted two decades ago. Vickers makes small amounts of handcrafted, barrel-fermented Chardonnay and sells the rest of his highly prized grapes to other wineries, most notably Pend d'Oreille Winery in Sandpoint and Phantom Hill in Ketchum.

BEST BETS

Chardonnay $$ A well-balanced wine showing buttery, toasty oak from barrel fermentation and rich, concentrated fruit. A showy, classy wine to pair with oysters, salmon, or chicken.

WHERE TO BUY: WINE SHOPS

15646 Sunny Slope Road, Caldwell, ID 93605; 208-454-7818. Not open to the public.

INDEX